The Saga of Coe Ridge

The Saga

of Coe Ridge

A Study in Oral History

BY WILLIAM LYNWOOD MONTELL

The University of Tennessee Press

Knoxville

Library of Congress Catalog Card Number 74–77846
International Standard Book Number 0–87049–096–6

Copyright © 1970 by The University of Tennessee Press
Manufactured in the United States of America
All Rights Reserved
First Edition 1970, second printing 1971

To Ruth Evelyn, Monisa, and Brad
and to the people, both black and white,
who found the good life along the upper Cumberland

Preface

Coe Ridge is the name of a tiny Negro colony that was nestled in the foothills of the Cumberland Mountains in Cumberland County, Kentucky, near the Tennessee line. Placed on the ridge as a result of Negro emancipation following the Civil War, the settlement withstood for almost a century the attempts of neighboring whites to remove this "scar" from the culture landscape of an otherwise homogeneous white society. During its existence, the Coe colony, sometimes called Coetown and Zeketown, produced a belligerent group of people who became a legend before the community died in the late 1950's. It became a place of refuge for white women rejected by their own society and the breeding ground for a race of mulattoes. Additionally, Coe Ridge had ranked first among the moonshiners of southern Kentucky and, consequently, became the chief concern of federal revenue agents. It was this occupation, this livelihood of the outcasts that eventually was to bring about their downfall. After years of raids, arrests, and skirmishes, the revenuers succeeded in driving the Negroes from Coe Ridge into the industrial centers north of the Ohio River. Thus the colony died.

Historical events in the life of this Negro colony provide the basis for this book. *The Saga of Coe Ridge* is not an ordinary reconstruction of local history, however, for only a very few written records pertaining to this settlement remain. The major source materials are the inveterate oral traditions collected from former members of the colony and their white neighbors. A work of this type is founded on the premise that the story of any local group, as viewed by its people, is worthy of being recorded, for it can serve as a historical record in those areas where written accounts have not been preserved. One must be prepared to defend a thesis which holds that folk history can complement historical literature. This study proposes such a defense.

THE CONTROVERSY OVER ORAL TRADITIONS

The utilization of oral traditions as undertaken here represents an area of open controversy and is severely attacked by some scholars who are accustomed to more conventional methods of documentation. A less hostile attitude claims that oral traditions can be utilized in historical writings, provided that these recollections are approached with proper caution. Still another line of thought holds that folklore is a mirror of history. That is to say, history can be viewed through folklore. A fourth position contends that the tales and songs of a people are grounded in historical fact. Inasmuch as *The Saga of Coe Ridge* is patently built upon the utilization of oral tradition, these various positions are worth examining in some detail. Let us look, therefore, at the thinking behind all four positions, beginning with the totally negative approach.

Folk Tradition as Historical Fallacy. Legends and traditions of the people should be avoided, according to Homer C. Hockett, who claimed in 1938 that "the historian can make nothing of them of any positive value, in the absence of corroboratory evidence of a documentary, archaeological, or other kind, for the simple reason that they cannot be traced to their origins. And without knowledge of origins the ordinary critical tests cannot be applied." [1] Hockett renewed his attack on oral tradition in 1955 when he defined history as "the written record of past or current events"; he gave some credence, however, to certain devices such as utensils, structures, weapons, and artifacts as items that the historian could use to supplement the absence of written records.[2] Hockett saw no potential in myths, legends, or traditions as informative channels which might be utilized as aids to the historian. Yet in a chapter on "New Trends," Hockett recognized a recent rapprochement between local history and folklore.

Allen Johnson, writing in 1926, also enumerated a list of "remains," some three dozen in number, which could be included as source materials for historical research. Oral tradition was not listed because it was "handed on from generation to generation by word of mouth without being committed to writing." Johnson immediately contradicted his attack on oral tradition, however, by attaching some weight to the Icelandic sagas. "Under certain conditions," he stated, "where the professional raconteur has a pride in keeping the conventional tradition intact, the tale may have a fixed content and a stereotyped form, and eventually may be

1 *Introduction to Research in American History* (New York, 1938), 90.

2 *The Critical Method in Historical Research and Writing* (3rd ed., New York, 1955), 3.

3 *The Historian and Historical Evidence* (New York, 1926), 5.

4 Richard M. Dorson, "The Debate over the Trustworthiness of Oral Traditional History," in Fritz Harkort, ed., *Volksüberlieferung : Festschrift für Kurt Ranke* (Göttingen, 1968), 21. This work hereafter referred to as "The Debate."

5 "Oral Tradition and History," *Journal of American Folklore*, XXX (April–June 1917), 165.

set down in writing substantially unchanged. On these grounds, the essential historicity of the Icelandic sagas is defended." [3]

Robert H. Lowie, an anthropologist, criticized the veracity of oral tradition a few years earlier than either Hockett or Johnson. He made what has been termed "the strongest statement against traditional history on this side of the Atlantic." [4] In 1915, Lowie published a short comment in the *American Anthropologist* on "Oral Tradition and History," objecting to the prohistorical position taken in that journal the previous year by John R. Swanton and Roland B. Dixon. Lowie's most biting comments were issued two years later to the American Folklore Society on the occasion of his presidential address, which was published in the *Journal of American Folklore*. He illustrated his thesis by using the traditions of North American Indians. "Indian tradition is historically worthless," he charged, "because the occurrences, possibly real, which it retains, are of no historical significance; and because it fails to record, or to record accurately, the most momentous happenings." [5] He further stated that stories of war and quarrels are not records of actual occurrences but are folklore, as attested to by their geographical distribution. Lowie conceded the point that traditional narratives are significant in the understanding of psychological, social, and religious phenomena associated with a tribal culture, but he categorically refused to allow any historical credence to the details of the narratives.

Lord Raglan, a recent student of comparative folklore and a clamorous champion of the skeptics of oral traditional history, studied both the classical and medieval bodies of traditional narrative and concluded that the great folk epics, the cherished sagas, the heroic legends and ballads, even the Christ story itself were ultimately drawn from ritual drama, not from historical fact.[6] The heroes of tradition, Raglan contended, were originally not men but gods, and the whole body of folk legend is a detritus of mythical accounts connected with ritualistic rites. After the rites ceased, the narratives remained and entered the realm of folk tradition where they were perpetuated as accounts of historical experiences. Raglan felt that a nonliterate people could not orally preserve the record of a historical event for more than 150 years and that any belief in the historicity of tradition stemmed from the desire to believe rather than from a critical analysis of the facts.

Edwin Sidney Hartland and Alfred Nutt, both talented Victorian folklorists, displayed negative attitudes toward the authenticity of oral historical narratives at an earlier date than Lord Raglan. Hartland studied *The Legend of Perseus* and was able to contend persuasively that certain African traditions are basically void of trustworthy history. Like Raglan, Hartland could allow only a brief time span to the limits of historical reliability in oral tradition. Among African peoples, he would concede one hundred, or at the most, two hundred years. In an article, Nutt attacked Sir William Ridgeway's *The Early Age of Greece,* which contained a strong plea for the acceptance of the Homeric poems as history. Nutt posed the question whether historic myths ever existed among barbaric peoples living in an oral-traditional mythopoetic stage of culture.[7] To Nutt's credit he at least called for an accumulation of more evidence before the thorny problems on the relationships of heroic legend and historic fact could be properly attacked.

Folklore as Embellished History. Joan Wake, a British

6 *The Hero: A Study in Tradition, Myth, and Drama* (New York, 1956).

7 "History, Tradition, and Historic Myth," *Folk-Lore,* XII (1901), 336–39.

8 *How to Compile a History and Present-Day Record of Village Life,* cited in Donald D. Parker, *Local History: How to Gather It, Write It, and Publish It* (New York [1944]), 25.

9 "Folklore and History," in Mody C. Boatright, ed., *Singers and Storytellers* (Dallas, 1961), 58, 61.

10 "History and Folklore: A Suggestion for Cooperation," *Journal of The West,* IV:1 (Jan. 1965), 95–96.

11 *Understanding History: A Primer of Historical Method* (New York, 1950), 114.

historian, deemed folklore to be embellished history. She noted that although the old English village traditions are "liable to fluctuations and variations without end . . . there is much that is valuable in them. . . ." [8] And Américo Paredes wrote that "folklore does not always make a complete wreck of historical facts." He further stated, "Where documents are available for comparison, one may actually trace the process—the reshaping of history to conform with the folk group's own world view, the embellishment of bare historical detail with universal motifs." At that point in the accumulation of historical data, the historian should be familiar with the research methods of the folklorist, Paredes continued, for "some knowledge of the frequency with which motifs of this kind occur in folk narratives would put the historian on guard." [9] Merle W. Wells, historian and archivist, similarly wrote, "Historians who are not interested in folklore ought to have their work examined regularly by good folklorists . . . . Only a skilled folklorist, thoroughly familiar with several hundred folklore types and several thousand folklore motifs, has the competence necessary to distinguish folklore from history in scholarly historical accounts." [10]

Louis R. Gottschalk conceded that oral tradition, when utilized with proper caution, can supplement the efforts of the formal historian. He wrote that the legendary stories of William Tell, the imaginary hero of the Swiss war for independence, and Dr. Faustus, the sixteenth-century necromancer, "are good examples of folklore that may tell about the aspirations, superstitions, and customs of the peoples among whom the stories developed, provided the historian (or folklorist) is able to distinguish between the legendary embroideries and their authentic foundations." [11]

Despite occasional deviations from fact, Russian historical songs have been excellent sources of history when approached by the discerning scholar. Y. M. Sokolov described how the tendency of the people to idealize Ivan the Terrible led to a departure from historical truth in one of their songs. In the year 1581 Ivan the Terrible, in a fit of wrath, murdered his son Ivan, but in the historical song describing the incident, the anger of Ivan was vented on another son who had been accused of treachery. Other than this one radical departure from reality, Sokolov contended, the song preserved a great many of the real circumstances surrounding the event.[12]

Folklore as a Mirror of History. Allan Nevins, the founder of Columbia University's oral history program in 1948,[13] is among those who feel that folklore mirrors history, and he points out that folksongs and legends should be considered in the study of American history. After first challenging historians to record systematically the personal reminiscences "from the lips and papers of living Americans who have led significant lives," Nevins notes that "in our more recent history the legends of pioneer settlements, mining camps, lumbermen, and the cowboys of the western range, whether in prose or ballad, are by no means devoid of light upon social and cultural history." [14] Nevins advocates oral history as a means of documenting decisions in recent history that otherwise would be unrecorded. He uses oral testimonies narrated by members of the Ford family and household servants in *Ford: The Man, The Times, and The Company,* and praises their testimonies as "pure gold for the historian." [15] M. Gorky, an authority on Russian literature, also writes that the oral creations of the people provide excellent material for ascertaining the popular historical opinions on the

12 *Russian Folklore,* trans. by Catherine Ruth Smith (New York, 1950), 350–51, et passim. The basic historicity of the Russian historical songs has commanded the attention of Carl Stief, *Studies in the Russian Historical Song* (Kφbenhavn, 1953; New York, 1957).

13 The increasing popularity of both university and private oral history projects is especially pleasing to folklorists, for the private interview is thus recognized as the basic unit of transmission in oral history. And, again in the mold of the folklorist, the oral historian uses the same tools and methodologies in field collecting. Some typical methodological descriptions would include the following works: Elizabeth I. Dixon, "Oral History: A New Horizon," *Library Journal,* 87:7 (April 1, 1962), 1363–65; Charles T. Morrissey, "The Case for Oral History," *Vermont History,* XXI:3 (July 1963), 145–55; and Helen McCann White, "Thoughts on Oral History," *The American Archivist,* XX:1 (Jan. 1957), 19–30. Charles T. Morrissey's "Oral History and the Mythmakers," *Historic Preservation,* XVI:6 (Nov.–Dec. 1964), 232–37, contains a brief but workable bibliography of the subject.

14 *The Gateway to History* (Boston, 1938), iv, 66. Wyman D. Walker, "Western Folklore and History," *The American West,* I:1 (Winter, 1964), 45–51, noted the strong relationship between folklore and the history of the American West, especially in the beliefs held by the pioneers concerning water, weather, and animals and in their stories of Indian fighting and in the lore of miners, cowboys, and sheepherders.

15 Cited in Morrissey, "Case for Oral History," 151.

16 *On Literature*, cited in Sokolov, *Russian Folklore*, 347.

17 *Grass Roots History* (Minneapolis, 1947).

18 "The Folklorist as Social Historian," *Western Folklore*, XII:3 (July 1953), 194–201.

phenomena of history. "From remote antiquity," Gorky states, "folklore persistently and with originality attends upon history. It has its own opinion of the doings of Louis XI, of Ivan the Terrible, and this opinion differs sharply from the evaluation made by history, which is written by specialists who are not very much interested in the question of what the conflict between the monarchs and the feudal lords actually contributed to the life of the laboring people."[16]

Certain American historians have directed their efforts toward producing works that point out the need for genuine cultural histories as a background for historical syntheses. One historian holding this view is Theodore C. Blegen, who feels that in order to understand the American people, historians should utilize folk documents, such as letters and diaries, which are the genuine indicators of history. In the past, our failure to define the American culture has been caused by what Blegen called "inverted provincialism"—that is to say, historians have scorned the simple and steered clear of the near-at-hand.[17] Philip D. Jordan, another cultural historian, writes that unless social stimuli are investigated, the contributions of the common man to historical movements cannot be articulated. American history has been written, he continues, but the full story is not to be found by a study of population statistics and historical documents; such channels of research are available to anyone, but the folklorist can bring to the formal historian knowledge of deep-lying cultural patterns. Folklore grows out of the national experience, Jordan states, and an understanding of oral traditions would greatly contribute to those who wish more clearly to understand the historical narrative.[18]

Research Opportunities in American Cultural History, a collection of twelve essays, sounded the clarion call to historians. Leading cultural historians and folklorists pointed out that too much stress can be placed on our nation's political and religious institutions, thus jeopardizing consideration of the human element in history. A more rounded approach, the contributors felt, would be to focus attention on the people who lived during the major movements in American history. Among the more common words used throughout the book were "grass roots," "everyday life," and "folkways." [19]

Folk Tradition as Historical Fact. The fourth view, that "traditions often have a basis in historical fact," is supported by an article which appeared in the *Journal of American Folklore.* In reporting the investigations of a historical tradition among the Southern Paiute Indians of southern Utah, David M. Pendergast and Clement W. Meighan disclosed that casual comments made by the Paiute revealed history that was consistent with archaeological evidence some eight hundred years old.[20] The traditions, which dealt with a prehistoric people, the Puebloids, were specific and generally accurate concerning the Puebloids' economic institutions, physical appearance, material culture, and Paiute-Puebloid relationships. The authors concluded that "archaeologists in particular should explore the possibilities of correlating historical traditions with archaeological data, since the historical information may substantiate, and in some cases broaden, inferences based solely on archaeological materials." [21]

The Southern Paiute example of the persistency of oral traditions was one of many emphatic rejoinders against the anti-historical pronouncements of Lowie and others who held to his school of relentless dogmatism. Frederica de Laguna, for example, issued a strong

19 John F. McDermott, ed. (Lexington, Ky., 1961).

20 "Folk Traditions as Historical Fact: A Paiute Example," *Journal of American Folklore,* LXXII (April–June 1959).

21 *Ibid.,* 132.

22 "Geological Confirmation of Native Traditions, Yakutat, Alaska," *American Antiquity.* XXIII (1958), 434; also cited in Dorson, "The Debate," 23–24.

23 *Folklore as an Historical Science* (London, 1908). See especially Ch. 1, "History and Folklore," 1–122.

24 *The Heroic Age* (Cambridge, England, 1912). The comments about this work were drawn from Richard M. Dorson, *American Folklore* (Chicago, 1958), 209; the Chadwicks' three-volume study of *The Growth of Literature* is summarized by Dorson in "The Debate," 20–21.

positive statement in 1958, writing that when a 1957 geological survey team reported habitable periods of the Icy Yakutat Bay area, the team was thereby confirming by means of radiocarbon tests native traditions dating from 1400. De Laguna concluded by saying, "Other natives' statements about the stages in the retreat of the ice in the Yakutat Bay during the late 18th and 19th centuries are in complete accord with geological evidence." [22]

The English folklorist, George Laurence Gomme, approached the question of the validity of oral tradition with what can be termed the extreme approach. He asserted that every folk custom and belief has roots in a historical event.[23] Closely akin to this stand, but not as dogmatically so, were the positions taken by the Chadwicks and Knut Liestøl. Hector M. and Nora K. Chadwick totally differed with the Raglan thesis by maintaining that folk heroes are rooted in history. During the process of cultural evolution experienced by a people, there was a historical Heroic Age characterized by a semi-nomadic, warring, raiding type of existence. At this stage of phylogeny, a great hero rose up to assume the leadership of his people. In some instances, the hero's exploits then entered the printed page and were thus perpetuated, but prior to that a great deal of fiction had already crept into the oral recountal. The painstaking scholar can winnow the historical from the unhistorical elements in that event, and this was one of the tasks undertaken by the Chadwicks.[24] If, for some reason, the hero's feats did not reach print, then the legends about him devolved into a cycle of songs or tales carried on in oral tradition. But historical traditions, whether oral or written, are authentic records of history, and the recurrent thesis postulated by the Chadwicks looks upon many of the persons and events described in the Teutonic, British, and Irish Heroic Ages as historical actualities.

The folklorist Knut Liestøl studied the origin of the Icelandic sagas and persuasively argued that under favoring conditions oral history can preserve its core of reality over long periods of time.[25] By a close analysis of oral traditions that originated during the period 930 to 1030 and later were written down in the period from 1120 to 1230, he showed that oral traditions could serve as a form of record-keeping, distinct from written historical accounts. Liestøl tested the reliability of the episodes recorded in the sagas by (1) comparing variant examples of the same incident in different sagas, to ascertain the original content and form of the oral tradition; (2) analyzing stylistic devices of oral narration, to see which of the written pages reveal the marks of oral style; (3) evaluating the amount of recognizable folklore material in the sagas; and (4) assessing the social *milieu* and the common historical background from which the sagas stemmed. In a society of more advanced peoples unshaken by wanderings and uprootings, according to Liestøl, historical recollections and folklore elements mingle to a considerable extent, but these two channels can be positively identified. The more advanced peoples utilize oral traditional history as a form of historical record-keeping that is separate and distinct from written historical records. Students of history, Liestøl contended, should not apply the rules of evidence belonging to documentary history in their evaluation of oral history.[26]

This was virtually the same stand taken by many Folk-Lore Society members who could not agree with Hartland and Nutt. Lach-Szyrma felt that the basic historicity of oral traditions in the West of England could be ascribed to the selective process of folk mem-

25 *Origin of the Icelandic Family Sagas* (Oslo, 1930). Dorson presents a brief but succinct summary of Liestøl's work in "The Debate," 26–30.

26 Liestøl's persuasive arguments met with strong opposition in the analyses of Sigurdur Nordal, *The Historical Element in the Icelandic Family Sagas* (Glasgow, 1957), Peter Hallberg, *The Icelandic Saga*, trans. by Paul Schach (Lincoln, Neb., 1962), and Theodore M. Andersson, *The Problem of Icelandic Saga Origins* (New Haven, 1964).

27 W. S. Lach-Szyrma, "Folk-Lore Traditions of Historical Events," *Folk-Lore*, III (1881), 157–68; David MacRitchie, "The Historical Aspect of Folk-lore," in Joseph Jacobs and Alfred Nutt, eds., *The International Folk-Lore Congress 1891, Papers and Transactions* (London, 1892), 105–6; and John L. Myres, "Folkmemory," *Folk-Lore*, XXXVII (1926), 12–34, but especially p. 28.

ory; David MacRitchie pointed out that archaeological findings in Wigtownshire verified local traditions which claimed that a cave in the vicinity had been occupied fourteen centuries earlier by Saint Ninias; and John Myres gave much credence to folkmemory in such isolated, stable, homogeneous, and preliterate societies as the Icelandic and the Polynesian, where family, community, and even regional history were matters of practical concern and common knowledge.[27] When a people share a common historical experience, according to Myres, the events in this experience become a tenacious part of folkmemory and may be perpetuated for centuries.

THE NATURE OF ORAL TRADITIONS

Through the years the American continent has witnessed the birth and flowering of an immense body of local historical legends arising in response to actual occurrences, usually of a sensational nature. These traditions may vex the historian of the articulate classes, and he may continue to have nothing to do with something as elusive as folk tradition. Yet, no historian who is aware of the ways of the people on a local level, especially in rural areas where ties with the land are strong, will question the importance played by oral traditions in the lives of the people. Accuracy of local historical legends is not the most important question to be faced by the person who gathers and analyzes them, but rather the essential fact is that these folk narratives are believed by the people who perpetuate them. Even in the more literate societies, folklore records the joy, humor, pathos, and indestructible spirit of the local group. In the preface to their book on Mormon folklore, Austin and Alta Fife state that "we have sought the authenticity not of history but of folklore . . . . We have tried to view the materials less as historical data than as legend—not as they actually were, but as they have been viewed by the folk." [28]

Richard M. Dorson made a similar point in his concluding comments on the trustworthiness of oral traditional history. He noted that blanket judgments regarding the historicity of oral traditions should be avoided, and added, "It is not a matter of fact versus fiction so much as the social acceptance of traditional history." [29] And in another article Dorson astutely wrote, "If the event is historically false, it is psychologically true, and its incorporation into tribal histories is something for the American historian to note." [30]

Ethnohistorians specializing in African history have approached the idea of historical truth from a perspective which stresses a periodical or cyclical rhythm of eternal repetition within the life-cycle of the individual. They note a direct correlation between the time perspective recognized by the society and the social structure.[31] One ethnohistorian, Paul Bohannan, writes in "Concepts of Time Among the Tiv of Nigeria" that repetitive natural or social events recorded in Tiv myths and legends explain the social process, not the historical past. Specifically, he remarks that "The most common incidents all cluster about a standard situation which arises time and again in the dynamic Tiv social process: particularly fission and fusion of lineage territories, which are the modal points in Tiv political process." [32]

Jan Vansina, pursuing these ideas in a book-length historiographical outline on nonliterate African societies, examined in depth the processes and functions of oral traditions in African societies. He pointed out the contrast in attitudes toward historical knowledge displayed by societies even in the same culture area. Be-

28 *Saints of Sage and Saddle: Folklore Among the Mormons* (Bloomington, Ind., 1956), xi.

29 "The Debate," 34.

30 "Oral Tradition and Written History: The Case for the United States," *Journal of the Folklore Institute*, I:3 (Dec. 1964), 230.

31 See, e. g., Meyer Fortes, *The Dynamics of Clanship Among the Tallensi* (New York, 1945), xi. G. I. Jones, "Oral Tradition and History," *African Notes*, II:2 (Jan. 1965), 7–11, uses narratives from eastern Nigeria and, in particular, origin myths of the Kalabari of the eastern Delta to show how oral traditions change in response to different social requirements and attitudes.

32 *Southwestern Journal of Anthropology*, IX (1953), 260–61.

33 *Oral Tradition: A Study in Historical Methodology*, trans. by H. M. Wright (London, 1965), 170–71; also quoted by Dorson in "The Debate," 35.

34 The theme of a conference on oral history in Africa, held at Northwestern University in 1965, was methodology as attested by the papers published in the *African Studies Bulletin*, VIII: 2 (Sept. 1965) : Aristide R. Zolberg, "A Preliminary Guide for Interviews," 3–8; Jan Vansina, "The Documentary Interview," 8–14; Ronald Cohen, "Quantification," 16–19; and Raoul Naroul, "Data Quality Control," 19–23.

cause of a coherent political structure, the Rwanda were rich in family and local historical traditions, Vansina explained, but the Burundi were restricted in their oral communication because of an incohesive political framework. In conclusion Vansina stated, "Each type of society has in fact chosen to preserve the kind of historical traditions suited to its particular type of structure, and the historical information to be obtained by studying these traditions is restricted by the framework of reference constructed by the society in question." [33] Vansina's statement may well summarize the case for African ethnohistory.[34]

American folklorists, on the other hand, are concerned with a literate people who have produced bodies of oral traditional narratives which may reflect social conditions but certainly not reflect political organization. By utilizing methods of research peculiar to his discipline, the comparative folklorist can study these narratives in societal context and thus function as a cultural historian. In addition, he can come to the aid of the formal historian, whose analysis of statistical data and historical documents seldom permits conclusions regarding the ways of life on a local level.

In the interests of formal history, therefore, a summary of the history of the immediate area surrounding Coe Ridge is presented in the Prologue of *The Saga of Coe Ridge* as a complement to the oral traditions of the people themselves. Data for this summary are drawn almost exclusively from the federal census and from other sources which in turn were based on generalized data. The use of data, however, does not make it possible to take a personal approach to history—that is, to consider the people as a living force. This is the critical distinction between folk history and history written by orthodox methods of research.

Folk history, as applied in this book, can be defined as a body of oral traditional narratives that are told by a people about themselves, and, therefore, the narratives articulate the feelings of a group toward the events and persons described.[35] Folk attitudes are included as a part of this definition because they are an integral part of almost every narrative recorded from the informants. In this account of Coe Ridge, these attitudes occasionally become the primary consideration, for local history is often intricately tied with the subjectivity of the people.[36]

I am in great debt to the many persons whose cooperation and inspiration made this study possible. Foremost among these are my informants. They are recognized by name in Appendix A, but I feel that a special note of thanks is due for the trust and confidence they placed in me as steward of their priceless and time-honored oral traditions. Certain professors at Indiana University also deserve major credit for this book—Richard M. Dorson, Warren E. Roberts, Felix J. Oinas, Oscar E. Winther, and J. Fraser Hart. They steered me through my doctoral program which combined folklore, history, and geography and resulted in the dissertation that was the nucleus for this book.

I am especially grateful to Dr. Dorson, for it is primarily his teaching which points the way to the synthesis of history and folklore. It is this combination of methodologies that permits the narratives of oral tradition to be placed into meaningful linear context.

35 Benjamin A. Botkin, *Lay My Burden Down: A Folk History of Slavery* (Chicago, 1945), xiii, defines folk history as "history from the bottom up, in which the people become their own historians." From the study of folk history, Botkin contends, one is able to consider "the inarticulate many as well as the articulate few."

36 In Chapter 1, for example, it is demonstrated that oral tradition offers rich insight into Negro attitudes toward the insecure status on the plantation experienced by slave ancestors. Additionally, these narratives provide ample documentation of the socio-economic aspects of plantations located along the upper Cumberland River.

Contents

Illustrations

The Saga of Coe Ridge

Prologue:
Lost Pages of History

Like most legends, the story of Coe Ridge and its people has enough in common with history to give it credence, enough of fiction to give the historian pause, and enough of mystery to make anyone wonder where lies the truth.[1]

Coe Ridge Negroes once served as slaves to the white Coes in the valley along Kettle Creek, one of the numerous small streams in Monroe and Cumberland counties, Kentucky. After their emancipation following the Civil War, these refugees were put on Coe Ridge, a desolate spur amidst almost inaccessible ridges and sharply incised valleys. Here they were virtually ignored in physical and cultural isolation. Few links existed with the outside world, and these usually came as a result of brushes with the law or as the ridge residents sought to earn a few dollars. The colony soon became a mecca for the transient misfits, the outcasts of society.

Aside from physical isolation, the Coe Ridge Negroes

1 Quinn Pearl, "Legendary Coe Ridge," *Louisville Courier-Journal Magazine*, Dec. 12, 1954, p. 8.

were further isolated socially and culturally, set apart from the white communities within the general area of the ridge. The whites wanted no part of the outcasts or of their haven, demanding, in fact, the obliteration of the settlement. Because legal authorities also largely ignored the colony prior to 1930, fearing to ride horseback through the friendless stretch of countryside surrounding Coe Ridge, bootlegging and other criminal offenses committed by the Coe Negroes usually went unpunished. For their part, the Coes, a people governed by clan meetings under the direction of chosen leaders, surrendered a guilty member of their colony only at their will.

But with the coming of graded and improved roads in the 1930's, the physical and cultural isolation of the Coe colony was weakened, and within twenty years the settlement ceased to exist. The colony survived only as a product of its own time, favored by the conditions of poor communications and transportation typical of the entire surrounding area.

There is a paucity of historical documents relating to the Coe colony, for it has been historically associated with a three-county area of the upper South where few written records remain. In Cumberland and Monroe counties, Kentucky, and in Clay County, Tennessee, the usual newspaper files, court records, and other such sources normally utilized by historians are no longer extant. None of the pioneers of the area left personal accounts of day-to-day occurrences—at least no diaries or manuscripts of significant age have been recovered. In addition, this geographical area cannot boast of an early newspaper circulation like that of Mark Twain's Hannibal or other frontier towns of the early West.

But some statistical and generalized data do remain. Therefore, in the interests of formal history, this information is herewith presented as a complement to the oral traditions of the people themselves.

The first newspaper in this tri-county area began publication in Burkesville, Cumberland County, in 1870, as the *Cumberland Courier*. Burkesville has had a history of continuous newspaper publication since that date, but only scattered copies of the issues are extant prior to 1903. In the adjoining county of Monroe, *The Banner* came into existence in Tompkinsville in 1885. There, too, a newspaper has been published since that time, but a 1931 fire destroyed the old file copies.[2] In neighboring Clay County, Tennessee, numerous attempts to begin a newspaper have met with failure because of the lack of financial support from the public.

Court records of all three counties have been destroyed at least once since the Civil War. While Clay County was still a part of Jackson County, Tennessee, a band of Union guerrillas from southern Kentucky rode into Gainesboro, the county seat, and burned the courthouse. A retaliation raid was erroneously made against Monroe County, Kentucky, during 1863. The Confederate raiders crossed into Monroe County and moved up the Cumberland River to Turkey Neck Bend where they murdered the county court clerk, then rode on to Tompkinsville and set fire to the courthouse. Monroe County again lost its public records in 1888 when fire razed the new building.

Cumberland County had preserved intact its public heritage until the courthouse in Burkesville was destroyed by fire on December 30, 1933, just before a new group of elected officials took office. Some will and deed books and court records were saved, but everything else was lost in the blaze.

2 A brief history of newspaper publication in Burkesville can be found in the *Cumberland County News*, Aug. 18, 1960, Sec. B, p. 4. For a mention of early Tompkinsville papers, consult "Newspaper Service in Monroe Since 1885," *Tompkinsville News*, 50th Anniversary Ed., Aug. 28, 1954, Sec. 7, p. 1.

3 *The History of Cumberland County* (Louisville, 1947).

4 W. H. Perrin, J. H. Battle, and G. C. Kniffin, *Kentucky: A History of the State* (Louisville, 1886), 763–92. It is claimed (by some local people whose families are represented in the sketches) that someone came through their section of the county in the early 1880's gathering data on the family of anyone who would pay a deposit and agree to purchase a book when it was published.

5 Byrd Douglas, *Steamboatin' on the Cumberland* (Nashville, 1961).

PREVIOUS WRITINGS ABOUT THE AREA

In 1947 Judge J. W. Wells published *The History of Cumberland County*, a rather dry and somewhat incomplete history that utilized what remained of Cumberland County's early court records, plus statistical figures on file in Frankfort.[3] A portion of the gaps in coverage was supplemented by oral traditions, but Wells did not give credit to his oral sources. Another work, written by outsiders, contained a brief historical description of Monroe County, including a genealogical sketch of some of the early families. Information about each family was drawn from Bible records, tombstone inscriptions, family recollections, but, like the work of Wells, no attempt was made to distinguish the various sources.[4]

One other source book of local history blends oral tradition with documentary sources in a very commendable fashion. That work, *Steamboatin' on the Cumberland*,[5] draws heavily on the word of the people, listing two pages of informants with whom the author conferred during thirty-five years of research. As the title implies, however, the book concerns the entire Cumberland and contains only one chapter which is really pertinent to the upper Cumberland around Celina and Burkesville.

Beyond the works mentioned, everything else written about the tri-county area is based solely on oral tradition, thus being suitable for utilization in *The Saga of Coe Ridge* as corroborative material. The basic article found in this group is "Early Days of Monroe County," written in the 1920's by J. E. Leslie, editor of *The Tompkinsville News*. Leslie draws heavily from his own mental storehouse of traditional history.

Not one of the aforementioned writers gives consideration to the Coe Negro colony, except for Wells, who devotes one-half page at two different places in his book.[6] Seven newspaper sketches and feature stories, written by visiting newsmen and revenue men, have been published since 1932. All are based on oral tradition and tend to repeat the same episodes in the colony's history.[7] A portion of the Coe story has been included in the pageant, *Mine Eyes Have Seen the Glory,* written and produced at Burkesville in 1960 to commemorate the county's 150 years of existence.

The most important work dealing with Coe Ridge was written by Samuel Coe, a former member of the colony, in collaboration with a white man. Published in Kansas City, Kansas, in 1930, *The Chronicles of the Coe Colony* is based solely on the author's childhood recollections in the colony. The accounts recorded in Coe's book are extremely prejudiced against the white race. This present study draws heavily on the *Chronicles* by constantly citing it in footnotes as corroborative evidence. For the most part, oral traditions recently collected closely parallel those in the *Chronicles,* yet none of the informants had read that work.

ORAL NARRATIVES UTILIZED

Three groups of oral narratives provide the basis for this book. First, there is a slim number of tales whose parallels are recorded in the indexes prepared by Stith Thompson[8] or in recently published collections of folklore. Some local historical legends are true without qualification, but even then a degree of embellishment may be present. Historical fact can be virtually smothered by distorted and folkloristic elements in some extreme cases. When local folk history plus exaggeration entwines with universally told folktales and migratory

6 *Cumberland County,* 105–6, 363.
7 "Interesting History of the Coe Outlaws," *Glasgow Times,* Dec. 1, 1932; Howard Hardaway, "Coes of Cumberland Were Born to Fight," *Louisville Courier-Journal,* Jan. 28, 1940; "The Coe Clan of Pea Ridge," *Glasgow Times,* Feb. 29, 1940; Quinn Pearl, "Legendary Coe Ridge," *Louisville Courier-Journal Magazine,* Dec. 12, 1954; "Coe Ridge Gained Fame as Hideout of Moonshiners," *Cumberland County News,* Aug. 16, 1960; "Calvin Coe," *Burkesville Sesqui-Centennial* brochure, Aug. 13–20, 1960, p. 85.
8 *The Types of the Folktale* (Helsinki, 1961) and *Motif-Index of Folk-Literature* (Bloomington, Ind., 1956).

9 Dorson, "Oral Tradition and Written History," 228, cites an excellent example of a book from Michigan's Upper Peninsula which publishes as fact numerous anecdotes and folktales that have been identified in the Thompson and Baughman indexes by Dorson.

legends, only a trained folklorist with a background in American civilization can unravel the various threads. If folk narratives can be identified, then regular folktales can be distinguished from local historical legends, thus permitting the latter to be utilized by the folk historian on a more rational basis.[9] In cases where historical narrative has been determined to be, in reality, a bit of universal folklore with a local flavoring, it has been utilized herein as a portion of the chronological sequence, but its folkloristic aspects have been indicated in a footnote. Such a manner of presentation permits attention to be focused on the interaction of folktales and local history.

The tales included in the second group contain a basic narrative element which resembles a motif and gives the stories cohesiveness, yet the tales have no exact recorded parallels in Southern Negro tradition. These narratives, totally dependent on the spoken rather than the written word and strongly bound by racial solidarity, perpetuate oral accounts of sufferings and triumphs and occasional bits of humor. Physical feats and cunning are constant themes found in these tales, which are concerned mainly with the moonshiner versus the revenue man, and with logging activities. An example from the moonshiner-revenuer cycle tells of a Negro youth who outraced an automobile containing revenue men and reached the Coe colony in time to warn the Negro moonshiners. In the logging cycle is found a narrative about a Negro man who held up one end of a wagon loaded with logs while others replaced a broken wheel. Such tales, always told for the truth, are documented, when possible, through the use of the indexes by Thompson.

The third class of oral narratives in this book is composed of local historical legends and makes up the bulk of the materials collected. Portions of each legend were known by most informants but always in varying detail. Presentation of these legends is based on the method of collation described by Richard M. Dorson:

> For a local legend, which has various shapes and fragments lodged in the minds of the townspeople, the collector may have to ask several leading questions, much in the form of an interview, and piece the data together into a connected whole, after he has queried many people in order to establish the group knowledge of the *Sage*.[10]

The local historical legends gathered from the descendants and friends of the white Coe family provided valuable information for *The Saga of Coe Ridge* because these traditional accounts contained some genealogical history which identified the early Coes. Further, this association with specific people gave vitality and force to family recollections that otherwise might have been lost. Genealogically oriented narratives apparently owe their continuous existence to the fact that they are not only accounts of unique incidents, but also accounts centered upon personalities whose identities are important to the narrator. Without this personal association the narratives have no real meaning. Although family history is generally restricted to family circles, these tales occasionally do enter community traditions.

Surprisingly, the Negro informants, who were queried about the genealogy of the white Coe family, knew little about that phase of their ancestral history. They recalled hearing, however, that the master's name was John Coe and that his wife was extremely kind and considerate to the slave children, but her first name was never mentioned during the Negro interviews. But even though the Negroes did not remember names of the white Coes, they did know their own genealogy and

10 *Bloodstoppers and Bearwalkers: Folk Traditions of the Upper Peninsula* (Cambridge, Mass., 1952), 5.

could recall specific physical characteristics of their early ancestors.

Strangely enough, the white Coes appear to remember the earlier Negro generations much better than those of their own family. Perhaps this was partly because human memories are genealogically focused on unusual events that stand apart from the routine of everyday life. For example, Charlie Coe, a descendant of the white plantation owners, could vividly recall Aunt Mime, an old Negro woman who was once a slave on his grandfather's plantation. As a young lad, Coe used to play with Mime's daughter at her cabin, usually cooking things in tin cans placed on a foundation of field rocks. It was the tin can episode that allowed Coe to bring Aunt Mime into mental focus when her name was brought up for discussion. Personal association with the former slaves by some of the older informants was another reason the Negro families were recalled. For the most part, however, the informants were from three to five generations removed from that of the slaves. Still another factor which aids in genealogical reconstruction is the desire by some individuals to see the early history of their family preserved in the minds of their descendants. Uncle Calvin Coe, once a clan leader in the Coe Negro colony, pleaded with his daughter to listen to him tell about the family's early generations. "Sissy," he would beg, "you mustn't forget what I tell you; some day you'll want to know these things."

Uncle Calvin's interest in preserving the history of his clan has provided what is perhaps the only existing statement relevant to the slave generations in North Carolina, who never lived to make the trek to Kentucky. The clan leader's undisputed wit and intelligence add weight to the validity of his recollections. Further, his genealogical traditions are strengthened by the scarcity of information known by the other informants who were contacted, and his recollections are in agreement with earlier corroborative sources that were available. Without Uncle Cal's statements, particularly his explanation concerning the origin of the Negro-Indian-white blood mixture evident in the present generations, a portion of the Coe colony's history would pass unexplained into the annals of time.

THIS VOLUME

Because of the absence of historical records, it has not been possible, for the most part, to parallel the oral accounts with written sources that describe the same episode. In the few instances where printed sources were available, the correlation between oral and written history has been indicated, sometimes in juxtaposition but generally in footnotes. Gaps in historical coverage are evident in this study. No attempts have been made to force conclusions when these were not forthcoming from the lips of narrators or from corroborative sources.

Such matters as tale structure and styles of narration are outside the scope of this volume. Other *genres* of folklore, such as beliefs, songs, and customs, are also not considered, except when they directly relate to legend. For example, one local historical event is used because it blossomed into ballad as well as legend, and in another instance the story of the drowning of a Negro man is repeated to reflect the belief that a drowned person's body will surface in nine days. Belief tales such as these, plus the actual historical events which gave rise to them, are utilized here inasmuch as both of them constitute a considerable portion of the folk history of the Coe colony.

Each of the seven chapters that follow represents a major phase of the social and economic life of Coe Ridge, beginning with its *raison d'être*. The ultimate task has been to depict the life and death of the Coe settlement, beginning in the days when its occupants were slaves on a nearby plantation and ending in the late 1950's when the colony finally succumbed to economic pressures.

The accounts utilized were gathered over a four-year span, beginning in 1961. The bulk of the materials was obtained by tape recorder, but numerous additional visits were made to record the traditions with a pencil and pad. Some telephone calls were placed when a random bit of information was needed. So that a prejudiced view of the colony's history would not be recorded, both Negroes and whites were visited and asked the same leading questions, which had been formulated previously after a reading of the available literature on the Coe settlement. The historical traditions related by both Negroes and whites varied little in basic detail, a factor which greatly enhances the validity of these oral recollections. Since the interviews were structured through the use of leading questions, the oral responses usually assumed the form of texts. It was thus possible to utilize them in this study as historical documents.

The oral accounts have been faithfully preserved in the same form in which they were collected from the people. Their words at all times have been transcribed as they sounded to this writer's ear. Although the reader may occasionally find it difficult to discern the words or word clusters reproduced on paper, any other manner of transcription would detract from the folk quality of the texts. Thus, for example, "was" becomes "wuz," "it would have been" sounds like "it'd a-been," and "just" is reproduced as "jist" and "dist." Informants may utter the word "just" in all three mentioned forms during one brief narration.

Throughout the course of gathering these historical traditions for half a decade, care was taken by the collector to treat the informants with respect during the interviews and to leave them with collector-informant rapport firmly established. There was never any hesitation or fear of returning on additional visits in order to secure needed bits of information. We were working together as a team, as it were, in order to preserve for the generations to come a bit of the area's history which otherwise might one day be erased from the memories of the local people.

Some of the recollections shared by the informants were candid concerning certain people and events included in this book. Complete informant identity has been withheld in connection with certain statements if a knowledge of the authorships of such statements might tend to strain relations between the informant and the persons mentioned in the narratives. The informant in question is thus identified, for example, as a merchant in the Judio community, rather than by his actual name.

The writer was not primarily concerned with sensational matters in human relations discovered during the period of research, but on the other hand he had no disposition to gloss over the personal reputations of the persons described, whether black or white. One cannot do a study to demonstrate that oral statements may be adequate for historical writing without acquiring an intimate knowledge of his subjects. But rather than cause possible embarrassment to the persons involved, the writer chose to use fictitious names in certain instances. Such changes are indicated by footnotes. The pseudonyms have replaced the real names even within

11 Comments in this paragraph are based on information derived from a study of the Black's Ferry Quadrangle of the Kentucky Topographic Series, published in 1954 by the United States Department of the Interior, Geological Survey.

the quotations from informants so as to retain continuity of the historical narrative. This action does not detract substantially from the historical value of the book, yet indicates that the writer is in no way desirous of invading the privacy of the persons involved.

PHYSICAL AND CULTURAL ANTECEDENTS OF COE RIDGE

The near absence of written records or accounts of the activities of Coe Ridge was not the only reason for its anomalous exclusion from historical annals. Its very isolation in the southern mountains of Kentucky further condemned it to become a "lost page of history." As a minor topographic feature of the Cumberland Plateau, Coe Ridge is in the transitional zone of southcentral Kentucky, where the mountains to the east give way to a broad belt of hills and ridges. More precisely, the ridge is situated one mile east of the Cumberland River in the isolated southern portion of Cumberland County, eight miles south of Burkesville, the county seat. With the exception of the nearby river bottoms, much of the area on and adjoining Coe Ridge is composed of critically dissected terrain, characterized by sharply incised valleys and almost inaccessible ridges. Relative relief in this area varies greatly even within small portions of the landscape. Topography on Coe Ridge has an average relief of 240 to 300 feet, but in some nearby communities these figures exceed 500 feet, especially around Ashlock on the Tennessee line, and at Stalcup, two miles north of Coe Ridge.[11]

Geologically, Coe Ridge is a western spur of Pea Ridge, a dominant structure which takes shape in the Highland Rim portion of adjoining Clay County, Tennessee, and moves across the Kentucky state line into the

Coe Ridge in geographical focus.

14

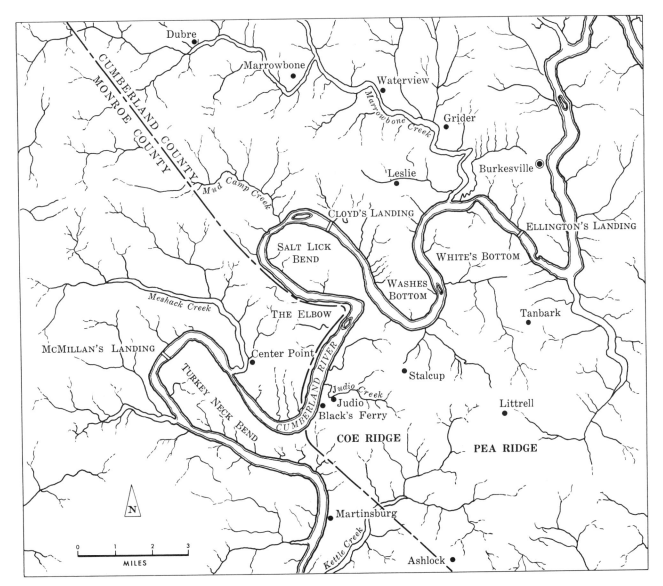

The Cumberland River as it winds through Monroe and Cumberland counties, Kentucky.

12 The Highland Rim, the name given to the lower plateau on Mississippian rocks at the foot of the Cumberland Plateau, surrounds the Nashville Basin; for more detail, consult Nevin M. Fenneman, *Physiography of Eastern United States* (New York, 1938), 415–16. An excellent study of the Eastern Pennyroyal can be found in Carl Ortwin Sauer's *Geography of the Kentucky Pennyroyal* (Frankfort, Ky., 1927).

13 Kentucky Conservation Needs Committee, *Kentucky Soil and Water: Conservation Needs Inventory* (Frankfort, Ky., July, 1962), 127. See also "Land Areas of Kentucky and Their Potential for Use," a land classification map published by the Agricultural and Development Board of Kentucky, Frankfort, 1953.

14 See, for example, the map in Frederic B. Loomis, *Physiography of the United States* (New York, 1938), 183.

Eastern Pennyroyal region of Cumberland County.[12] This section of Kentucky and Tennessee comprises the marginal zone between the Highland Rim and the Eastern Pennyroyal. While these geological provinces are clearly distinguishable elsewhere, their general features are identical in the area under consideration, and only the political state line divides one province from the other. Soils in the area have continuing limitations that cannot be corrected, such as steep slope, severe erosion hazard and effects of past erosion, shallow rooting zone, and low-moisture capacity. The uses of the soils are limited largely to pasture, woodland, or wildlife food and cover.[13]

Because of the homogeneous aspects of the physical landscape, it is the Cumberland River that dominates the topography of the area. The river flows in great loops in a southwesterly course across Cumberland County, then passes through eastern Monroe County before disappearing into Clay County, Tennessee. Erosional action of the river has cut down through the rock strata to the limestone beds of low resistance, the same formations from which the Nashville and Blue Grass basins were formed. Incidentally, the river and its larger tributaries are at work extending the Nashville Basin upstream, and already some geologists classify the Cumberland River flood plains as far north as Burkesville, Kentucky, as an extension of the Nashville Basin.[14] The flood plains are suited to a wide range of plants and wildlife, and may be used safely for cultivated crops or for pastures and woodlands. The soils are nearly level and erosion hazard is low. Moreover, the soils are deep, generally well drained, and easily worked. Along Kettle Creek, where the older Coe Ridge Negroes once served as slaves, the soils have gentle

The birthplace of the Coe legend is an area of rugged terrain, isolating the ridge inhabitants both physically and culturally.

15 *Kentucky Soil and Water*, 123–24, et passim.

slopes, and thus are moderately susceptible to water erosion.[15]

Smaller streams empty into the Cumberland all along its route, but the river's tributary pattern is dominated by larger creeks which receive the smaller ones as they drain from the fluvial divides. Coe Ridge forms the divide between the Judio and Kettle Creek systems, and provides numerous headstreams for these two creeks. The stream pattern on Coe Ridge, accompanied by severe sheet and gully erosion, raises the question as to how the ridge soils supported the Coe Negro colony for almost a century. There is not a level field on the entire ridge, and the eroded lands do not appear capable of crop production in their present state. The logical answer is that the colony's continued existence, after the timber resources had been exhausted, was dependent on the presence of numerous headstreams flowing from the ridge. These streams provided the water necessary to maintain the many moonshine stills operated by the ridge inhabitants. Without these streams the colony would have ceased to exist long before it did.

Settlement Along the Cumberland. During the early years of settlement in Cumberland, Monroe, and Clay counties, the Cumberland River served as the only transportation link with the outside world. This particular geographical area was peculiarly adapted to steamboat transportation. In fact, this method, along with flatboats, remained the only practical one available for almost a century. During the pioneer years there were very few, if any, land routes capable of handling heavy loads or connecting the scattered river communities with a market. This area remained one of the last frontiers in the eastern portion of the United

States, unexcelled in natural beauty and unadorned by modern improvements. Railroads never attempted to conquer the deep ravines and endless hills in this portion of the upper South, where the steamboats found hidden wealth along the banks of the river.

The commercial and cultural significance of the steamboat era lasted until the late 1920's, at which time the arrival of motor trucks caused the disappearance of river boats. The trucks could traverse and conquer most of the rugged terrain, especially when modern highways were finally built in the territory in the 1930's. Before the packets left, however, they had established a record of continuous service for a century, and had annually hauled to market products whose value totaled thousands and thousands of dollars. With the passing of the steamboat, the curtain was closed on the pioneer phase of upper Cumberland history.[16]

Notwithstanding its unifying role in the economy and culture of these three counties, the Cumberland River was the chief factor in a cultural cleavage among the white people of the area, the effects of which have carried over to the present. This cultural dichotomy can be traced back to the days of pioneer settlement, although it took the Civil War to reveal the pattern clearly. The fertile lands along the river were attractive to the earliest white settlers from Virginia, North Carolina, and East Tennessee. Pioneers from these states moved into the great loops of the river where, with slave labor, they engaged in farming practices that could not be approximated by the farmers who moved into the upland areas a few years later. Since the first settlers took up all the choice lands, the farmers who came later had to go inland from the river and establish

16 The steamer *Celina*, in 1929, was the last boat to go up river as far as Burkesville. For additional information, see "Steamboats Played Important Part in History of City of Burkesville," *Cumberland County News*, Sec. B, p. 1, Aug. 18, 1960. Douglas, *Steamboatin' on the Cumberland*, devotes a chapter to the decline and passing of the steamboat on that river; see "Packets Leave the Cumberland," 247–82.

17 *The Population of the United States in 1860, Eighth Census* (Washington, D.C., 1864), 229.
18 Oral traditions bear out the effect of geography in terms of Monroe County slaveholding. In collecting local historical traditions from every section of Monroe County, this writer found that a mention of the Civil War in most communities removed from the river generally produced stories about military musters and guerrilla foraging parties, and a mention of the war in the river country brought stories about slaves and closely related topics.

homes on or between a series of ridges which, even today, are practically inaccessible.

Slaveholding in Cumberland, Monroe, and Clay counties multiplied over the years preceding the Civil War. Statistics for Monroe County, from 1820 to 1860, reveal a proportion of slaves to total population that may be applied generally to the three-county area during that period.

POPULATION FOR MONROE COUNTY, KENTUCKY

	1820	1830	1840	1850	1860	1870
Whites	4,453	4,690	5,811	6,902	7,612	8,442
Slaves	498	645	703	831	922	0
Free Colored	5	5	12	23	17	789
Totals	4,956	5,340	6,526	7,756	8,551	9,231

Abstracted from *The Statistics of the Population of the United States . . . Compiled from the Original Returns of the Ninth Census, June 1, 1870* (Washington, D. C., 1872), I, 31–32.

In 1860 there were 191 slaveholders in Monroe County, but fifty-seven of them owned only one slave. The majority of slaveholders possessed from two to ten Negro servants, although one man owned between forty and fifty, and another between fifty and seventy.[17] Most of the slaves in Monroe County were located in the vicinity of the Cumberland River, where the richness of the soil attracted the original settlers. Although the soils in northcentral Monroe County are also good, being among the best in the county except for the river bottoms, only three of the 191 slaveholders in 1860 lived in that portion, an area consisting of approximately ten miles square.[18]

A cleavage developed between the settlers who came first, choosing the rich river bottoms, and the latecomers who were forced to seek land inland, a division

The rich river bottom land in Turkey Neck Bend was grabbed by the first white settlers.

19   James Simmons, a Civil War authority from nearby Glasgow, Ky., stated that although Monroe County had only 654 men enrolled in the militia, it furnished approximately 1,200 soldiers for the Union cause. Records do not permit an exact count, but it appears that Monroe County supplied no more than thirty men to the Confederate Army. That figure would probably increase in Cumberland and Clay counties, especially in Clay which was a hotbed of Southern sympathy.

20   "Those things" probably refers to the intensity of guerrilla activities throughout the area during the war years.

that was emphasized by the Civil War. The river farmers fought for the Confederacy, while those who lived in other portions of the county entered the ranks of the Union Army, although a few of the latter did own slaves.[19] This loyalty cleavage was also painfully expressed in the history of the Coe Negro colony. In fact, Civil War animosities were a chief factor in the feud which erupted in 1888 between the Coe Negroes and local white men. Today, the rift among the whites of the area is still expressed on voting days. Monroe and Cumberland counties are predominantly Republican in political sentiment, except in the river precincts where the Democrats form a majority. The following commentary by Tim Coe, a grandson of slaveowners, illustrates the nature of local political sentiment:

> You know, they's lots of people still fighting the Civil War today. I see it right down here at election. People have not forgotten those things[20] that happened to their folks back there. And that is why some people vote the way they vote today—both sides, Democrats and Republicans. I told a Republican at the election down there one day, I told him, "I guess if we would own it, we're both still fighting the Civil War." And he laughed and said, "I guess you are right."

The historic communities mentioned frequently in this study are those found mainly along the river between Celina, Tennessee, and Burkesville, Kentucky. Celina is located at the mouth of the Obey River, the largest navigable tributary of the upper Cumberland, somewhat back from the junction of the two streams. Historically, this proud town was in the commercial heart of the area's hardwood timber belt and contributed greatly to the prosperity of steamboats on the upper Cumberland. In addition, Celina generally served as the river landing for the Tennessee back country consisting of Jamestown, county seat of Fentress County, and Byrdstown, county seat of Pickett County, a fact which substantially enhanced the commercial significance of Celina.

Around 1900 there were four principal river landings between Celina and Burkesville, all of which figured prominently in Coe Ridge's history. Going upstream, these were, in order, Martinsburg, McMillan's Landing, Black's Ferry, all in Monroe County, and Cloyd's Landing in Cumberland County. Martinsburg, founded about 1800, had blossomed into a sizable village by 1850 with about thirty houses, two or more stores, a grist mill, and some warehouses. Although surrounded by the Martinsburg Hills, this community was able to serve a hinterland of some ten miles to the east by means of the Martinsburg Gap, a narrow pass through the hills which provided access to the river for the communities located on Pea Ridge and more distant areas.

McMillan's Landing became one of the choice steamboat landings on the upper Cumberland. Located on the west bank of the river, it frequently surpassed all other landings, especially in the shipment of corn, hogs, and tobacco. Along with Black's Ferry, McMillan's Landing served Tompkinsville, the county seat of Monroe County, plus other communities more removed from the river. Cloyd's Landing, along with Burkesville, served much of Cumberland County, and was significant for early timber shipments.

At one time, ferry boats crossed the Cumberland River at several points between Burkesville and Celina. Today, only McMillan's Landing in Monroe County has a ferry still in operation. When other ferries were discontinued, bridges were not constructed to replace them. Thus, these river communities, once proud centers of local commerce, are now more isolated than ever. Elling-

During the early years of the clan settlement, the Cumberland River served as the only link with the outside world. Shown here is McMillan's Landing on the river.

ton's Landing, for example, was only seven miles from Burkesville via ferry; now it is fourteen miles away since it is necessary to travel over the newly constructed gravel road which intersects Kentucky 61, the main artery from Burkesville to Celina.

Other local communities, especially those removed from the river, are occasionally referred to in this study, but the history of the Coe Ridge colony is not intimately associated with them. Two possible exceptions would be Center Point, located on Meshack Creek about one-half mile from the river, and Leslie, a community located on the fluvial divide between Mud Camp and Marrowbone creeks. Exact locations of all the places mentioned, in relation to their proximity to Coe Ridge, can be seen in Map 2.

Kentucky 61, which follows the crest of Pea Ridge, bridged the Cumberland in 1961 in hopes of "getting the obscure sections of the county out of the mud." [21] Parallel with the west bank of the river, but about two miles away from the stream, Kentucky 100 dissects the rugged Meshack Hills to connect Burkesville and Tompkinsville. But like Kentucky 61, this road misses the river communities, leaving them in an isolated position. Some of the roads branching off these two state highways are sufficient and passable on a year-round basis. But especially in the upland areas, roads are barely traversable most of the time. They generally follow the courses of least resistance, such as ridge crests and creek beds. The road from Red Bank across Coe Ridge to Kettle Creek is impassable by automobile except during the hot summer months when the road dries quickly after rains. In the early 1950's, this road was graded and stoned with creek gravel by the Cumberland County road crew. Because of the heavy outmigration, there were virtually no occupants in the Coe colony by the late

21 *Cumberland County News*, Sec. A, p. 1, Aug. 16, 1960.

1950's; thus, the road was neglected and once again mud holes and rock ledges formed by limestone outcroppings are characteristic sights all along its route.

1 *Mahster Coe's Plantation*

"Now you can find in there that one of my great, great, great, I don't know just exactly how far back it was, come in there from England and settled in Surry County, North Carolina." So runs the recollection of Tim Coe, a descendant of the white Coes, who lives near the original family homestead on Kettle Creek in Monroe County, Kentucky. Although correct about the country of family origin, Coe incorrectly stated that his ancestor first settled in North Carolina. Virginia was the first American home of the white Coes, for Timothy Coe I settled in Accomac County between 1642 and 1652.[1] His four children had to leave Virginia because of their Quaker faith, and during the late years of the seventeenth century they were living in what is now Sussex County, Delaware. Timothy Coe III was born there in 1715, but migrated southward to Rowan County, North Carolina, where he died in 1763. Three years earlier a

[1] The genealogy of the white family which figured so prominently in the history of the Negro Coes is easier to trace than that of their slaves. Descendants of Timothy Coe married into other local families, whose slaves, after manumission, married some of the Coe slaves. Such intermarriages created problems of identification, for the Negroes took the family names of their former white masters and usually named children for them.

2 Only the date is missing from the testimonies of Tim Coe and his brother Charlie concerning the birthplace of their great-grandfather. Thus, the white Coe genealogy can be traced rather easily through family traditions and recorded history. Both of these channels of history, however, have criss-crossed so many times that it is difficult to tell the specific source at any given time. The two brief published sketches of the Coe family by Wells and Perrin are based on documentary sources and oral family traditions. Mrs. Howard Peden of Glasgow, Ky., a white Coe descendant now compiling a history of that family, has done considerable research for recording the criss-crossing of oral and written history. Some of her genealogical findings, therefore, are incorporated in *The Saga of Coe Ridge* to supplement gaps in documentary coverage and in my own investigations. During the course of her research for local traditions, she passed along recently discovered facts to Coe family members, and they in turn fed some of that information into tape recordings made in preparing for this study. For information concerning the early years of John Coe, consult the Peden ms; Wells, *Cumberland County*, 363; and Perrin, *Kentucky*, 768.

3 Dates of the Jackson County sojourn are recorded in Wells, *Cumberland County*, 363, and in Perrin, *Kentucky*, 768. Mrs. Sarah Coe Tooley is a former member of the Coe Ridge colony. Charlie Coe asked to go along when the writer interviewed Mrs. Tooley during Aug. 1961.

4 Information was obtained from Tim Coe, Aug. 1961. Corroborative data based on tombstone inscriptions are given in the Peden manuscript.

son, Isaiah, was also born in North Carolina, but in Surry County in the famed Yadkin River country of the northwestern section of the state. There he married, became the father of three sons, and the owner of four hundred acres of land. He died in 1836 at the age of seventy-six, and was buried in the county of his birth.

John Coe, one of Isaiah's sons, was to become the great-grandfather of the informant Tim Coe. John Coe was born in 1784, in Surry County.[2] Like countless other frontiersmen from that area, he migrated westward across the valleys and plateaus of East Tennessee to the Cumberland River country of northern Tennessee and southern Kentucky. In 1809 he moved to the hill country of Jackson (now Clay) County, Tennessee, and remained there until harvest time in 1811. The dates of John Coe's migration were not known orally by the present generations, but they did know of his brief sojourn in Jackson County. "They come out of Tennessee," commented Sarah Coe Tooley, a Negro descendant of the slaves who accompanied John Coe from North Carolina. Present at the same interview, Charlie Coe (white) immediately added, "Yessir, first come to Tennessee and then they moved up into Cumberland County." [3]

When he moved to Cumberland County, Kentucky, John Coe settled on Kettle Creek, on a site located about one mile east of the Cumberland River. A portion of the Coe lands was included within the bounds of Monroe County when it was carved from Cumberland and Barren counties in 1820. Coe died in 1854 at the age of seventy and was interred in the family cemetery, located near the house he had built on the Kettle Creek homestead. Four years later, his wife was placed at his side.[4] John Coe was a man held in high esteem by his friends and neighbors; for approximately thirty-five years, he served Cumberland County as high sheriff and magistrate and also served in other public offices.[5]

About 1806, John had married Nancy Scott of Surry County, North Carolina,[6] and they had three children—a son whose name is unknown, Fanny, and Mary ("Polly")—prior to their move to Jackson County, Tennessee. A second son, Jesse, was born during the sojourn in Jackson County. Three additional children—Jemima, John Jefferson, and Malinda—were born after John and Nancy settled in Cumberland County, Kentucky. One year prior to his death, John Coe made his final will, which mentioned the last six children by describing their inheritance and calling them by their married names. These names were also known orally to the present generations.[7] Fanny Coe, the first daughter, married a Poindexter of Kentucky birth. The will indicated that she died before 1858, leaving seven children who were also remembered in their grandfather's will. Polly married Elisha Deweese of Cumberland County and, like Fanny, preceded her father in death. By 1858, Malinda had become Mrs. Bill Short, and Jemima, Mrs. William D. Spearman. Both of their husbands were from the Kettle Creek area. The will specified that money was to go to the children of Fanny and Polly, while Malinda Short was to receive 150 acres of land and a Negro girl. Jemima was to receive three slaves—a Negro man, a Negro woman, and a Negro girl. Jesse was to get two Negro boys and a Negro man, and "Mahster" John Coe's will also left John Jefferson a Negro woman and two Negro boys.[8] John Coe's wife, Nancy, was to get the remaining portion of the old plantation for as long as she lived, and he explicitly stated that "she is not to want for anything." In 1900, the will went on,

5 Tim and Charlie Coe knew something of their great-grandfather's public life, but did not recall the dates when he served in office. The corroborative sources are in conflict about the length of his term as sheriff. Wells, *Cumberland County*, 363, claims that he served two years, while Perrin, *Kentucky*, 768, states four years.

6 None of the informants knew the name of Coe's wife, but after consulting various documentary sources, Mrs. Peden determined that her name was Nancy, a daughter of Jesse Scott of Surry County. Scott apparently accompanied John Coe from North Carolina to Kentucky. Their dates of migration coincide, and documentary sources, plus oral testimonies, claim that the Scotts as well as the Coes located on the waters of Kettle Creek.

7 None of the descendants could recall the name of John and Nancy's first son, who probably died at an early age, but other names were remembered by Tim and Charlie Coe. From that generation forward, these two informants could easily recall the names of spouses and list the children of each marriage. Other white Coes also recall the names of the children of the John Coes, but most frequently mention Jesse and Malinda. Jesse, the oldest of John's living sons and perhaps the best remembered of the seven children, carried on the plantation tradition of his father until the slaves were manumitted in 1865. Malinda is remembered today for her marriage to William "Bill" Short, for this union made her the stepmother of Beanie Short, a Confederate guerrilla who became a legend along the upper Cumberland. Moreover, Malinda's marriage tied her closely to the Short and Taylor families who were the chief forces in the attempts to put an end to the Coe Ridge colony.

8 Although his slaves passed into the hands of his children, John Coe is the "Mahster" referred to by the Negro informants contacted during the course of collecting materials for this study. Rare exceptions find the son Jesse referred to in that capacity.

The word "master" was generally pronounced "mahster" by the informants. On one occasion,

Aunt Kate Tooley, a Negro informant, used the form which sounds like "marster." "Marse" was used once by Leslie Coe, Jr., one of the Negroes born in the colony; my father, Willie Montell, stated that "massa" was used by the older Negroes of central Monroe County, Kentucky, and Dr. Gordon Wilson, professor emeritus at Western Kentucky University, told that in his home county of Calloway in the Purchase area of western Kentucky all four of the above forms were spoken by Negroes. It would appear that there is no uniformity of pronunciation, even within small geographical areas.

9 Both Charlie and Tim Coe knew of the family's racing tradition; I discussed it with them during my first interviews in Aug. 1961, and again later with Charlie on July 22, 1963, and with Tim on Dec. 8, 1963.

10 Information about Jesse's wife was provided by Charlie Coe, July 22, 1963.

11 Their names were Isaiah, 16, Milton, 14, John Jefferson, 12, Margaret, 10, Nancy, 8, Ben, 4, and Jesse, 1. These names were known by Charlie and Tim Coe, but it was necessary to obtain the ages from the federal census of 1850, which verified the names given by the informants.

12 Charlie Coe provided this information on July 22, 1963; the Peden manuscript corroborates the account.

Jesse and Caroline were buried on Kettle Creek on lands then belonging to them, but now called the Squire Logan place after their son-in-law.

13 For the most part, the traditional stories told about the Coe store at Martinsburg omit mention of the owner's name, referring simply to the name of the community in connection with the occurrence of certain events there.

those lands left to her were to be sold, and the proceeds divided among the descendants of Jesse, John Jefferson, Jemima, and Malinda.

Jesse was very fond of race horses, and shared that love with his father. Together they built a racetrack, still known as the "Racetrack Field," on the eastern edge of the Coe plantation at the foot of Pea Ridge. Some of the finest racing stock found in the area was brought to the Coe plantation where exciting races were held, usually on Sunday afternoons. Jesse would frequently take his horses to races held on Obey River, north of Celina.[9]

While in Lexington, Kentucky, about 1830, in quest of racing stock, Jesse met and later married Caroline Murley, a beautiful twenty-year-old Virginia girl who was then from Fayette County, Kentucky.[10] Caroline became a devoted wife and mother who showered constant attention upon her husband and seven children.[11] One instance of her affection for her children was demonstrated during the Civil War when one of her sons, Isaiah, fought for the Confederacy. During the Battle of Nashville, Isaiah was injured and placed in a hospital; his mother, hearing that he had been wounded, rode horseback from Kettle Creek to Nashville to see him, a distance each way of approximately ninety-five miles. One final tribute was accorded to her husband after his death on February 28, 1899, for she died one day later.[12]

John Jefferson Coe, another son of Jesse and Caroline, was a merchant at nearby Martinsburg for many years. His milling center and general store were the late nineteenth-century focal points for the commerce of the Coe Ridge Negroes, who frequented this river-landing community in quest of river employment as well as to buy groceries and staples.[13]

The fourth son, Benjamin Franklin Coe, was born in

1846. At the age of twenty-seven, Ben married Martha Smith, the twenty-two-year-old daughter of Sperry and Nancy Moore Smith.[14] Before the Civil War, Sperry Smith was one of the most prominent slaveholders in Turkey Neck Bend, according to Coe tradition.[15] Smith's wife had a sister, name unknown, who married into the white Andrews family of local history fame. This Andrews family owned a group of slaves who assumed the family name after manumission[16] and who then married into the Coe Negro clan on Coe Ridge. In addition to the intermarriage of families that had previously owned some of the Coe Ridge progenitors, Mrs. Andrews and Mrs. Smith had a brother who held a portion of the Coe slaves at the time the Civil War erupted.[17] He was Dr. Samuel Moore, a general physician whose office was located at Black's Ferry in Monroe County. Moore's nephew, Charlie Coe, told the following story about one of the slaves who was studying medicine under Moore:

> There's a little story about Dr. Moore and a Nigger boy he had working with him, you might like to hear. Dr. Moore, he was an old-timey pilldoctor that lived in that old house up here at Black's Ferry. And he had this Nigger boy that he had been kinda training to help him in his practice, don't you see.
>
> Well, one night this man sent word that he was sick and wanted Dr. Moore to come to see him, and doctor him, you know. Well, Dr. Moore took that Nigger boy along to this sick man's house. When they got there, Dr. Moore looked him over—examined him; set there a few minutes, and finally told him that he was sick because he had been eatin' boiled eggs. He give the man some pills and they left.
>
> On the outside, the boy wanted to know, "Dr. Moore, how come you knowed he had been eatin' boiled eggs?"
>
> Dr. Moore told him, said, "I looked under the bed and seen some egg shells, and reckoned he had been eatin' eggs."
>
> Well, a few days later, another man got sick. This time

14 Charlie Coe, July 22, 1963. This same information is found in the Peden manuscript and in Perrin, *Kentucky*, 768.

15 Smith was not listed as a slaveowner in either 1850 or 1860, according to the Monroe County Slave Census for those years.

16 Almost everyone questioned claimed that the Andrews family owned many slaves. The 1860 slave census for Monroe County shows that William Andrews owned ten slaves, while Varney F. Andrews owned four.

17 Coe's *Chronicles* (p. 28) is the only source to claim that Moore owned more than one of the Coe slaves. Actually, the oral informants fail to specify the number of slaves in his possession. The slave census of Monroe County for 1860 specifies that Moore had only one slave, a male.

18 Recorded with pencil and pad, Aug. 7, 1963. This story is tale type 1862C, *Imitation of Diagnosis by Observation: Ass's Flesh* [Motif J2412.4]. It is typical of the group of anecdotes which are very popular in jestbooks and collections of medieval tales. This is the first report of this folk narrative from American tradition.

19 Wildcatters poured into the Kettle Creek area when oil was discovered there in the 1920's. A more recent strike occurred in Aug. 1963. Neither strike was too significant, although three wells are presently pumping on the former Coe lands, according to Charlie Coe during a telephone conversation on Mar. 28, 1964.

20 This tract represents no less than one-fourth of the original tract, according to John Coe's will. By superimposing a pattern of one-mile square grids on the Black's Ferry Quadrangle Map, which contains the area from the Tennessee line to Coe Ridge, a fairly accurate idea of the size of the John Coe landholdings can be obtained. From any vantage point a conservative estimate would place between 5,000 and 6,000 acres within the bounds of the Coe plantation. The boundaries of the northern portion have been roughly delineated on an aerial photo of the area.

Dr. Moore told the Nigger boy to go over there and give him some pills. (You see, he give most all the patients the same medicine, and he knowed the colored boy could give them pills like he could.)

He said, "Now, you go on over there and diagnose his trouble and give him these pills," said to the Nigger boy.

Well, this boy went over, and directly he come on back. Dr. Moore wanted to know what the man's trouble was. The Nigger told him, "He had eat a horse," and said, "I told him so."

Well, that kinda set Dr. Moore back! Said, "How did you know he had eat a horse?"

The Nigger boy said, "Well, I looked under the man's bed and they wuz a saddle under the bed. I figured he had eat a horse." [18]

THE MAHSTER'S PLANTATION

"It begin about a mile before you get down to the state line, and went clear up to what they call Red Banks, all the way up that creek like we went the other day." Thus, Charlie Coe attempted to voice the limits of the Coe plantation, but the exact boundaries of the original tract could not be determined—either from oral or court-recorded sources. Tim Coe agreed with his brother concerning the vastness of the old plantation:

> I heerd some of the oil men say,[19] "They's not a piece of land on Kettle Creek that's not been owned by a Coe," . . . and my grandfather himself has owned at one time or another practically every piece of it on Kettle Creek. The place that I was raised on down there, my father bought that. That was his father's place. My grandfather died when I was two years old, and then my father bought that place there. Now the deed it calls for 850 acres more or less. And they wuz at least a 1,000 or 1,200 acres of it.[20]

Mahster John Coe's house, located on the upper reaches of Kettle Creek, was surrounded by fertile bottom lands, which were formed by the erosional action of

Mahster Coe's house now stands deserted overlooking the former plantation lands along Kettle Creek.

21 Oral traditions failed to record tobacco prices on the New Orleans market. An 1802 source claimed that prices ranged from $2.00 to $3.00 per hundred weight. See Reuben Gold Thwaites, ed., *Early Western Travels, 1748–1846*, Vol. III, *François Andre Michaux's Travels West of Alleghany Mountains, 1802* (Cleveland, 1904), 241. Crop names are found mainly in the oral traditional tales, but in connection with getting the produce to market. The cultural and commercial aspects of the Coe plantation have been lost to present Negro generations and, surprisingly, almost lost by the white Coe descendants. The types of crops grown and fields devoted to certain crops were known, but crop acreages, harvest output, cost of production, and the like were unknown. Indeed, it can be questioned whether this information ever passed into oral channels. Flatboating narratives alone form the slim core of legendary accounts which depict the commercial aspects of the Coe and neighboring plantations during pioneer days.

22 John E. Leslie's "Early Days of Monroe County," *Tompkinsville News*, Sec. 3, p. 6, Oct. 28, 1954, is a reprint of an earlier article (Aug. 28, 1954) in which Mr. Leslie drew entirely from oral traditions. For accounts of the coming of the steamboats, consult Douglas, *Steamboatin' on the Cumberland*, 35, and "Steamboats Played Important Part in Burkesville," *Cumberland County News*, Aug. 18, 1960.

the Kettle Creek fluvial system. Probably most of the original plantation was clothed in a dense blanket of forests, because even today not over 25 percent of that area has been cleared for agricultural pursuits. The bulk of the area occupied by the old Coe plantation consists of almost inaccessible ridges from the standpoint of modern transportation devices.

Cotton, oats, wheat, and corn were grown on the Coe plantation in early times, but the bulk of the agricultural activities was devoted to raising dark tobacco for sale on Southern markets, especially at New Orleans.[21] Flatboats were the chief mode of transportation from the upper Cumberland area from the late years of the eighteenth century until the Civil War period. Steamboats played an important role after 1833, absorbing much of the freight hauling from this isolated region of the upper South. The flatboating industry, however, remained an integral part of the commercial picture for many years. Just when flatboating began on the Cumberland River is not remembered, but a corroborative account written by J. E. Leslie placed the date about 1790. It was about forty years later when steamboats came into the area.[22]

Judge J. W. Wells of Cumberland County was rather specific concerning the nature of the products hauled to New Orleans on the flatboats: "The rafts of the trips that went to New Orleans was mostly tobacco and farm products. And they had a special place on the raft to put the valuable roots that they'd dig, like ginseng, yellowroot, and stuff. They'd take that to New Orleans; then they'd ship it from there to foreign countries." Leslie's account agrees with this testimony, and is a bit more precise as to the nature of the farm products transported. It claims that "a number of farmers would build a flatboat in the river, load it with corn, wheat, and tobacco, and then let it float down the river . . . ."

Both of the above testimonies are validated by an 1801 eyewitness account of flatboating on the Cumberland River:

> Cotton, corn, indigo, whiskey, hogs, horses, cattle, apples, pork, course linen, gunpowder, salt-petre, poultry, bacon, lard, butter, etc. are the articles which generally constitute the loading of a boat coming out of the Cumberland [onto the Ohio River], and which is frequently shipped in boats so badly put together, it is a matter of surprise how they ever get them to market.[23]

During early years, Nashville was by-passed by settlers on the upper Cumberland in favor of the New Orleans market. This market was preferred, according to Judge Wells, because "Nashville was so young, it wasn't established a good market—no market there. In fact, New Orleans was a big market for years and years for the Cumberland Country." [24] "Nashville, at that time, was a small village and did not afford a market for such products. New Orleans was the only market that could be reached by flatboat and the major part of the shipping was to that point." [25] The 1801 eyewitness account again validates these more recent traditional testimonies. Because the flatboats were "coming out of the Cumberland River," they were, in all probability, shunning Nashville markets, for that village had been passed many miles upstream.

Flatboat ownership in the upper Cumberland country was of three types. First, a group of small farmers, usually from fifteen to twenty, pooled their resources and constructed a communal raft; thus, each farmer "got his shipping free and was privileged to go with his products and to personally look after the sale of them on the market." [26] Second, ownership was by certain

23 Ethel C. Leahy, *Who's Who on the Ohio and Its Tributaries: The Ohio River from the Ice Age to the Future* (Cincinnati [1931]), 166, quoting from *The Navigator*, an almanac written in 1801.

24 Douglas, *Steamboatin' on the Cumberland*, xv, states that by 1819 Nashville had rapidly developed as a leading business and industrial town, but he makes no claim that Nashville was ready to receive the upper Cumberland trade.

25 Leslie, "Early Days of Monroe County," *Tompkinsville News*, Oct. 28, 1954. Tim Coe observed that "the only market they had was New Orleans."

26 *Ibid.*

27 The story of Hugh Kirkpatrick was told by Price Kirkpatrick, a descendant, and by Alvin Strode, a descendant of Henry Strode who was always the man in charge of Kirkpatrick's flatboats en route to the Southern markets. The slave census of Monroe County for 1860 verified that Kirkpatrick owned twenty slaves.

28 Leslie, "Early Days of Monroe County," *Tompkinsville News*, Oct. 28, 1954. Not any of the written accounts agree on the time necessary. J. Winston Coleman, Jr., *Slavery Times in Kentucky* (Chapel Hill, 1940), 42, claims that it took two and one-half months to go to New Orleans from near Louisville. Douglas, *Steamboatin' on the Cumberland*, xv, also lists that time and says that the round trip from Nashville took five months. Michaux, in Thwaites, *Early Western Travels*, 239, contends that it took only thirty to forty days to go from Louisville to New Orleans by flatboat.

29 Thirty days appear about right for the return trip. Michaux, in Thwaites, *Early Western Travels*, 240, states that it took from forty to forty-five days to make the trip from New Orleans to Lexington, which is about 125 miles north of Clay, Monroe, and Cumberland counties.

30 Alvin Strode, pencil and pad interview, June 27, 1960.

river merchants who purchased locally grown produce and then employed local men to make the annual flatboat trip to New Orleans for them. Such was the case of Hugh Kirkpatrick, who was a merchant at Meshack, Monroe County, for many years prior to the Civil War. At the onset of the war, Kirkpatrick, a Southern sympathizer, hauled his slaves and material possessions overland to Livingston, Tennessee, about forty miles away, and there caught a train to Texas, never to return to Kentucky.[27] The third category of flatboat ownership concerns those few planter-like farmers whose total agricultural output was sufficiently large enough to merit privately owned flatboats. This was apparently the case for the Coes of Kettle Creek, as attested to by all of the oral traditional accounts. Tim Coe, for example, stated that his "grandfather built what they called a flatboat—just a big barge. And then what farm products he had to sell, he'd put on there."

Oral testimonies did not specify the amount of time necessary to make the trip to New Orleans by flatboat. The corroborative source states that "it required from seven to eight weeks for boats in this section to float to New Orleans."[28] After the cargo and the boat were disposed of, the account continues, "the crew walked back home . . . . It required about thirty days to walk from New Orleans into this territory."[29] While describing his grandfather's experiences as the person in charge of the Hugh Kirkpatrick boats, Alvin Strode stated that "after his cargo had been sold, he would sell the boat, put his gold in a bag, and strike out across country on foot for Kentucky. He had to watch out for robbers; said they was as thick as hops."[30] Tim Coe remembered that his great-grandfather and slave Zeke had similar experiences. "They'd have to walk back from New Orleans," he stated, noting that "Zeke would carry the money in a sack. They wouldn't get 300 yards up the road [until] somebody would get that money."

After 1833, the local farmers usually rode back from New Orleans on the steamboats which traveled on the Cumberland as far north as Burnside, Kentucky, the terminus of navigation on the river. On the trips to New Orleans, Mahster Coe always took along Zeke to do the cooking.[31] During one return trip, Coe and Zeke traveled on the same boat with another white man and his slave. The *Chronicles* claims that the other "slave" was in reality a pro-wrestler accompanied by his master, while Charlie Coe claims that the Negro was a regular slave traveling with his master in the same status as Mahster Coe and Zeke. The account, repeated in the *Chronicles,* began with an introduction of the characters aboard the boat and then quoted the boastings of the two masters:

> Asking to see slave Zeke, the trainer then laughed and said, "Why, that little fellow would do well to wrestle with a rooster, but he would be no match for my man; why, he would put his head through the bottom of the boat."
>
> "Well," he continued, "if you are willing to take the chance, I'll let the champion take the whip out of him, and I'll carry off your hundred dollars and make you the laughing stock of the country."
>
> Laughing, Jack Coe said, "Wal, if your man can do all that I am willing to lose my money."
>
> So, the champion came and they entered the ring marked off on the deck of the boat, and the contest was on.
>
> There was great excitement, and for awhile it looked as if the champion would win. It was about decided that the master had played the fool and lost his money. When the contest was so close and amid excitement, the master called out, "Throw him, Zeke, by zounds!"
>
> It seemed that when he heard his master's voice calling to him Ezekiel gained courage and strength. He made a

31   Tim Coe, Dec. 8, 1963. The *Chronicles* (pp. 17–18, et passim) corroborates the statement that Zeke was considered a good and obedient servant and that he frequently made trips with his master to New Orleans. This account also mentions that Zeke walked alongside his master and carried the gold.

32 *Chronicles*, 19.

33 This narrative could be a folktale which has been totally adapted to local history. The element of textual variation characteristic of folktales is present, and the wager between the two masters belongs under Motif N10, "Wagers on wives, husbands, or servants." The strength of each slave can be compared to Motif F617, "Mighty wrestler." However, the episode on the steamboat sounds like a real happening with nothing incongruous in the episode. Events such as this may be the kind which gave rise to folktales about strong slaves being pitted against each other. See, for example, Richard M. Dorson's *Negro Folktales in Michigan* (Cambridge, Mass., 1956), 55–56, which contains a tale beginning with the words, "You take in the South, they always have one strong colored guy on all the plantations. He's given a lot of consideration by the boss—usually he be foreman."

great struggle; put forth his greatest strength, and finally pinned the champion's shoulders to the mat, won the match and saved his master's money.[32]

Charlie Coe's version of this same story is greatly abbreviated:

I'll tell you another thing I heard Cal tell, too. You know they used to take tobacco down on the river on barges. Sell it. And Cal said my grandfather and Zeke wuz comin' back from down there after delivering some tobacco. And some man on there had his slaves there, and about half drunk and wantin' to bet anyone that his slaves could throw the other'n. And finally he said my grandfather told him he'd put up that much money. That Zeke could throw his'n.

So they started wrestlin'. And Zeke, Cal said Zeke looked like he wudn't goin' to do it, and said grandfather said, "By damn, Zeke, throw him." Said when [*chuckle*] and when he said that, he really put him to the ground.[33]

2 *Back During Slavery*

Three slaves accompanied Mahster Coe from North Carolina to Kentucky. They were Betty and her two sons, Ransom and Ezekiel.[1] Not one of the three was born on the Coe lands in North Carolina, however. At an unknown date before the move to Kentucky, Coe had purchased Betty and her sons from a Cherokee Indian named Stove. It was from Stove that Indian blood entered the veins of the Coe Negroes, for these two half-breed sons were born as a result of Betty's sexual relations with Mahster Stove.[2]

The Indian-Negro blood mixture forms a vital part of the Coe legend. A prominent Tompkinsville businessman, who has known the Coes since childhood, points to this as a basic reason for the "bad streak of meanness" inbred in the Coe Negro line. Each of the informants agrees that certain physical characteristics distinguish the Coe Negroes from others of their race. In the words of the Tompkinsville informant:

1 Informants do not give the original number of slaves in Coe's possession, but a collation of their traditions places it at three. Data are unimportant to the informants—their interests center on personal attributes. Except for a mention in Coe's will and in the *Chronicles* (p. 9), Ransom was identified orally by only Calvin (Negro), Tim, and Charlie Coe. Ransom probably died on the Coe plantation, unmarried and without offspring, but Charlie Coe (white) stated on July 23, 1963, that his father went to visit Ransom as he lay dying in the Negro colony. Ezekiel, the youngest son, is well known in oral memories because he led the colony through its darkest hours.

2 Mary Ann Keen, Burkesville, Ky., personally interviewed Calvin Coe before his death, and in her unpublished manuscript reported that he alone knew the name and traditions associated with the name Stove. The Cumberland County Census for 1880 made no mention of Ransom, but listed North Carolina as the birthplace of Betty and Ezekiel.

Mrs. Anders claimed that Betty had a Negro husband, who was the father of her children. Her tradition seems associated with the Kettle Creek section of Monroe County, however. It appears that if Betty had a husband at all, she married after coming to Kentucky.

To start with, they were Negroes, you know, full-stock Niggers, and then they married Cherokee girls, and then married white women and, of course, you've got a cross-breed there of everything in the world. They don't look like any other colored people that you'd see anywhere. If you ever seen any once and know them, why, you'd know him whenever you'd see him! They was one over there the other day on the street, and I told my wife (we come out of Bradshaw-Hagan store), and I said, "You always said you'd like to see a Zeke or one of those Coe Niggers." You know, they was called Zekes; they're really Coes. I said, "There's one of them."

And another feller was standin' there that knew for sure, and he said, "How did you know?"

And I said, "Why, I can tell one as far as I can see him. He doesn't have features like a Nigger. He has a nose like a white man; you know, a kinda sharp, peaked nose and high cheek bones. And he isn't black; he's got kinda reddish-brownish skin."

These words echo the sentiments of other informants who also point out the high cheek bones and copper-colored skin so typical of the Indian race. George Allred, a Negro informant who once lived in the colony, claimed that "they all had high cheek bones like Indians. They claimed they wuz mixed with Indian. I don't know whether they wuz or not." Tim Coe noted that "they was one family in there that was real black. These others, they were kinda copper colored." Finally, C. B. Coe, one of the white descendants of the plantation owners, in describing Zeke Coe, the slave, stated that "he was a very bright copper color and from his appearance must have had Indian blood in his veins."

Granny Betty was a "very pretty woman," according to Ruthie Coe Anders, an elderly descendant, but she was "awfully black." She was quick-tempered, and when driven to anger, would yell out in a piercing voice, "Blast your eternal picture, I'll knock y'er head off." [3]

Betty may have had a sister, Sukey, who accompanied her from North Carolina. Indications are strong, however, that Betty and Sukey were not related, and that Sukey was already living in the Kettle Creek community when Mahster Coe arrived in Kentucky in 1811. Most likely, Sukey was owned by a white man named Lynch.[4] Sukey, whose mother was imported to America, was, in the words of Calvin Coe, "big and fat, just like a real African." The date that Sukey passed into the hands of John Coe must pass unexplained, but when the negotiation was made, she took along four mulatto children to the Coe plantation, Riley, Patsy Ann, Bill Burress, and Tom Softly. The mingling of blood lines in this instance resulted from Sukey's sexual relations with Mahster Lynch, which produced, according to the *Chronicles* (p. 9), a "people half-white and half-colored."[5] Recent Negro generations acknowledge their white ancestry without shame, but point the finger of guilt at the old plantation mahsters who used Betty and Sukey as they saw fit. Mrs. Ray Anders protests strongly:

The white man mixed with the colored in time of slavery. He made these colored people do what he wanted them to, you see. I'm coming with the truth! And that's how come these people mixed up like they are today. And they shouldn't be a-fightin' them for it, and jailing them for it, 'cause they come by it through hard time and tribulation.

Patsy Ann, described by a white neighbor as "a litty bitty humped-over colored person, and yellow,"[6] was born on Kettle Creek in Monroe County, Kentucky, about 1822, eleven years before "the stars fell."[7] A fitting tribute was paid her by C. B. Coe:

Patsy Ann was a kind, motherly old slave. She always had a kind word for all. She always looked on the bright side, no matter under what circumstances she was placed.

4 Some accounts have it that Sukey made the trek from North Carolina (see, e. g., *Chronicles*, 9). Ruthie Coe Anders could not recall that Betty had any sisters at all. Three of the informants—Tim Coe, Mrs. Etta Long, and Mrs. Mattie Davidson—had never heard of Sukey. Calvin Coe, cited in the Keen manuscript, claimed that Lynch was her owner.

5 Two of Sukey and Mahster Lynch's children, Bill and Tom, could be identified by only Calvin Coe. Because of the legends surrounding Riley and Patsy Ann, their names seem destined to be perpetuated indefinitely. Riley's importance in local tradition stems from his being "southed" by Mahster Coe. The Riley *sage* is centered around his escape from a cruel new master and his return to the Coe plantation where he hid for many months under the floor of Zeke's cabin.

6 Statement by Mrs. Richard Glass (a white informant), tape recorded in Aug. 1961.

7 Loman D. Cansler, Jr., in Aug. 1962, tape recorded some of the Coe traditions from Leslie Coe, Jr. (Negro), in Kansas City, Kan., and sent the recordings to me with a covering letter. The letter contained the statement "the stars fell," and further noted that Patsy Ann died about 1907 and was buried in the clan cemetery on the ridge.

The expression "the stars fell" owes its derivation to the occurrence of the great Leonid meteor shower that appeared over America on November 13, 1833. Astronomer Charles P. Olivier records in his article "Meteor," *The Encyclopedia Americana*, 1953 edition, that the shower furnished 200,000 meteors for a given location between midnight and dawn; numbers of the meteors were brilliant, and many left trains of light. The terror excited among the masses of the population was great, and thousands of people fully expected that the end of time was at hand. An 1881 edition of the *Americana* commented that this was perhaps the greatest display of celestial fireworks since the creation of the world.

8 Ruthie Coe Anders and the *Chronicles* (p. 11) both testify that Zeke and Patsy were married by jumping over the broomstick. Others who had heard of their peculiar marriage include Leslie Coe, Jr., and Mrs. Myrtle Kerr, a white informant who recalled that her mother had mentioned Zeke and Patsy's marriage.

Coleman, *Slavery Times*, 57–58, claims that broomstick marriages were common on Kentucky plantations and that the practice originated from some ancient ceremony in Europe and was handed down with many variations by the "white folk" over a long period of years. Orville W. Taylor, *Negro Slavery in Arkansas* (Durham, N.C., 1958), devotes an entire chapter (pp. 189–202) to the various forms of Negro marriages, including jumping over the broomstick.

9 Zeke and Patsy Ann and all their children are listed as mulattoes on the Cumberland County Census for 1870 and 1880.

Even in her old age she stood in the cabin door and saw her own flesh and blood drop dead in her yard from assassins' bullets. Even then, her words were always kind. She was very religious and, being the old time slave that she was, I sincerely believe that she came as near living religion as any person I ever saw, white or colored.

About 1840 Patsy Ann "married" Ezekiel Coe, the half-breed son of Betty and Stove. It was a broomstick affair, typical of slave marriages in many parts of the South; the marriage was performed when Zeke and Patsy jumped over a broom handle, held by Mahster Coe.[8] Mrs. Sarah Coe Tooley, a descendant, claimed that Zeke and Patsy jumped backwards across the broomstick.

From this marriage were born twelve children whose blood was one-half Negro, with the other half being divided between Indian and white.[9] These children looked much like their parents, having a bright copper color and being small in physical stature. Few of the boys ever exceeded five feet or weighed more than 125 pounds. Their strength, however, was comparable to that of a bull, and they were absolutely tireless at work. C. B. Coe described them in the following manner:

> I have never in all my life known one of them to flinch under any circumstances. They are quiet and cool, never showing any signs of nervousness. They have nearly all worked for me at various times, and I have always found them very obedient and ready to do anything I ordered them to do. I have always found them true to any trust or duty confided in them. I never knew them to spare an enemy, for no one who ever encountered them is alive to tell how it was done.

The twelve children of Ezekiel and Patsy Ann were Mary, Thomas, William ("Bill Zeke"), Ezekiel ("Crippled Zeke"), Jemima ("Mime Zeke"), Joe, Frank, Sarah, Sue "Suze," John, Calvin, and a daughter who died at birth.[10]

Although all names of Ezekiel's children are remembered by the present generations, only Mary (usually pronounced Murry), John, and Calvin won a durable niche in family tradition and assumed, more or less, a hero status to the Coe clansmen. Like their parents, these three children played their most important roles from 1885 to 1910, during the time the Coe colony experienced a period of racial feuding. According to oral tradition, all but one of the twelve children spent their lives in the ridge colony after emancipation. Only Mime Zeke continued to live near the Old Mahster's home, in a little log cabin. Just what her status was after slavery can only be conjectured. Most likely, Mime had served as the "Negro mammy" in the mahster's household, and thus received preferential treatment after being manumitted. Indications are strong that she lived alone in her little cabin, but that she was frequently visited by a black man, Danny Holman, who became the father of her four children, Mary Ellen, Bob, Wilse, and Frank. Charlie Coe remembered exactly where Mime's cabin stood and pointed out the spot to the writer during a ride through the area. Coe's memory was sharpened by his visits to her cabin as a small boy to play with her daughter Mary Ellen. In her late years, about 1895, Mime moved to Columbia, Kentucky, some sixty miles to the north, where one of her sons worked in a hotel as a shoe black.[11]

MAHSTER-SLAVE RELATIONS

"My mother said they's awful good to the darkies," stated George Allred, who grew up in Overton County,

10   Leslie Coe, Jr., claimed that the original number of children was thirteen, but it is generally felt that there were only twelve. After the names of the twelve children had been determined through oral tradition, the 1853 will of John Coe came into my possession. That document verifies the names, except for one named Monk. It is possible that he would make the thirteenth child, or that Monk was a nickname for either Frank or Joe, or that Monk was just another slave on the Coe plantation. At any rate, his identity has been lost to the present generations.

11   Mrs. Sarah Coe Tooley, Charlie and Tim Coe, and Mrs. Etta Short and her sister, Mrs. Mattie Davidson, all agreed on most points concerning Mime, including identity of the father of the children. There was some question about her son Frank's identity, but it was generally conceded that he was her son and that he now lives in Kokomo, Ind. At a later date, Ruthie Coe Anders definitely identified Frank as Mime's son.

12 In the Deep South, the institution of slavery was kaleidoscopic, especially in the matter of master-slave relations. In Botkin's *Lay My Burden Down*, many instances are recorded of cruel punishments. Some masters beat their slaves or subjected them to whips of overseers or meted out various other punishments, even the withholding of food. There are, however, equally numerous instances of amiable master-slave relations. F. A. Michaux, writing in 1802, described a Tennessee plantation located on the Cumberland River about thirty miles south of Celina where slaves lived in contentment and abundance; see R. G. Thwaites, *Early Western Travels*, 257.

Although slavery in the upper South was not unlike that found in the Cotton Kingdom of the lower South—in both areas the Negro was held in bondage—the varied economies of the two areas required different considerations for the slaves. With increased production of cotton, the lower South could not keep its plantations stocked with slaves, but in the upper South where production of other staple crops was the rule, the need for a large number of slaves diminished. Thus, in the upper South slaves were produced through natural increase at a rate in excess of the demands made on slave labor. In the early decades of the nineteenth century, the county seat towns in Kentucky became local centers for slave auctions.

13 The folk traditions of slavery times cover enough of the upper Cumberland to permit a comparison with those of the Coe plantation. While the traditions were gathered from former Coe Ridge Negroes and usually concerned the Coe plantation, some of the informants had backgrounds of slavery on neighboring plantations. In their stories about slavery days, the informants who were not historically associated with the Coe plantation quite naturally related their own ancestral traditions. Such accounts are utilized herein, for they supplement the Coe traditions and aid in the attempt to discern the total picture of slavery on the Coe plantation.

14 "Slaver" is a generic term used locally to denote a cruel master. The tradition that the "Pines" owned the earlier Coe Negroes was known only by Mrs. Ruthie Coe Anders. Leslie

Tennessee, about thirty miles east of Celina. "They would never sell her. People came there and wanted to buy her; they never would sell her," he added, thus pointing out that the master's attitude toward the use of the slave block was the chief factor in the creation of good relations between a master and his slaves.[12] For this reason, instances of cruelties toward slaves diminished in the minds of the informants if the masters kept the family intact. This same Negro informant, for example, acknowledged that a few local masters in the Overton County area occasionally resorted to rough tactics in dealing with their slaves, but that such treatment was justified on the grounds that many of the slaves were stubborn. In his own words, "They claim some of the owners was awful rough with them—but they had to be rough with lots of them, 'cause you find lots of colored people now pretty hardheaded." [13]

The Poindexters, a slaveholding family on Pine Creek, just across the Tennessee line from Monroe County, were inconsiderate, unpredictable, and extremely cruel to their slaves. Mrs. Ruthie Coe Anders told about the following incident between her great-great-grandfather and Bud Pine [Poindexter], the "slaver":[14]

> I was going to tell you a-while ago [about the time] when Mr. Pine sent grandpa down in the woods, or field, to cut his wood. Well, Bud Pine went down there and tried to chain him, and [make] him come up to the house and do a whole lot of stuff. He said, "Mr. Pine sent me down here to cut this wood today, and I'm a-going to cut it!"
>
> Well, Bud wouldn't go back to the house. He went on; finally he did go back to the house. And when he went back, he tells [lies to] Mr. Pine . . . about grandfather wouldn't cut the wood.
>
> And so Mr. Pine . . . said, "Why didn't you cut the wood?"

"You told me to cut that wood! And I cut the wood, and that's why I cut the wood. That's just 'zactly why."

And he said, "Well, you come on up a few inches," said, "I God, we come down here to give you a good lashing and whip you." Grandfather was a little short man. He said, "All right," said, "I'm going to tell you right now, if you come two inches nearer me," says, "I'll give ye the lash! I'll stick this ax plumb through you."

And him and Mr. Pine and the woman was back in their house and glad to get back.

Even worse master-slave relations existed on the Hugh Kirkpatrick plantation, located on Meshack Creek in Monroe County, not far from the Cumberland River. Kirkpatrick is remembered only as a very cruel, hard slaver who treated his Negroes in a manner reminiscent of the accounts found in abolitionist literature.[15] Kate Anders Tooley, whose mother grew up in bondage near the Kirkpatrick plantation, gave the following account of his cruel ways, and at the same time offered an insight into the daily routine of the field slaves:

Old Hugh Kirk he owned a bunch of Niggers. And the way he done them, they wuz a-working in the field—he'd build him a scaffold about middle ways of the field, and he'd get up on that with a big whip. And he'd put them in the field to working where he could see them from one end of the field to another.

And if they didn't work jist like fightin' fire, when they'd come back to the middle of the field where he's at, he'd shout, "Hey, you Niggers, you ain't a-doing nothing." Walked over and said he dist cut the blood out of 'um.

And they'd tell him they's going as fast as they could, but he'd make 'um jist get under lash and go on.

Oral traditions indicate that Jimmy Geralds was engaged in the nefarious practice of breeding slaves for export to the cotton states.[16] Geralds owned a large farm on Tooley Branch in Monroe County, Kentucky, near the Cumberland River. Although the geography of

Coe, Jr., did, however, contribute an interesting and corroboratory statement: "They took the name of the slaveowner. But see, their real name was Poindexter. But my great-grand-father went to town and had his name put in his mahster's name—Coe."

15 Kirkpatrick owned twenty slaves in 1860, according to the slave census for Monroe County.

16 Kentucky began early to export slaves, even after the Non-Importation Act of 1833 forbade the practice; see Frederic Bancroft, *Slave Trading in the Old South* (New York, 1959), 124. The practice was accelerated in 1849 after the Kentucky legislature repealed the act; see Coleman, *Slavery Times*, 155. Coleman devotes some pages (142–95) to the activities of slavebreeding and sales to Southern planters, but makes no specific mention of the upper Cumberland area.

17 The slave census for 1850 and 1860 reveals that the informant grossly overestimated the number of slaves owned by James F. Geralds—he had six slaves in 1850, and eleven in 1860.

that area negates the possibility of profitable slave-ownership, Geralds owned sixty slaves at one time, according to Kate Tooley, who is descended from one of the Geralds slaves.[17] She told a pathetic story about the sale of her grandmother by Geralds, and how he then beat the informant's mother over the head for crying after her departing mother:

> He sold my mother's mother. They wuz big Nigger buyers, my father and my mother said, come here, and buy Niggers and take them south, and work them just like mules. Sold my mother's mother to a big Nigger buyer, they called him, and sent her to the South.
> And mother said Old Uncle Jimmy Geralds he caught her crying, and he knocked her in the head. And my mother never could hear out of this left ear. She never could hear much where he knocked her in the . . . hit her with a chair because she cried because she seen her mother go off with these Nigger buyers.

Kate Tooley's sister, Lucy Coe, who married Robert Coe and spent sixty-one years in the Coe Ridge Negro colony, carried the story one step further. She claimed that their own mother was also auctioned off to a Southern buyer:

> My mother was sold. They said they . . . southed her . . . . She come back from the South—back to this country, somehow. I don't know how she got back, but she came back. They sold her mother [too], and took her away. Said she [i. e., informant's mother] was about five years old when they took her mother away. And she stayed with these Geralds. They raised her up 'til she got big enough . . . . put her on a stump and auctioned her off.

George Allred further contributes information about the sale of slaves in the upper Cumberland area as he describes a group being driven to a slave market:

> [They would] drive them off and sell them, buy them, you know, just like you would a bunch of cattle—maybe

a drove of cattle. Maybe you would take them to . . . Louisville or somewhere and make big money of them. They would just drive them along the road just like they would a bunch of stock [with] a big man riding along behind them driving them along the road. Take them to a place and hike them up on a rock and bid them off.

Traditional history, recorded in a corroborative source,[18] relates that buyers from the Deep South would gather in Burkesville, where they would purchase locally produced Negroes. These slaves usually were never heard from again. Mrs. Ray Anders, one of the Coe Negro descendants, described Burkesville as a place where the slave auctioneers would "just stand them up on a stump and cry them off like crying off stock or something." Her husband, Ray, affirmed her statement by adding, "Just go to a sale or something that-a-way and recommend them [as] good workers and sell them to the highest bidder. Take them and work them as you would a mule, I guess." Leslie Coe, Jr., charged that the slaves were sold like "cattle, hogs, or anything else."

The prices paid for slaves varied, but according to Ray Anders, a "lot of them brought four or five hundred dollars!"[19] George Allred claimed, "They brought a lot—now they never did say for certain—said they brought lots of money, brought a big price. Course, they wanted them stout, you know, able to work . . . . One good, strong, healthy woman or man brought good money. And one weasley one wasn't no 'count didn't sell for much."

The slave owners in the Kettle Creek area had trouble keeping their slaves on the plantation and had to resort to the mounted patrol or "patteroller" system utilized universally throughout the Southern states.[20] When queried about the duties of the patterollers, Bill Poin-

18 Wells, *Cumberland County*, 104. Coleman, *Slavery Times*, devotes an entire chapter (pp. 115–41) to the "Auction Block." General accounts of slave markets and slavebreeding can be obtained from various historical sources, but folk traditions such as those presented in this study are the grassroots accounts of these institutions. Quite naturally, the informants themselves do not realize that they convey such valuable historical data that can synthesize regional history. To the informants, these accounts represent community and family history and therefore are totally worthy of oral perpetuation.

19 Wells, *Cumberland County*, 103, claims that slaves on the Burkesville market brought up to $1,500.

20 Coleman, *Slavery Times*, 85–114, describes the patteroller system in Kentucky, but again makes no mention of the upper Cumberland area. That system's background began with a slave code of 1798, specifying that "the slave was not to leave the farm of his owner without a pass from his master, the main purpose being to keep the Negroes from congregating on any one farm." This code was enforced, commencing in the 1830's, when emissaries from the North started schemes to stir up the slaves. In some parts of the state, mounted patrols were organized and went about at night to watch the movement of slaves. But such a system of county patrols did not prove sufficient when the slave population grew and when towns where whiskey could be found grew larger and more attractive to the country slave. Ivan E. McDougle, "Slavery in Kentucky, 1792–1865," *Journal of Negro History*, III:3 (July 1918), 41. Caleb Perry Patterson, *The Negro in Tennessee, 1790–1865* (Dallas, 1922), 38–43, traces the evolution of the patrol system in Tennessee. Botkin's *Lay My Burden Down* contains eleven oral accounts of patterolls, and one is found in Dorson, *Negro Folktales in Michigan*, 85–86. See Dorson's note 52, p. 217, for additional oral references.

dexter, whose father was a local patteroller, made the following statement:

> Well, that was when these darkies wuz all under bondage—all slaves. Why, if a patteroll caught them out away from home without a pass, why, they had to whup them —give them so many stripes. And that wuz their duty to do that.
>
> They dist had to watch these darkies that wuz under bondage. And if they caught them away from home without a pass from their mahster, why, they had to give them so many stripes.

Mr. Poindexter told about the time his father caught a runaway slave at the mouth of Kettle Creek, near the close of the Civil War:

> Said he got after one once—I've forgot the darkie's name—and he'd come out without a pass. And said he got after him and was a-running him, and this darkie ran over a cow. And she jumped up and pitched him out in the field, and he [the patteroll] caught him.
>
> Said, "Oh, Mister Pine, please don't whup me," said, "I've done broke my toe."

Thus, it was necessary for the slaves to have a written permit before they could leave the plantation. The necessity of possessing this paper was confirmed by the testimony of Aunt Kate Tooley, although she erroneously gave the Ku Klux Klan label to a patteroll who beat up her own parents during their courting days:

> And my mother said they wudn't allowed to get out nowhere unless they had a paper from their mahster. And if they caught 'um out away without a paper from they mahster, why, the Ku Klux would pick 'um up and beat 'um up.
>
> One night, my mother said, her and my father wuz going to a dance—slipped off and went to a dance. So when they come back (they didn't have any paper from they mahster. They's afraid to ask him. They knowed he wouldn't let 'um go, and they slipped off and went any-

how). But these Ku Klux caught 'um on the road and like to 'uv beat 'um to death. They didn't have no paper from they mahster. And the Ku Klux beat 'um up.

From both Negro and white traditions, it was learned that only the most amiable master-slave relations existed on the Coe plantation. Those conditions began under Mahster Jack Coe and were continued by his son, Jesse Coe, who assumed the reins of the plantation upon the death of his father in 1854. Leslie Coe, Jr., summed up the servitude of his ancestors with the words, "There wasn't nothing so awfully bad about it— only they were jist slaves." Coe proceeded, however, to describe the wrath inflicted against the slave children by Mahster Coe's second wife:

He was a kind man until he married his second wife. His second wife, she was a young woman and she was mean to the slaves, so the older people tell me. But the first wife and Jack Coe were just beautiful to the slaves. But the new wife he married like older men do, they marry a young woman—she was mean and ugly to the slaves. She'd whup the little ones, but the bigger ones, she didn't bother them.

Calvin Coe, himself formerly a slave on the Coe plantation, constantly expressed his love, devotion, and great respect for the Jesse Coe family and the white Coe descendants. Calvin seemed to have not only love for them, but a deep sense of loyalty and an ardent desire to praise them whenever an occasion offered the opportunity. Of his mahster, Calvin Coe stated:

We could not have had a better master. He was kind and good to all of us. We was taught to love Master Coe and all his family. I have loved him, and I loved all his family, his children and his grandchildren. I just love the name "Coe," and I would want to do anything I could for one of them. It would just make me happy to know that I had done something for one of them.[21]

21 Quoted in Keen ms, 2.

49

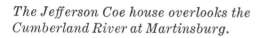

The Jefferson Coe house overlooks the Cumberland River at Martinsburg.

The Coe descendants, both white and Negro, remember the Coe mahsters as people who would never "sell a child away from a mother" nor "separate a husband from a wife." [22] The Coe descendants also remember that Mahster John Coe's will specified that Zeke should never be hired out for "more than five miles from home so he could return to his family on Saturday night and Sunday." [23] An additional factor endeared Mahster Jesse Coe to the Negroes on his plantation. He would never let anyone, not even his own children, mistreat the slaves. "He always told us," testified Calvin Coe, "if one of his children hit us for us to hit them back." Such knowledge was especially reassuring to the slaves who were constantly susceptible to teasing and ridicule. On one occasion, Cal Coe and his brother John were helping Bill Garner, one of Mahster Coe's sons-in-law, gather corn on the Coe plantation. Garner "aggravated" Cal and John to the extent that the two young slaves reported the affair to Mahster Coe. Coe then made Garner continue gathering corn by himself, and permitted Cal and John to assume a new job for the day.[24] Charlie Coe tells it this way:

> He said my grandfather never would let nobody run over them. And he wouldn't have white ones out with him. He said they was helping Bill Garner (that's feller that married my aunt) gather corn, and aggravating Cal and John. They told grandfather about it. He made him go back by hisself and gather corn and sent the boys to other places.

The consideration shown by Mahster Coe to his Negro slaves was not without its reciprocal qualities, as described by Tim Coe in the following narrative which tells of a moment of danger experienced by Mahster Coe:

> Take Old John and Cal and all that bunch there, why,

22 Calvin Coe, *ibid.* Charlie Coe (white) similarly testified to his grandfather's desire to keep his slave families together.

"Virtually everybody preferred to be humane," according to Bancroft, *Slave Trading*, 197, "when it was not financially disadvantageous or inconvenient to do so." McDougle, "Slavery in Kentucky," 79, claims that the practice of separating slave families was not very common in Kentucky because of the storm of public disapproval over such an event.

23 Calvin Coe quoted in Keen ms, 2. Master John Coe's will specifies: "I want said Negro woman Patsy to live near her husband, say no farther than five miles so long as they remain as they are now. . . ." *Chronicles*, 14, states that "Jack Coe, though a slave owner, was a man of integrity, and was humane in dealing with his slaves. . . . He would not separate husband and wife by selling either from the other; nor would he sell a baby from its mother's eyes, nor the mother from her child, no matter what the circumstances . . . ."

Slave hiring was a restricted kind of slave trading common to all Southern states, according to Bancroft, *Slave Trading*, 145. James B. Sellers, *Slavery in Alabama* (University, Ala., 1950), 195, claims that the practice was prevalent in Alabama, especially in times of depression. Slave hiring did not allow title to the slave, but gave the slave's labor for a definite period of time or purpose, usually at a specified price. Prestige of some degree went with the ownership and hiring of slaves, and although it has been rather ignored historically, that factor is important to the understanding of the slave period.

24 Since Cal would have been only four years old, even at the end of the Civil War, tradition here has apparently confused the names of Cal and John with two older brothers. Because of the legendary roles later ascribed to Cal and John, it is understandable how this traditional tale centers upon Cal and John as the chief actors.

51

25 The instances of the few slave sales from the Coe plantation were never mentioned when the humane character of Coe was being considered. Although the motive was not specified, it was probably Coe's need for ready cash that motivated him to sell three of four of his slaves.

26 Carol has been almost forgotten by the oral traditions associated with the early history of the Coes. Only three informants knew of him—Ray Anders, Mrs. Sarah Coe Tooley, and Tim Coe, Aug. 23, 1963—and all these claimed that he was sold to a Southern slave buyer. "He never did return back from where they took him to," claimed Ray Anders. Carol's actual identity is unknown. There is no indication that he stemmed from Betty or Sukey.

27 Botkin, *Lay My Burden Down*, 134–40, records a similar incident where a mistress kept a Negro child by buying it.

they thought so much of my grandfather [Jesse] because he was so good to them during slavery. And they would have fought for any of his people.

See they was a bully—I don't remember his name—back there on Pea Ridge. I don't know what he got mad at my grandfather Coe about, but he sent word down there that (down in front of the house near the road they was a gate, and they was two huge posts—gate posts put in there; they was about eighteen inches square . . .) he was going to come down there and cut his head off and set it on one of them gateposts.

Well, when these Niggers heard that, why, they sent him word that when Massa Jess' head set on one of them posts, that his head would set on the other.

And this fellow never did bother grandfather.

Mahster Jesse Coe occasionally resorted to the slave auction block, despite his reputation as a kind and considerate master.[25] Traditions collected from both Negroes and whites state that Carol,[26] Riley, and Bill all were sold from the Coe plantation. John Coe, a Negro lad of four years, was under negotiation when the Civil War came to a close, according to Ray Anders, and he was to be sold to Frank Lollar of Judio, Cumberland County, for $400. When John learned of the proposed negotiations, he went to Mahster Coe and pleaded, "Oh, Mister Coe, oh, Mister Coe, buy me," related Mrs. Sarah Coe Tooley in a throaty voice of imitation. Coe then bought him for $450, for he "would have paid a thousand or more for him before he would have let him gone."[27] Thus, there is a contradiction in the accounts by Anders and Mrs. Tooley concerning the sale of John: one says that Mahster Coe was ready to sell John; the other claims that Mahster Coe then bought his own slave. Charlie Coe later explained that John was being sold to settle the estate of John Coe, deceased. When Jesse Coe saw the disappointment in the young boy's eyes, he purchased the boy himself from the estate of his father.

Charlie Coe's testimony is most likely correct. Another informant, Mrs. Myrtle Kerr, said that her grandmother, who was a Coe, came into possession of Mary, a daughter of Zeke and Patsy Ann Coe, because Patsy told her that Mary was to be sold and thereupon Mrs. Kerr's grandmother went to Mahster Coe to tell him not to sell Mary. Coe then agreed that she could take Mary as her own, by deducting her cost from her portion of the estate. In Mrs. Kerr's own words:

> I've jist heerd her say that when he sold Mary Wilburn —she was the baby one of 'um. And when she come, she wuz a-weaving—grandmammy wuz—when Old Aunt Pats, now understand, come. Why, she wuz a-weaving, and she told her, says, "Massa is a-going to sell my baby today." And she says, "No, he ain't neither." Said, "Dad ain't going to sell yo baby." Said, "I've got some babies, and I know how you feel—he ain't gonna sell yo baby. Where's he at?" "About a mile up the creek." Says, "I'll just get out of this loom and me and you will go up thar." And says, "He ain't going to sell your baby." And she went up thar, why, he's jist a-bossing around. She jist walked up, said, "Dad, Pats tells me you are going to sell Mary today." "Yeah, I'm going to sell her." "No, you ain't neither." Says, "I've got some children," says, "I know how she feels." "Well, do you want me to take a hundred dollars out of your estate for Mary?" "Yeah, take her out of my estate." "You take Mary, then!"

THE ESCAPE OF SLAVE RILEY

Riley's name is synonymous in folk memory with the term "slave sale," and his adventures dealing with his sale and subsequent return to the Coe plantation constitute a vital core of plantation memories held by the present generations.[28] Riley was sold by Mahster Jesse

28 It should be pointed out that most of the traditions concerning slavery times are purely historical in nature, and are told by the Negroes as a part of their ancestral history. Some of these oral traditions have weathered with age, however, and are beginning to show variations characteristic of folktales and migratory legends. An example of the development of a legend is perfectly illustrated in the Riley *sage*.

29 Charlie Coe affirmed his brother's claim: "My grandfather and his brothers could not get along with Riley."

30 Mrs. Etta Short spoke from memory of her parents' testimony.

31 *Chronicles*, 10.

32 *Chronicles*, 14–15, et passim.

33 In quoting the $1,500 figure, Charlie Coe emphatically stated, "Now this is true, too! I've heard my daddy tell it," thus showing the validity placed in the family traditions by Mr. Coe. Leslie Coe, Jr., also specified $1,500.

34 This statement of Ruthie Coe Anders is corroborated in the *Chronicles*, 15.

Coe, of that there is no question, but the reason for selling him may never be fully explained. "He was the only mean one in the bunch," claimed Tim Coe, "and he give grandfather so much trouble he finally sold him." [29] "They said he was . . . almost a white man, and passed for a white man," claimed another white informant. "And he'd run off, and they'd go get him and bring him back, and he'd run off again. So finally . . . he sold him to somebody and they took him to the South." [30]

The *Chronicles,* more or less in agreement with these accounts, contends that Riley was "bright," a term which meant that a slave was too white, proud, and difficult to subdue, rather than a meek and humble slave who accepted orders and carried them out as commanded.[31] The *Chronicles,* however, disagrees with the oral accounts on the reason for the sale of Riley, claiming that the whole affair was negotiated due to economic necessities. After the marriage of Zeke and Patsy Ann began producing many children, an overpopulation of slaves on the Coe Plantation resulted within a few years. Mahster Coe decided to sell off one of the slaves, and the lot fell to Riley, a bachelor, since the mahster would never separate husband from wife, or mother from child.[32]

Riley and his new master, who had paid $1,500[33] for him, left the Coe plantation on horseback and began a four-day journey to the south. Riley felt very lonely and dissatisfied after reaching his new home where the people were not good to him. Difficult tasks assigned him, along with treatment that was far different from that received from his former master, tempted Riley to run away and return to Kentucky.[34] Toward that aim, the slave secretly secured information concerning the most expeditious route for return to his Old Mahster's home on Kettle Creek.[35]

Riley escaped around midnight because he knew that he would have to be as far away as possible when his master discovered that he was gone. Riley also realized that the bloodhounds and patterollers would be after him at daybreak.[36] The slave made rapid progress and had been on his journey for two days before his pursuers got near him. They came so close at one time that Riley was forced to crawl into a hollow log, although he was afraid poisonous snakes would be there. Riley later reported that he had feared his pursuers and the treatment he would receive from them far more than he did any poisonous snakes that might have been in the log. He was much relieved when he heard his pursuers pass on by, and after waiting a few minutes, he crept out of the log and started again on his journey home. An uncanny sense of direction revealed the correct way to turn at all of the crossroads.[37]

For the most part, Riley traveled at night and hid by day.[38] The last three days of the journey were accomplished without food and water. At last Riley silently slipped into the little cabin of Sukey, his mother, where he revealed to her and his sister, Patsy Ann, that he had run away from his new master.[39]

In the meantime, Zeke saw and recognized the footprints of Riley, while walking with Mahster Coe along the banks of Kettle Creek, near the Tennessee line. Zeke did not reveal Riley's presence to Mahster Coe. Instead he went to Sukey's cabin, found Riley there, and immediately pledged to help hide him, regardless of the consequences.[40]

Riley was concealed in the barn, unknowingly to Mahster Coe and family, after the fugitive told his rel-

35 The plans for escape and return were recorded only in the *Chronicles*, 15.

36 No reference was found to indicate how many slaveowners kept bloodhounds to track down runaway slaves, but apparently at least the big plantations kept bloodhounds for this purpose. See, e.g., William Wells Brown, *Narrative of William W. Brown, A Fugitive Slave* (Boston, 1847), 22; Francis Fedric, *Slave Life in Virginia and Kentucky: or, Fifty Years of Slavery in the Southern States of America, by Francis Fedric, An Escaped Slave* (London, 1863 [Microcard]), 76. Oral accounts which describe the use of bloodhounds in tracking slaves can be found in Dorson, *Negro Folktales in Michigan*, 86–87, and in Botkin, *Lay My Burden Down*, 168–69.

37 *Chronicles*, 15–16, et passim.

38 Ruthie Coe Anders stated, "He slipped off and walked back. He'd walk at night; through the day he'd hide." The *Chronicles*, 16, also maintained that he would hide during the day.

39 *Chronicles*, 16. Details of Riley's escape are very similar to those of slave John Bennett, recorded in Dorson, *Negro Folktales in Michigan*, 86–87. In both instances, the slaves traveled by night, were pursued by bloodhounds, evaded detection by hiding in a unique manner, and were given aid at the end of the successful flight.

40 Charlie Coe told of the footprint episode on two or three occasions during my visits with him. This episode is also recorded in the *Chronicles*, 13.

41 *Chronicles*, 16.

42 Tim Coe and Charlie Coe claimed that the hiding place was under the floor, but Ruthie Coe Anders and the *Chronicles* (p. 17) specify the place of concealment as a small cellar or basement under Zeke's cabin. I prefer the former claim since a known cellar would be a suspect place of concealment.

43 Ruthie Coe Anders.

44 See also *Chronicles*, 17.

45 Tim Coe related this portion of the story on at least two occasions during Aug. 1961.

46 Ruthie Coe Anders claimed that it was for twenty-four months.

atives that he was being followed and that his pursuers would probably come to the cabin to find him. His owner soon did come to the cabin, but he found no traces of Riley. In anger, the owner vowed that he would find Riley if he "stayed on top of the earth," and then left.[41]

Fully aware that Riley could not remain undetected in the barn, his relatives decided that the safest place to conceal the runaway was under the floor of Zeke's cabin.[42] To make the place of concealment sufficiently large and fairly comfortable, they decided to remove some dirt from beneath the cabin.[43] Disposing of the fresh dirt raised a problem for Riley's kinsmen. They decided that it would be safe to carry the fresh diggings to the creek and dump them in during the rainy periods, so that the already muddy waters would not betray their activities. This plan worked successfully, for sometimes Mahster Coe sat in the cabin above Riley, never knowing that under the floor Riley was digging away. Tim Coe relates the story in these words:

> He hid out 'til the war ended. I couldn't tell you now just how long that was, but it was quite a while. And well, nobody never did know that he was there but his own people. And, of course, they was people a-lookin' for him all the time; he belonged to the other man, don't you see. And he would have paid a reward for him. But no one ever found him. But after the war was over, they didn't care to tell them where they kept Riley. They kept him under the floor! And they'd dig and carry the dirt to the creek and put the dirt in the creek so as not to leave any sign—and made a place for Riley under the floor.[44]

During his sojourn, Riley was given food and water through a plank in the floor. Each night he would come out and exercise his stiff limbs.[45] For eighteen months, Riley hid in his improvised home.[46] Meanwhile, his master from the south, willing to pay a reward for his return, determinedly searched for his lost slave but to no avail.[47] Finally, the new master and Mahster Coe agreed that Coe should pay the new master $500, and if Riley should ever be found, he would again become the property of Mahster Coe.[48] Before confirming the plan, however, Mahster Coe went to Zeke's cabin, explained the plan to him, and asked Zeke if he thought Riley could be found. Zeke would not betray his kinsman whom he had kept hidden all these months, but he also wanted the good will of his mahster. In the belief that he could trust his mahster and in the desire to be relieved of the strain under which he had been for so long, Zeke said to his mahster, "You buy him, I'll bet you Riley will come back." [49] Upon the word of Zeke, the contract was closed with Mahster Coe confident that Riley would be found.

One afternoon soon afterward, Riley was "found" in a little patch of woods not far from the cabin. He seemed to be a happy slave, for he was smiling and whistling as if nothing had ever happened. Although considerable inquiry was made as to where Riley had been all those eighteen months, neither he nor his loyal kinsmen revealed their secret until years later.[50]

SLAVE BILL ZEKE

Bill Zeke was born on the Coe plantation to Zeke and Patsy Coe, about 1845. Though only five feet tall and weighing 145 pounds, Bill possessed the strength of Samson.[51] "He was a regular giant," claimed Tim Coe in describing Bill's physical strength. George Allred remembered that Bill was an "awful stout man." Ruthie Coe Anders claimed that "when it come to these corn fields and log hauling and everything, he was there! That was a good man!" Because of Bill's apparent size and strength, later Coe generations ascribed almost su-

47 Tim Coe.

48 *Chronicles*, 12.

49 Charlie Coe, Aug. 1961, while at the home of Sarah Coe Tooley.

50 This episode of the late 1850's constituted the first link in a chain of stirring events that illustrate the indomitable spirit of loyalty and tribal cohesion that distinguished the Coe clan throughout its history. Riley was never mentioned after this episode, and he is not recorded as moving to the Coe Ridge Negro colony after the Civil War. It is felt that he spent his last years with the white Coes on the Kettle Creek homeplace.

Botkin, *Lay My Burden Down*, 174–90, contains several accounts of runaway slaves. Dorson's *Negro Folktales in Michigan*, 86–89, prints two accounts of slave escapes. In note 53, p. 217, Dorson refers to an early collection of runaway slave experiences published by Benjamin Drew in *The Refugee: or the Narratives of Fugitive Slaves in Canada* (Boston, 1856). These narratives purportedly were written by slaves, but Dorson states that "they read too smoothly."

51 *Chronicles*, 28.

52 Charlie Coe, grandson of Mahster Coe, claimed that Moore *sold* his slaves to a Texas slaveowner.

53 *Chronicles*, 28–29, et passim. The account cited in the *Chronicles* does not identify the slaves who traveled with Bill, and there is no oral evidence that Bill traveled with others or that Dr. Moore owned any slaves except Bill. The 1860 slave census of Monroe County shows that Moore had only one slave, a male.

54 Unlike the single *sage* associated with Slave Riley, which is still traditional, Bill was the hero in a cycle of legendary tales that apparently have been dropped from oral tradition in their original form. Just one of the Bill narratives was collected from oral sources, yet these tales possess all the ingredients necessary to capture the fancy of a storyteller and his audience. The only Bill narrative that has persisted in oral tradition concerns the strong woman wrestler who could pin the shoulders of any man to the ground.

It is my belief that the Bill tales have not disappeared. Characteristic of folk narratives, these stories have displayed a dynamic quality —the chief actor and role have been adapted to more recent characters and situations. The names of Tom Wilburn and other Coe Ridge occupants have been substituted for Slave Bill, and, in this form, have remained in oral tradition. A dichotomy in the Bill story cycle can be seen. Those stories associated with his sojourn in Texas seem to represent the typical plantation culture with which the Negro slaves were associated. There appears to be a generic relationship between these and the tales found in the Old Marster and John cycle, commonly associated with the Plantation South. On the other hand, those narratives dealing with logging experiences have no parallels in Southern Negro tradition, but follow the patterns which extol the physical prowess of the rip-roaring frontiersmen.

55 *Chronicles*, 28–29. The introductory comments in this tale indicate that other such stories about Bill were told by him in a fashion similar to the Muenchhausen tales of the nineteenth century.

perhuman feats to him, thus allowing a cycle of strongman stories to develop. These stories deal with Bill's trip to Texas, his escapades there, and with logging activities after he had returned to Coe Ridge.

At the age of ten, Bill Zeke passed into the hands of Dr. Sam Moore, of Black's Ferry. Moore reckoned, with the outbreak of the Civil War, that the slaves would be freed in Kentucky before they would be any other place in the South. With that thought in mind, Moore sent Bill to Texas for safekeeping.[52] En route to Texas, Bill and some fellow slaves traveled in wagons and on horseback, according to the *Chronicles*. At one point along the way, the thought of fleeing came to Bill's mind, but he thought better of it and continued on with the others. The new Texas master was a man named Stephenson, whom Bill served until the end of the Civil War.[53] Bill returned to Kentucky in time to join his relatives in their venture to establish the colony on Coe Ridge.[54] Dr. Moore was wrong in his belief that Kentucky would be the first state to free its slaves because, in the words of Leslie Coe, Jr., "Texas freed the slaves before Kentucky. Kentucky was three years later. When they freed him he came back—walked and caught rides and hoboed all the way back from Texas to Kentucky."

The *Chronicles* contains only one account of Bill's experiences during his journey to Texas:

> Another of Bill's experiences was in Arkansas. As is related by Bill, they had pitched tents near a canebreak, and he was sent to get a bucket of water. He had to go through the dense growth of canes to reach the spring, and out jumped some kind of large animal and sprang at him, at the same time making a loud noise.
> And Bill laughed afterward, and declared the folks in the tent did not have to wait long for the water.[55]

Four stories told by Bill Zeke about his experiences

after arriving in Texas are mentioned in the *Chronicles*. The first claims that Bill had a fight with the master's son, the second notes that he wrestled with a strong woman slave who had been able to throw every man with whom she contested,[56] and the third tells that on one occasion Bill became so excited that he slapped two stones together in the master's face and yelled, "If you try to hurt me, I'll fight you as quick as I'll fight any man." The fourth narrative is summarized as follows:

Bill saved his own life when attacked by a furious bull. Bill was carrying a tanned hide, when he was met by a herd of cattle. He was charged by a bull, but Bill stepped aside and threw the tanned hide across the back of the charging animal. The bull becomes [*sic*] frightened and changed its course.[57]

56   Both Charlie Coe and Mrs. Sarah Coe Tooley, without being questioned on the matter, volunteered information about an awfully strong woman who could throw a man flat on his back. This story can be compared to Motifs F610.0.1, "Remarkably strong woman," and X973(a) "Lie: Girl as remarkable wrestler," although none of the references call attention to a parallel situation.

57   This story is strikingly similar to "The Devil and Strap Buckner," printed in J. Frank Dobie, ed., *Legends of Texas* (Austin, 1924), 121–22. When a huge black bull appeared mysteriously in Austin's Texas colony, Strap Buckner threw a red blanket over his shoulder and walked out on the prairie where he challenged the bull to single combat and won. There is a strong resemblance here to Motif F618, "Strong man tames animals."

3 The Early Years of the Coe Colony: 1866–1885

Coe Ridge was located on the back part of the Coe plantation, situated in the hill country of Cumberland County, and the entire area was clothed in a dense blanket of virgin forests. The ridge lands passed into the hands of Coe slaves in 1866 and became the scene for some of the most fascinating legends to evolve in the upper South.

THE BEGINNINGS OF ZEKETOWN

Time has obscured the early history of Coe Ridge, so named when the Coe slaves took their master's family name and gave it also to their new home.[1] It may be that the ridge was once the location of an Indian village which served as a haven of refuge for runaway slaves, but that portion of the ridge's history, mentioned only in a newspaper account,[2] has been lost with the passing of time. Present traditions tell only of a nearby Indian village, once located on Pea Ridge. Some

1 The Coe colony is often referred to as Zeketown and sometimes Coetown. In the words of Mrs. Etta Short, "People didn't call them [the Negroes] Coe; they went by Zeke."

2 "Coe Ridge Gained Fame," *Cumberland County News*, Aug. 16, 1960. In Alabama it was common practice during the early days for runaway slaves to seek refuge in Indian villages rather than attempt flight to the North. See Sellers, *Slavery in Alabama*, 273.

extremely old descendants of that village still live in the immediate area, and are characterized by their longevity. Ray Anders offered the following:

> They live a longer life than ordinary people. I was in the hospital two or three months ago. They's one said he was about half Indian come in there in the hospital. I believe he said he was eighty-seven years old; had every one of his teeth that he was born with in his head—jist as sound as yore teeth is. I set there and talked with him. Lived down here at Pea Town somewhere.

There is no reason to believe that there were direct historical connections between the Indians and the Coe slaves, unless such ties are alluded to in an unexplained tradition claiming that Slave Ransom lived on Coe Ridge before his fellow slaves from the Coe plantation joined him in 1866.[3]

The most logical tradition about the ridge's early occupants alleges that a white man, John Jeff Webb, and his family were the first ever to locate on the ridge, and were occupying it when the Coes first moved there.[4] The whites lived in what the Coes later called the Webb Field, situated on the southern portion of the ridge. Webb is remembered as the person responsible for the beginning of the cemetery on Coe Ridge. When a daughter died, Webb obtained permission from the Negroes to bury her on their land. Afterwards, the Coes buried their own dead on the same site,[5] a high hill from which one can scan the countryside in all directions. The graveyard now contains about fifty graves, marked for the most part by uncarved fieldstones. Webb is remembered, secondly, as the person who pulled bad teeth by tying a string around them. With the other end of the string attached to a limb in a peach tree, Webb would jump to the ground, leaving the tooth dangling at the end of the suspended string.[6]

3 Tim Coe, Aug. 23, 1961; he did not date the move, however. The date 1867 is given by Howard Hardaway in "Coes of Cumberland," *Louisville Courier-Journal*, Jan. 28, 1940, but the *Chronicles* (p. 29) sets 1866 as the year when the Coe settlement was established. Not one of my own informants was able to date the event precisely.

4 Mrs. Ray Anders made this claim Aug. 18, 1961, on the basis of information earlier received from her mother, Molly Coe Holman.

5 Ray Anders told about Webb during our trip together across the ridge in his truck on Dec. 23, 1961.

6 *Ibid.* No additional recollections of the Webbs were recorded. It can be assumed from the above traditions that good relations existed between this family and the early Coes.

7 The logging phase was so important to the economy of the ridge that a whole chapter is later devoted to this pursuit; see "Woods and River," Ch. 6.

8 Mrs. Myrtle Kerr recalled it in this manner: "After Old Aunt Patsy and Zeke came back, granddaddy gave them this land over on top of the ridge for them to live on. And had it set out in a big orchard out there. I can remember that orchard myself. We were told that he give that land to Old Pats and Zeke." Mr. and Mrs. Richard Glass also remembered hearing that the Coe slaves had been given the land on Coe Ridge. It may be that the land on the ridge was never deeded to Zeke, for his granddaughter had the court records of Cumberland County searched to no avail in an effort to obtain a clear title to lands inherited from Zeke and Calvin Coe.

The Coe slaves were reluctant to leave the plantation when the day of manumission arrived. They had no place to go, and no money with which to finance the beginning of an independent existence. But Jesse Coe understood the predicament of his black people and made provisions for them. He felt that they could go it alone on land under their own care. They could cut the trees on the ridge, use the logs for building purposes, and plant crops in the newly cleared land. Throughout the growing season they could raise sufficient crops to feed their families, and during the cold seasons they could engage in logging activities as a means of raising much needed money.[7] With the welfare of his slaves at heart, Coe deeded his favorite slave, Zeke, some land located on Coe Ridge.

So runs the essence of four oral testimonies, the most interesting of which was offered by Ray Anders:

> It wudn't cleared up. It'uz all jist in woods. And so they told 'um if they wanted to live on it, they would deed it to 'um.
>
> When they freed 'um, you know, they give 'um a place to stay. Some said they didn't want to be freed, that they didn't have no place to go. And they give 'um a place to go, see. Like if you had a colored person and you thought lots of him, you'd give him a place to go, wouldn't ye? A place to stay? A piece of land to live on? That's the way they did.
>
> Well, after they give them that land in thar, they went to work. Logged and accumulated enough to kindly add a little more and buy a little more. Finally, they bought up I think it was 1,400 or 1,500 acres.[8]

Rather than making a gift of the land, however, it seems most likely that Master Coe sold the land to Zeke. Leslie Coe, Jr., claimed: "After they had got free, my grandfather went to where the Coe colony is located. His master let him save money. He raised tobacco and

The impassable road, heavy growth of weeds, and primitive hand-made headstones of the clan cemetery belie the fact that almost annually a native son or daughter comes home for the last time.

9 These testimonies are corroborated by Hardaway, "Coes of Cumberland," *Louisville Courier-Journal*, Jan. 28, 1940.

A third version of how the Coe Negroes came into possession of the lands on Coe Ridge is associated with the white Lollar family instead of Master Coe. The Lollars probably never owned any of the Zeke Negroes, and it is not likely that they would have given them land after the Civil War. The following text, told by Frank Murley of Ellington's Landing in Cumberland County, is interesting, nevertheless, for its folktale qualities:

> Now, my people always said that when the word came that they were freed, my great grandfather, Druie Lollar, told them Niggers that they are free.
>
> They said, "We are already as free as we want to be."
>
> But he told them that they might need a little patch of land for themselves.
>
> They said, "No," but later decided that they might need the land sometime, and decided to take the land. Old Aunt Patsy went with my grandfather Lollar when he was to show the little square patch of land he was going to give them.
>
> And Aunt Pats took four of her boys and gave them a corner apiece. She took her a great long switch and stood a boy in each corner and then just cut the blood out of their legs. She always said that a-way the boys would remember the four corners of the land that my grandfather give them.

The whipping Patsy Ann gave each of the four boys is strikingly similar to the ancient English custom of beating the bounds. The latter consisted of bumping persons to make them remember parish boundaries. See T. Sharper Knowlson, *The Origins of Popular Superstitions and Customs* (London, 1930), 60.

10 In most of the Southern states some of the more energetic slaves worked for pay during their idle hours and thus eventually secured a sufficient surplus to buy their own freedom. Such was not the case generally in Kentucky, however. Most Negroes there were content with their bondage, according to McDougle, "Slavery in Kentucky," 73.

different things. He had $400 saved up, so he bought 400 acres of land. He give a dollar an acre for it." Mrs. Cornelius Allen, a great-grandaughter, stated that Zeke "bought that little home for his family. He had to buy himself from his master and pay for his home all at the same time." Mrs. Ruthie Coe Anders emphatically declared, "Grandpa bought this home and paid for it! They didn't give it to 'um! They bought it! Grandfather and them, they hauled logs and things and paid for this ground. They bought it tract by tract, little by little." Finally, both Charlie Coe (white) and Mrs. Sarah Coe Tooley (Negro) jointly agreed that Zeke purchased the land:

> Coe: Zeke bought that!
> Tooley: Yeah, I know that's what Daddy said. They bought this little tract, you know, where they could have a home. They went in there and cleaned it up.
> Coe: And Uncle Zeke would make baskets. And my grandfather would let him have so much tobacco ground every year and give him all he'd make. That's the way they paid for that land out there.[9]

Zeke had been saving his money for over twenty-five years toward the day that he could manumit himself and Patsy Ann.[10] Zeke's personal income came from three chief sources—basket-making, rebottoming chairs, and growing tobacco crops on free acreage granted by his master. Tim Coe told about the importance of a tobacco crop in Zeke's economic scheme:

> Grandfather always give Zeke so much tobacco ground, and he cultivated that. And then he made this trip to New Orleans with 'um. And Zeke had all the tobacco he made on that spot of ground. Well, they'd run that to New Orleans, and, course, Zeke had no expense. Well, then when the war was ended, why, Zeke had a little over $600 in cash. Amount to $6,000 today; equal to $6,000. And when

the war was ended, why, they went out there on this ridge and bought this ridge.[11]

Zeke's baskets, made in bushel, half-bushel, and peck sizes, can be described as inverted heart-shaped containers minus the half containing the apex. Some of them were made from flat hickory strips, which provided the frame, and from willow switches that were interlaced to make up the sides and bottom. Other baskets were made totally from the hickory strips.[12] The material for Zeke's chair-rebottoming industry consisted of bark taken from hickory trees in the springtime in sufficient quantity to last all year.[13] Although the informants did not explicitly say so, Zeke did not use the bark itself, but rather the woody lining of the bark, which could be removed from the trees in long strips. He picked up chairs in need of repair while he peddled his baskets at the white neighbors' houses or placed them for sale in the local stores.

When freedom came after the Civil War, Zeke had a cash accumulation slightly in excess of $600. With the money, and acting upon the advice of his former master, he purchased three hundred acres of land on Coe Ridge at $2.00 per acre.[14] The deal was closed sometime during 1866, and Zeke began constructing log buildings to shelter his family and possessions.

The ridge home served as the focal point for the former Coe slaves. When the new home was ready to be occupied, Zeke re-gathered his offspring who had been willed off to the children of Master Jack Coe in 1853.[15] Leslie Coe, Jr., related a portion of the search in this manner:

> He left for 200 miles from where we lived. One of his daughters, Aunt Jemima, was in Louisville. One of the Coes—white Coes—had moved to Louisville, and they carried her with them. Every one of them, they'd take

11 Tobacco, sweet potatoes, and watermelons were the most common crops grown by the slaves for personal profit. See McDougle, "Slavery in Kentucky," 73. Slaves throughout Kentucky made additional money from making brooms, baskets, and chairs. See Coleman, *Slavery Times*, 79–80, et passim.

12 Charlie Coe recalled during the Coe-Tooley interview, Aug. 20, 1961, that Zeke made baskets as a source of income. Lucy Robert Coe described how the baskets were made, Sept. 24, 1962. Richard Glass mentioned the basket-making procedure during a tape-recorded interview, Aug. 14, 1961.

13 Zeke's chair-rebottoming activities were described by Charlie Coe and Ruthie Coe Anders and are corroborated by the *Chronicles*, 19.

14 These figures stated by Charlie Coe are corroborated by Hardaway, "Coes of Cumberland," *Louisville Courier-Journal*, Jan. 28, 1940. Tim Coe, on two occasions, claimed that the acreage was six hundred. Leslie Coe, Jr., contended that the money saved was $400 and that four hundred acres of land were purchased. The disputed traditions of these informants cannot be settled in the absence of written documents.

15 Mary Coe, about twenty-five, came from the home of Malinda Short; Patsy, about forty-seven, Jemima, about eighteen, and Monk, age unknown, were given up by Jemima Spearman; Thomas, about twenty-two, Joe, about fifteen, and Ransom came from Jesse Coe's farm; William, about twenty-one, Zeke, about nineteen, and Betty came from the home of John Jefferson Coe; others, including Zeke himself, had remained at the old Coe plantation home. The foregoing data were summarized from the 1853 will of Master John Coe.

16   If this tradition is correct, Patsy Ann had Frank by a white man prior to her marriage to Zeke.

17   Mrs. Moore is a great-granddaughter of Sammy Smith. Her historical tradition runs at variance with the one that claims Jesse Coe was the last person to own Zeke and Patsy.

Dog-trot house.

wherever they went, they took one with them. And so he went to get all of them back together.... He got most of it done ... except one. He didn't find one.

Now one of them, the oldest one, Frank, he was born by this white man. Well, he sold him. When they married, he sold this one out of the family. And they never did hear from him any more. Old man Ezekiel he went out and found them all but this one. He couldn't find him, 'cause he'd been sold south. And no one ever heard from him any more.[16]

Although some of Zeke's children lived with the Old Mahster's children, others may have been sold outright sometime prior to emancipation. Shortly before Calvin Coe died, he made a statement to Mary Ann Keen which may bear out this assumption: "I don't know why, but we was living on the Sam Smith farm on Kettle Creek when we was freed. I don't know whether we had been borrowed by Smith or not, but I know we hadn't been sold to him." Susie Taylor Moore[17] gave a similar testimony:

Sammy Smith lived on Kettle Creek. He bought Aunt Pats and Zeke .... Paid a thousand dollars for her. And he bought Zeke; paid a thousand dollars for him, and kept them 'til they freed the darkies. And then they left him and went to Zeketown and bought that place, and lived thar 'til their death.

I don't know whether they had any children when he bought them or not. But he first bought her, and then he bought Zeke, you know, to live with her. And they worked fer him 'til they freed them, you know.

A roll call of the first Negro settlers in the colony would have included at least sixteen names. These were Zeke and Patsy Ann, and eight of their children, Tom, Joe, Crippled Zeke, John, Calvin, Sarah, Susan, and Mary—many of them grown and ready for marriage. Betty and Sukey, the old grandmothers, were there also along with their other boys, Ransom, Tom Softly, Riley, and Bill Burress.[18] By 1869, three of Zeke's children had taken mates and had built homes in the colony. Mary was married to Tom Wilburn, Tom Coe to Lucetta King, and Bill Zeke Coe, who had returned home from Texas bondage, was married to Mandy Kirkpatrick. Additional marriages by Zeke's children, or cohabitation rather than marriage, rapidly increased the population of the ridge settlement.[19]

EARLY BUILDINGS ON COE RIDGE

The first Coe cabins on the ridge had only one room, typical of those found across the South. As the families grew, however, another room was added to the one-room cabins, thus forming a dwelling unit composed of two distinct, rectangular pens connected by a roof over an open breezeway. These structures, sometimes called "dog-trot" houses, were like those utilized by the whites of the area. On the process of house construction, Ray Anders said: "Them houses was all logs. They would take a pair of steers to the woods and cut down a tree and trim it up. They'd snake it back to the house and chip out the ends, and lay them logs down on top of each other. They'd fit, too! Yessir! Jist as snug as ye please." [20]

The logs were heavy and therefore did not need to be pinned together or tied down, except for the top or plate log. This log was secured to the second log by a wooden pin so that the wind would not blow away the roof. Between the logs was placed a trimmed pole, which was daubed with a chinking mixture composed of clay and hog's hair. The hog's hair was included to keep the clay from drying too rapidly and cracking.

Chimneys were located at each end of the houses, and were constructed from "jist old picked up field rock,

18 The *Chronicles*, 20, runs at slight variance with the names listed above. It lists as the original settlers Betty, Zeke, Patsy, Sukey, and ten of Zeke's children.

The Cumberland County Census for 1870 lists the following inhabitants of Coe Ridge: Bill Coe, Mandy Coe, and Catherine Coe comprised one household, while Zeke's home held Betsy, Patsy, Thomas, Zeke, Mike, Joe, John, Sarah, Susan, and Calvin. A daughter, Mary, is not listed. Perhaps during the very first years of her marriage to Thomas Wilburn she lived away from the ridge.

Although genealogical traditions tend to become confused in some instances, and the wrong names creep into the wrong slots, the traditions of a genealogical nature are surprisingly accurate for the most part.

19 By 1900 the colony contained approximately 100 inhabitants, living in a dozen or so houses. Royce Cary, a Negro informant from Mud Camp, on Aug. 21, 1961, stated that in about 1935 there were roughly twenty-five to thirty houses on the ridge, either standing or in decay. That figure appears somewhat high, however. Mrs. Myrtle Kerr, on Aug. 15, 1961, claimed that at its zenith, Zeketown contained about a dozen occupied houses. Mrs. Cornelius Allen, Jan. 24, 1964, agreed with Mrs. Kerr as to the date and number of houses. Leslie Coe, Jr., Aug. 18, 1962, claimed that "they told me that my great-grandfather had eighty grandchildren [in 1907]." This testimony did not make mention of the great-grandchildren Zeke had. The Cumberland County Census for 1900 and thereafter is not yet available for viewing.

20 Recorded with pencil and pad while riding across Coe Ridge in a pick-up truck driven by Anders, Dec. 23, 1961. The other statements in the next two paragraphs are also derived from that same interview.

The clay and hog's hair chinking mixture was commonly used in pioneer house construction throughout the South. Other oral accounts on this building mixture can be obtained from Botkin, *Lay My Burden Down*, pp. 79, 84.

21 In addition to helping identify early generations, folktales also provide valuable data concerning the early native and cultural features of Coe Ridge. Three tales mention wild animals that were found at one time on the ridge, while this tale commences with a description of the first log houses built in Zeketown. In these instances, introductory information is as important as the belief in the validity of the narratives. That is, belief tales can be valuable sources of historical information, as they tend to be introduced with statements which point out identities of people no longer living and which describe buildings no longer existent.

22 Narrated by Mrs. Ray Anders. The panther was the favored animal, according to Mody C. Boatright, "for a story placing a human being in jeopardy." See "The Family Saga and Other Phases of American Folklore," in Mody C. Boatright, Robert B. Downs, and John T. Flanagan, *The Family Saga and Other Phases of American Folklore* (Urbana, Ill., 1958), 7.

Two versions of "Panther on the Roof," and five versions of the panther in pursuit, may be found in J. Frank Dobie, *Tales of Old-Time Texas* (Boston, 1955), 181–94. Boatright, in "The Family Saga," gives a summary of a text from the "Panther on the Roof" and states that it may have come from Tennessee tradition prior to 1822. (I collected a version of the latter from Green County, Ky., white tradition in July, 1965.)

or maybe knocked off a ledge. They wudn't hewed out." Again, clay was used for cement, along with hog's hair or sticks.

In the interior of the earliest Coe Ridge houses, the kitchen and hallway were usually floorless, as shown in the introductory comments in the following panther legend.[21]

The Painter in the Yard

My grandmother told, said, "Aunt Til, you better quit that."

They lived in an old log house and they's a—you know, they always have a hallway, and they may dist have a kitchen. Wouldn't have no floor in it. That's the way they did back in olden times. They didn't have no floor in the kitchen nor in the hallway like that.

And said she was in there washin' dishes and whistlin' away. She said, "Tilda, you'd better come out of there, it's gettin' near sundown. That old painter will be here directly." (Said the old painter would come every night and scratch and eat bones.)

Said she jist went on about her business, whistlin' and washin' dishes and fiddlin' around and wudn't payin' no attention to what Mammy was tellin' her. So directly said grandmother said she'd done went and carried her wood in. (See they was two girls. They mother and father had died and left them two girls by theyself. They had to make it by theirselves, you know.) She hollered out to Til, "Til, the painter's in the yard." (See, she couldn't get in the house where her sister was at.)

Well, she slammed the door. And when she slammed her door, grandmother slammed her door. She had to stay in there all night and throw bones and things over, up at the top, out through the top logs, you know, let 'um fall down so he'd eat 'til he got full. He'd dist scratch; try to get in there to get her. And scratch, he would, and growl.

And grandmother they set up all night feerd that he was gonna break in on 'um—that painter. She was skeered to death.[22]

This quaint log structure on Coe Ridge is a mountain stable which bears a forward projecting roof more reminiscent of early smokehouses. It now functions as a hog house for the ridge's lone occupant.

23 This description was given by Ruthie Coe Anders on Sept. 2, 1961. All informants who knew Sett agreed that she came from the area above Celina, Tenn.

24 *Chronicles*, 23.

25 Some of the ancestors mentioned in this chapter have found a place in folktales which are now told as history. Such narratives are good sources of historical information that otherwise would be unrecorded. Aunt Til is also the chief character in the panther legend previously documented. At first, this writer considered her to be a traditional stock figure in the tales told about her, but intensive investigation showed that she was a real person.

Double log pen barn.

Along with the log houses, two additional buildings—a smokehouse and a barn—usually were included in the structures making up a homestead in Zeketown. The smokehouse was a small one-room log building with one door, and the barn, constructed of roughly hewn logs, contained two stories. On the bottom floor of the barn were livestock stables and a combination gear room-corncrib; the second story was used solely for the storage of hay and corn fodder.

In the words of Mrs. Edith Williams, who spent most of her life near Zeketown, "It was not a very prosperous looking place, but they had homes, and they were clean and neat around their homes. Their homes was clean and their families and children were always kept clean."

THE OLDER GENERATIONS OF ZEKETOWN

Tom Coe. Shortly after the inception of Zeketown, Tom Coe, one of the sons of Zeke and Patsy Ann, married Lucetta "Sett" King and brought her to live among his people. Sett's mother, Mary, is remembered as "a little short, dark woman," who owned her own home in the Obey River area, just north of Celina, Tennessee.[23] Sett never lived under bondage, for her mother had been freed before the Civil War.[24] When Sett came to Coe Ridge, she was accompanied by her sister, Fertilda, who lived with Tom and Sett the rest of her life. "Til," as she was called, was a ferryboat operator at one time during her life, if the information contained in the following belief tale is correct:[25]

> My mother's sister she used to ferry across the river. So my grandmother kept tellin' her, says, "Now you better quit that settin' people across the river every night. Somebody will fool you some of these nights and you are liable to get drowned or something another."

Said she said, "No, I ain't afraid."

Said one night, something 'nother called her, "O Fertil, O Fertil."

She said, "What?"

Said, "I want to cross the rive-r-r-r."

Said, well, she went on down. Said she got down there and said she didn't see nobody. Said she said, "Where are ye?" Nobody didn't answer, and said she said, "Where are ye?"

Said they answered on the other side of the river then, "Whooo." Said she went on across the river; got up there and said something another hopped on the other end of the kunue [canoe]. Said it had a head as big as a half bushel. Said its teeth was a long as its finger. And said its eyes was a big as ye fist. And said its neck wudn't big as a broomstick. And said he was just a-grittin' them teeth, "Eeehhh, Eeehhh," and said it was a-settin' on the other end of the kunue. And she paddled backerds plumb across the river and said in reason it looked jist like a ghost.

Said when he, when this thing, hopped in the river to leave—just something another like a ghost. And it hopped in, too. Said she fell backerds right backerds across the river in the skift. Said when she got to the bank she jumped out backerds and said she shoved her skift out in the river, and said that thing hollered, "tooddle-opp, tooddle-opp," made two of the funniest noises ever she ever heerd in her life, and that skift jist as fer as she could see it said he wuz grittin' his teeth going on down the river out of sight.[26]

Tom did not live long after his fourth child was born, for Sett is remembered as a widow by the oldest living generations. She managed to raise her children by taking in washings from the white families who surrounded the Coe colony. Sett carried her wash water from a nearby spring, three bucketsful at a time—one bucket in each hand and one on top her head.[27]

Tom and Sett's four children were Molly, Robert, Josephus, and Sarah Ruth. Of the four, only Sarah

26 Told by Mrs. Ray Anders. Motifs F500-529, "Remarkable persons," contain mention of the basic descriptive motifs found in this tale, but no motif contains reference to parallel accounts. In medieval concepts of the devil, according to George Lyman Kittredge, *Witchcraft in Old and New England* (Cambridge, 1929; reprinted, New York, 1956), 175 ff., the devil often assumed hideous forms. This tale has been included as a revenant, however, because the creature has basic attributes of a human and was called a ghost by the narrator.

27 Information in this paragraph was obtained in 1961 from Mrs. Etta Short, Bill Poindexter, and Mr. and Mrs. Ray Anders. Portions can be corroborated by the *Chronicles* (p. 23) and by the 1880 census of Cumberland County.

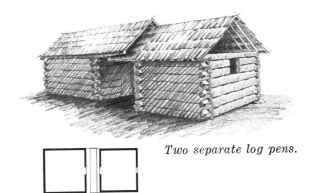

Two separate log pens.

71

28 Sarah Ruth ("Ruthie") was born in 1877, according to her personal testimony on Sept. 2, 1961. She married Frank Anders, a brother of Lucy Robert Coe. Frank preceded Ruthie in death by several years. She died in Oct. 1962, only two weeks after the writer interviewed her with a tape recorder. The names of Sarah Ruth and her sister and brothers, as stated above, were verified by the 1880 census of Cumberland County.

29 His daughter, Mrs. Ray Anders, provided a little information concerning her father in a tape-recorded interview, Aug. 18, 1961. Tombstone inscriptions in the colony cemetery show that Wilse was some twenty years older than his wife, Molly Coe. He was born on Oct. 17, 1853, and died on Sept. 28, 1915.

30 Tim Coe, Mrs. Etta Short, and Mrs. Mattie Davidson, during the interview at Tanbark, Ky., Aug. 24, 1961, related most of what is known of Wilse Holman's background. On March 29, 1969, Mrs. Ray Anders disagreed that Mime Coe was her grandmother—she thought her name was Mary.

31 According to Mrs. Ray Anders, the children were Lawyer, Henry, Esau, Calvin, Oscar, Tom, Isabelle, Lizzie, Cassie, Lucy, Fannie, and Lottie Beatrice.

32 Mrs. Ray Anders, Aug. 18, 1961.

Ruth, who married early in life and moved to Indianapolis, failed to leave a lasting impression on the colony's history.[28] The other three have been remembered for their deeds, both good and bad. Molly was remembered as a midwife, herb doctor, fortuneteller, and as one of the colony's chief storytellers. Robert was considered to be one of the few stabilizing influences in the colony—he had an almost irreproachable character and was hard-working and extremely industrious. Josephus, commonly called "Sephus," was the exact opposite of his brother, being a hot-headed, drunken troublemaker who was always in the middle of any fracas.

Molly married Wilse Holman, a Negro from Monroe County with a virtually unknown background.[29] Wilse, the son of Danny Holman and Mime Coe, grew to manhood along the banks of Kettle Creek, just north of Tennessee. He had a sister, Mary Ellen, who married Molly's first cousin, Little John Coe.[30] Thus, with Danny and two of his children injecting Holman blood into the Coe line, the Holman element was important in the colony's population. Molly and Wilse had twelve children,[31] but only Fannie (now Mrs. Ray Anders) was born on the ridge. With the exception of two years' residence in the colony and five years on Judio Creek, Wilse and Molly spent the rest of their married years on the Johnny Overstreet place, near Celina, Tennessee.[32] With the death of Wilse while they lived on Judio Creek, Molly took her children and moved back to Zeketown, in 1915, and spent the rest of her life among her own people. It was during this period in her life that Molly began her duties as midwife, fortuneteller, herb doctor, and storyteller.

Molly's brother Robert was the oldest of Tom and Sett's children. He was born September 21, 1874, and died December 7, 1946, on Coe Ridge, in a house which stood on the identical site once occupied by his father's original cabin. In 1895, Robert had married Lucy Anders, the sixteen-year-old daughter of slaves from Monroe County. (She was generally identified during later years as Lucy Robert Coe.) Her very light colored mother, Jennie, whose father was Isom Stephens, a white man, was the property of Marster Jimmy Geralds of the Tooley Branch section. Lucy Robert's father was Mart Anders, a very black Negro man who was the property of Marster Varney Anders (actually Andrews) of Turkey Neck Bend.[33] Robert and Lucy had thirteen children, all born and raised in Zeketown.[34] Eight of these children are dead; five died in the colony and were buried in the clan cemetery. Two grown daughters, Ruthie Calvin and Mary Susie, died on successive days during the influenza epidemic of 1918 and were buried in the same grave. Three of the surviving children live in Indianapolis, while the other lives in Chicago.

Tom and Sett's youngest son, Josephus, has been dead for many years. Although Sephus grew to manhood in the Coe colony, he moved to Indianapolis and spent his last years there. He married Lou Williams, a daughter of Billy Williams who lived in the Meshack section of Monroe County. After they moved to Indiana, three children were born to Sephus and Lou. Their only daughter, Hazel, died in Indianapolis, in 1956, but a son, Frank, still lives there. The other child, Tom, now lives in Chicago.[35] Sephus is remembered as an extremely "mean" Negro, one who was constantly in trouble during the middle years of the colony's history.[36] One Negro informant claimed that her own brother was "as mean as Sephus," thus using the latter as a means of comparison.

Joe Coe. This son of Zeke and Patsy Ann married Tilda

33 On Sept. 24, 1962, the writer visited Lucy Robert Coe for the second time. It took considerable effort on her part, aided by my pencil, to arrive at 1874 as the date of Robert's birth. The date of birth is apparently correct, for he is listed on the 1880 census as being five years old. The census was taken in Aug. 1880.

34 According to Lucy Robert, on Sept. 24, 1962, the children were Joe, born on July 30; Clay, born on Feb. 11; Jack, born on Oct. 22; Annie, born on Mar. 28; Ollie, born on May 11; Ivie, born on Feb. 11; Grace, born on Oct. 5; Kate, born on Feb. 21; Lucie, born on Dec. 28; Willie, born on Sept. 22; Mattie; Ruthie Calvin, born on June 14; and Mary Susie, born on Mar. 5, 1900. Lucy knew the dates of birth, but only in the instance of Mary Suzie could she recall the year of birth. Tombstone inscriptions verify the birth and death dates of Ruthie Calvin and Mary Susie.

Time is rather meaningless to the informants and is reckoned in terms of major events that occurred on a personal, community, or national level. "I was about ten years old when that happened" and "My father died when I was two" are typical comments of the informants when they were queried about dates. The actual year when an event took place was seldom known.

35 Information provided by Lucy Robert Coe, Sept. 24, 1962.

36 The white informants constantly referred to Sephus as a troublemaker, yet no stories were collected about his actions, indicating that he was never involved with the trouble between the Negroes and whites. It was this racial clash that gave tenacity to the traditions associated with the Coe colony.

37   The information stated about Joe is common knowledge. His death is described in detail at another point in this study.

38   This description came from Mrs. Sarah Coe Tooley, on Aug. 20, 1961. Other comments in this paragraph were written on the basis of information supplied by Mrs. Etta Short and by Mrs. Ruthie Coe Anders, who also said: "Uncle Zeke, the one that's crippled that makes them baskets, wudn't able to do no kind of work. But he could make and bottom baskets—lovely baskets. Uncle Zeke done that and sold and made him money."

39   The informants identify their ancestors by associating them with some physical characteristic. Thus, quite naturally, the crippled son of Zeke and Patsy is remembered as "Crippled Zeke"; another son, John, who was very yellow in color, became "Yaller John" when a nephew, John, was born. Sometimes the former is referred to as "Old John," while the younger is variously designated "Racer John," "Little John," or "Slick John" because of his speed, age, and black color.

40   Most of the information about John Coe is community knowledge. Tim Coe supplied the information that John died at the age of ninety.

Virginia Warren is a pseudonym, used in this text to avoid any possibility of invasion of privacy.

Black, a girl from the Mud Camp section of Cumberland County, and moved to that area sometime during the 1880's. Joe was killed by an assassin's bullet during a visit to Zeketown in 1888. No children were born to Joe and Tilda.[37]

Crippled Zeke Coe. Crippled Zeke was never married; he lived with his parents, Zeke and Patsy, until his death in his fifties. Described as a Negro who was "as mean as the dickens," [38] Crippled Zeke had to walk on crutches throughout his life, yet he was able to earn money from making baskets and rebottoming chairs—trades which undoubtedly were learned from Old Zeke.

Yaller John Coe. John Coe, or "Yaller John" [39] as he was frequently called, played a rather important role in the history of Zeketown. This son of Zeke and Patsy Ann is commonly associated with the legends about the white women and with the Taylor trouble which engulfed the Coe colony during the years around 1890. Sometime during the 1880's, John married Tennessee Black and moved to the community of her birth at Mud Camp, Cumberland County. At her death, John took up with Virginia Warren, a white woman who had wandered into Zeketown. Virginia soon died of tuberculosis, but not before she gave birth to John's son, Willie, who also died with that same disease at an early age. John himself lived to the ripe old age of ninety years, spending most of them in Zeketown. He was buried in the clan cemetery on the ridge.[40]

Calvin Coe. Calvin, the youngest of Zeke and Patsy's children, was born on May 20, 1861, according to the Keen manuscript. He died on April 21, 1955, at the age of ninety-three, and, as he had requested, was taken home to the ridge for burial.[41] Cal was described as a Negro who was yellow or light brown of skin, who had a flat forehead over which hung a bushy crop of dark hair, and who never weighed more than 135 pounds. He was remembered as a person who never bothered anyone unless extenuating circumstances drove him to it. Mrs. Edith Williams stated it this way: "He never bothered anybody. He never meddled in other people's affairs. And he was a person who wanted you to let him alone and he'd let you alone. And he was always nice and polite to anybody that was about him."

Calvin apparently catered to white girls only. On one occasion, he was foiled in an attempt to elope with Molly Ballard. That abortive scheme led to much bloodshed because Molly's father attempted to take personal revenge for the outrage. Sometime after his marriage plans went awry, Cal courted another local white woman and took her as his common-law wife. They lived together for the rest of her life, except for the period during which she was in jail for "living with a Nigger." She died in jail, but had already become the mother of "a houseful of children" by Calvin.

Calvin nourished hatred in his heart for many years for the legal injustices committed against the mother of his children; however, he was wise enough to know that he could not do anything about these wrongs. After the death of his companion, Calvin raised their children, and most informants admitted that he did a "pretty good" job of mothering his large family. As he grew older and his children moved away from the ridge, Calvin's living conditions depreciated considerably. In her manuscript, Mary Ann Keen described his home in 1954:

The living conditions in the home of Calvin Coe were of

41 His age and date of death were supplied by Mrs. Sarah Coe Tooley during the tape-recorded interview, Aug. 20, 1961. Uncle Cal's desire to be taken home for burial is reminiscent of the custom practiced by the Ibos of Nigeria, who always desired to be taken back to the place of their birth for burial; see Writers' Project, *Drums and Shadows: Survival Studies Among the Georgia Coastal Negroes* (Athens, 1940), 105–6.

42 Information in this paragraph came from various informants, including Ruthie Coe Anders, Mrs. Etta Short, Mrs. Mattie Davidson, Tim Coe, and Leslie Coe, Jr. The date that Bill died was established by Ruthie Coe Anders. Mrs. Anders said that Bill died when she was two years old and that she was born in 1877. The date of Mandy's death was obtained from her tombstone inscription. The Cumberland County Census for 1870 verifies that Mandy was born in Tennessee, but it did not yet include Tilda as a member of their household.

the poorest. His bedroom was furnished with two beds, a small table, a stove for heating the room, and two very old trunks. His banjo hung on the wall. On each side of the one small window stood a shot gun and another was hanging on nails above the door. The other room of Calvin Coe's cabin was a small kitchen and, like the bedroom, it was very untidy. The large cracks in the floors and walls made the writer wonder how anyone could possibly stay warm, even with a big fire, on cold winter days. Although the cabin was very dirty and the bedclothes were . . . filthy, Calvin Coe was clean and his clothing was clean. He sat on the side of the bed as he talked with the writer. He was unable to walk without the aid of canes.

Calvin Coe depended on his neighbors to help take care of his home. A distant relative stayed with him at night. Calvin Coe received thirty-eight dollars each month from the Public Assistance Program to meet his needs.

Bill Zeke Coe. Bill Zeke Coe, one of Zeke and Patsy's oldest sons, was married to Mandy Kirkpatrick, a slave girl who could read and write. Mandy was born and raised on the Chism Kirkpatrick plantation, located on the Obey River, north of Celina. When Bill Zeke and Mandy settled in the Coe colony, her sister, Tilda, came to live with them. Their first cabin was located in a deep ravine below the Coe cemetery. Later they built a house not far from the one occupied by Tom and Sett. Bill died in 1879, but Mandy lived on for many years, dying on February 9, 1913.[42] Seven children were born to Bill and Mandy: Little John, Thomas Ezekiel, Jesse, Cassie, Ada, Ora, and Samuel F.

Little John was extremely black and shiny. He was usually in the center of any fracas during the middle years of the colony's history. In the words of his cousin, Ruthie Anders, "That Little John was around here, children. Don't mess with Little John!" The first impression he made on the oral history of the colony came during the late 1880's when he and Calvin attempted to elope with teen-age white girls. But perhaps the most significant incident in the life of Little John occurred during the 1920's. In his presence, Leslie (Big Les) Coe killed Simp Smith,[43] and Little John was sentenced to the penitentiary because he would not turn state's evidence against Big Les. Little John's wife was Mary Ellen Holman, a sister of Wilse Holman who had married Molly Coe. Immediately after Little John was confined in connection with the murder of Simp Smith, Mary Ellen took their eight children[44] and moved to Indianapolis, never to return to Zeketown. Little John joined them in Indiana after his release in 1928, but he died soon afterwards.

Thomas Ezekiel, the son of Bill Zeke and Mandy who was commonly called "E" Coe, married his first cousin, Lucy Wilburn. E and Lucy built a large, weatherboard house in Zeketown, and there raised seven children who now live in Kansas City (Kansas), Indianapolis, Chicago, and on Kettle Creek in Monroe County. E Coe was a schoolteacher in Zeketown for many years and also a preacher and a peacemaker among his people. His qualities of leadership are still remembered and respected by all those who call his name, both Negro and white. E died shortly before Lucy, and both were buried in the family cemetery on the ridge.

Jesse Coe, a bachelor son of Bill Zeke and Mandy, lived most of his life in the Coe colony. While he was in Indianapolis in 1906, Jess killed two policemen, but he slipped out of Indianapolis and returned to Zeketown where he hid out for eighteen months. Eventually, however, Jess was betrayed and shot to death in a sheriff's ambush.

Cassie Coe, one of the daughters of Bill Zeke and Mandy, married Bill Asberry, usually called Raspberry, a drifter from Virginia who came into the Coe colony

43 Simp Smith is a pseudonym, used in this text to avoid any possibility of invasion of privacy.

44 According to Mrs. Ida Allen, a daughter, on Jan. 24, 1964, Little John and Mary Ellen's children were Ida, who married Cornelius Allen and who presently lives in Noah's Hollow, Cumberland County; Minnie, who married a Barksdale and who died in 1963; Levie, who married a McMillan girl and who died in Indianapolis in Nov. 1962; Ulah, a soldier who was killed in World War II; Samuel, Jr., who married a Moody and who lives in Indianapolis; and Laura (Hickman), Beulah (Action), and Lois (Cook), all of whom live in Indianapolis.

45   Information about Cassie and Raspberry was provided by Mrs. Cornelius Allen, Jan. 24, 1964. The 1880 Cumberland County Census records that Cassie was born in 1870.

46   Information supplied by Mrs. Cornelius Allen, Jan. 24, 1964.

47   Statistical information was provided in a letter from Loman Cansler to the writer, dated Aug. 19, 1962. The 1880 census does not list Samuel; thus he may be in error about this birth by one or two years.

48   Information concerning the time that Samuel left Zeketown and his marital status was provided by Mrs. Cornelius Allen, Jan. 24, 1964.

during the 1890's. Cassie and Bill were married about 1897 and left for Indianapolis that year. On his deathbed, Bill Raspberry told his children that his real name was Esselman and that he had lived for many years under an assumed name. The children immediately had their names changed and go by Esselman today.[45] Cassie became a preacher known as Mother Wagner and returned to Zeketown to preach a doctrine of peace and coexistence. To her goes much of the credit for the Negro Coes' laying down their guns to end the period of feuding with the whites.

Two other daughters of Bill Zeke and Mandy, Ada and Ora Coe, are rarely mentioned in connection with the oral history of Zeketown. Ada went to Indianapolis in 1900, found a job, and lived with Bill and Cassie. Eventually she married Hance Williams, a young Negro from the Martinsburg area of Monroe County. They raised several children who were born in Indianapolis and who are still living there. Ora married Chester Coe, the son of Yaller John. Ora and Chester lived their lives in the Coe colony, where she died rather prematurely at the age of forty-two. Their children were Big Les, Marjorie, Tim, Wallace, Prentice, and Tabitha.[46]

Samuel F. Coe was the last of Bill Zeke and Mandy's children. He was born on September 12, 1879, and died in Kansas City, Kansas, on May 12, 1962.[47] At the age of twenty-two, Samuel moved to Kansas City, where he later married but raised no children. It was Samuel who wrote *The Chronicles of the Coe Colony*, frequently referred to in this study.[48]

Sarah Coe. This daughter of Zeke and Patsy Ann never produced offspring, although she was twice married. Sarah first married Joe Kirkpatrick, a cousin from the Meshack section of Monroe County, and then married a Mr. Lewis and moved to Glasgow, a town in Barren County located about forty miles west of Coe Ridge. She lived there for many years, mainly among white people whom she served in the capacity of maid. Sarah managed to accumulate a modest amount of material possessions, but the whites with whom she lived "got everything she had." [49] She died about 1956.

Sue "Suze" Coe. Another daughter of Zeke and Patsy Ann, Suze was a very yellow Negro girl, and was the youngest of the children. She became ill with tuberculosis and died while still in school on the ridge. Her exact age at death is not known. [50]

Mary Coe. A faded tombstone inscription in the ridge cemetery testifies that Mary Coe Wilburn died on February 8, 1907. The birthdate on the stone appears to be October 29, 1848. [51] Sometime between 1865 and 1869, this daughter of Zeke and Patsy Ann married Thomas Wilburn, "a strange man who came from the head of the [Obey] River." Those words, voiced by Mrs. Ray Anders, were corroborated by other informants. Charlie Coe claimed that Tom was descended from slave parents who belonged to a white Wilburn clan on Obey River.

Both Tom and Mary played rather important roles in the history of the Coe colony. Although Tom is remembered as a rather eccentric person, he does not have the dubious claim to fame that Mary does—that of bootlegging. One white informant testified that he had "bought a few quarts of whiskey from Aunt Mary," but "Tom was not a moonshiner." It was the sons of Tom and Mary who did the whiskey-making and who were constantly in trouble with the law or with some of the local whites. Two of these six sons were drowned,

49 Quote uttered by Mrs. Sarah Coe Tooley, Aug. 20, 1961. In addition to that testimony, Ruthie Coe Anders, Sept. 2, 1961, provided the additional information concerning Sarah Coe.

50 Information concerning Sue Coe was provided by Ruthie Coe Anders, Sept. 2, 1961, and by Mrs. Etta Short, Aug. 24, 1961. Susan Coe was fifteen in 1880 and still living, according to the Cumberland County Census for that year.

51 The Cumberland County Census for 1880 lists Mary as thirty-six years of age; thus she may have been born as early as 1844. The age of an individual will generally vary on the census charts from one census period to the next, however, thus indicating that many people did not know their exact ages.

one was clubbed to death, and another was killed in a gun fight. Only one of the six lived beyond young adulthood. The survivor was Charlie, a man highly respected for his personal integrity and industriousness, but also a man who raised a brood of children who were reputedly into all sorts of trouble during the declining years of the colony.

4 *The Middle Years of the Colony: 1885–1910*

Oral testimonies in this chapter point up racial antagonisms that smouldered for twenty years along the upper Cumberland River after the Civil War and then finally erupted in a violent racial feud in 1888. The evidences of hatred shown by the whites did not extend to all members of that race, for among the families that surrounded the Coe colony only a certain segment resented the presence of an island of Negro culture in their midst. From these white families sprang a generation of ruffians who grew up during and immediately after the Civil War. It was that generation which caused havoc throughout the countryside, and in turn became famous in oral tradition for the roles they played during the years of the life-and-death struggle which gripped the Coe colony.

Any mention of the racial feud brings recollections of many white family names of the area. The Taylors are especially remembered, for they were the central actors in the gruesome drama. Other names, such as Short, Neely, Vaughn, Ballard, Capps, and Irvin, are frequently cited, but these assume secondary importance to the Taylors in the historical legends about the Coe colony. The role played by the Taylors, strangely enough, is no more significant in reality than that of the other families mentioned. The Shorts and Neelys were the apparent instigators of the feud; the Taylors entered the fight only at the urging of Fannie "Tump" Short [Neely]. And the other families were responsible for the death of one or more of the Coe Negroes, while the Taylors, themselves never able to kill anyone, met their own deaths at the hands of the Coes.

It now appears that the legendary prominence of the Taylors lies in the fact that they were defeated by the Negroes. For this reason the Taylors form the core of historical traditions associated with the feuding years. Although responsible for the deaths of Will and George Taylor, Calvin and Yaller John Coe played no part in the defense of the colony when it was attacked by an army of white men who intended to annihilate the population and to burn the dwelling structures in the ridge colony. During that trying incident in the history of the colony the burden of defense was shouldered not by Cal and Old John, but by Bill Raspberry, Tom Wilburn, Little John Coe, and three younger boys. Soon thereafter, four of the sons of Tom Wilburn met violent deaths, and Jess Coe was betrayed and killed in brutal ambush. Yet, it was Cal and Old John who became folk heroes to their clansmen. Their conquests of the Taylor boys have placed them in the same heroic roles as those enjoyed by Riley and Bill of slavery fame; Cal and Yaller John are remembered by the present generations as two legendary ancestors who were able to outwit their antagonists.

Additional comments which accompanied each historical narrative told by the informants, especially by the Negroes, were directed toward the Taylor boys. Practically everyone was willing to make observations about the Taylors, but, strangely enough, the other white families were left out of consideration. Even the members of the white Coe line did not hesitate to offer their views about the Taylors; they remained quiet, however, concerning other families participating in the feud. This silence can apparently be explained by the fact that many of the other families are related to the white Coes. The mahster's living descendants readily admitted that Ike Short, an illegitimate cousin, may have started the feuding, but they were cautious in describing Short's personal character. Events in which Short and others participated were related by the present white Coe descendants, but no further comments were offered pertaining to the roles of these men in local society.

All of the white informants placed the entire blame for the feud on the white troublemakers of the area, except for the niece of the Taylor boys, who naturally blamed the Negroes. Although the white informants could not place the exact source of the feud, they unknowingly alluded to the cleavage in the white society that took form during the Civil War and that continued into subsequent generations. These informants noted that there were whites who accepted the presence of the Negro colony, but also whites who did not want the Negroes in their midst.

The nature of the early relations between the races was adequately demonstrated through oral family tra-

1 Mrs. Jesse E. Coe, Burkesville, Ky., interviewed by Miss Mary Ann Keen.

2 Of the younger Negro generation, Coe added at another point, "The further away from Old John and Cal and that bunch you get, why, the meaner that bunch got."

3 The white troublemakers were closely related to Mrs. Short, both by birth and marriage. Her mother was a Coe before marriage.

ditions. All testimonies claimed that the older Negro generations in the colony were careful not to interfere with local occurrences which did not concern them. The neutral stand of these early Zeketowners was respected by the majority of the whites who lived near the colony. Statements gathered from the white informants attested to an attitude of kindness and honesty on the part of the older Negro generations and pointed the finger of guilt for the period of feuding at the group of white troublemakers who apparently were as much despised by members of their own race as by the Negroes whom they provoked and incited.

"The older colored Coes were good, honest, hard-working people," stated the widow of Mahster Jesse Coe's grandson, "and they would treat anyone fair and right. But these people who tried to run them off the ridge, they really made the Coes kill them." [1] Tim Coe, another grandson of Jesse Coe, staunchly defended the character of the older Negroes, but could speak only bad things about the younger Negro generations: "Now, I'll tell ye, if people [have] got in their head that this old bunch of Coes out there wuz blood-thirsty and wanted to kill, they're jist wrong. Now the latter ones along at the last, I wouldn't risk one of them for nothing. They'd soon kill ye as not." [2]

During the interview at Tanbark, Kentucky, Coe again defended the former slaves of his grandfather: "They never was any trouble back there on that ridge 'til the whites started it. They never would have bothered the white people if they'd let 'em alone." Mrs. Etta Short added her agreement: "All of them colored people wuz all right. I have to tell the truth! And the white people were the ones that caused all the trouble. I remember how my mother used to talk to them boys and try to keep that trouble down." [3]

A lifelong resident of the community adjoining Coe Ridge testified: "They said when they entered Coe Ridge, they wuz as harmless as doves." His wife, also born near the ridge, said: "The first generation that growed up there was jist as nice as anybody. Good neighbors, good, clever, honest people as anybody. Them darkies wuz honest back then; jist as honest as any white man."

Hascal Haile, a former merchant in the river area, attested in a different vein to the honesty and integrity of the older Coe Negro generations:

> When they bought anything in the store, they always paid for each article as they bought it, don't you see. They wouldn't never let you add up a big column of groceries or anything. Why, they'd get the money out and pay you for that [single item], they'd then look to see how much they had, and they'd buy something else—they'd pay you for that.
>
> . . . When I was a boy . . . I've waited on them many a time. And all those old colored people over there was mighty honest. They could be trusted with a debt. If they promised anything, you could depend on it. Very superstitious and things like that, but they were honest.

Needless to say, former members of the Zeketown colony placed all the blame on the whites for the trouble between the races. In two typical instances, Negro attitudes in the matter were expressed by informants who pointed out that the Negroes were wrongly accused and that the bad name received by the feuding generations carried over to the present time, thus casting a shadow on the names and lives of the present generations who no longer live in the ridge colony. According to Mrs. Sarah Coe Tooley, "They mistreated them over there. You see, the Coes got a bad name, and it hurts me! But, of course, they ain't nothing much I can do about it. They'd holler about 'em being bullies

4   The Taylors had a sister, Jane, who married Tom Kerr, according to Mrs. Mattie Davidson and Tim Coe, at Tanbark, Ky. The parents of the Redheads were not identified by these informants. Since their names are not important for this study, neither informants nor census schedules were consulted in an effort to learn their identity.

5   Mrs. Coe had expected trouble between the two due to an old grudge which began when Jesse Coe shot Babe Taylor five times in the chest at the Kettle Creek schoolhouse, which is described later in this chapter.

bad. But that older generation, they didn't bother nobody unless they bothered them. But it's a poor frog that won't holler fer its own pond, and try to take care of hisself."

Mrs. Ray Anders also defended the right of the Negro Coes to take up for themselves: "They wudn't a thing in the world the matter with the people on Coe Ridge. . . . They jist took up for themselves like you would, if you, if somebody was to come around your home and try to run over you."

THE TROUBLEMAKING REDHEADS

Called the "Redheads" because of the fiery red color of their hair, the three white Taylor brothers,[4] Will, George, and Babe, were born and grew to manhood at Rock Springs, located in the rugged southern portion of Cumberland County near the Tennessee line. All three boys were "mean," according to Ruthie Coe Anders, but were especially notorious for peddling bad whiskey which "poisoned and killed lots of people." Mrs. Jesse E. Coe (white) of Burkesville remembers the Taylors as a family of troublemakers:

> They were a bad group of people. You never knew when they were going to cause trouble. They really wanted to and tried to run the colored Coes off Coe Ridge.
> I remember very well when my husband and I lived on Kettle Creek in 1891, and George Taylor came to our house and called for Jess. After telling Taylor that Jesse was in the field working, I ran in the house, got a pistol, and took a short path to the field and gave the pistol to Jess so he could be prepared if trouble should arise. However, there was no trouble.[5]

The Redheads were not a despised group, for the most part, and they were not criminals in the true sense. Beyond their escapades with the Coe Negroes, their legendary fame lies in their rowdy and boisterous actions. Perhaps Tim Coe best summed up the true picture of the Taylor boys: "Never heard of them doing anything like that [i.e., robbing stores and the like]. They jist wanted to be in trouble with some man."

No one questioned the bravery of the Redheads, for they never retreated from the greatest of odds. Commenting on that admirable quality, Tim Coe said, "You couldn't scare one of them Taylors. There was no way to scare them." That statement was borne out in 1888 and 1892 when Will and George Taylor met death at the hands of Cal and Old John Coe. In both instances, the incident was precipitated by foolish but daredevil advances against the Coes by the Taylor brothers.[6]

The first incident—at least the earliest recorded in oral tradition—in which the rowdiness of the Taylors was shown occurred at the Kettle Creek schoolhouse about 1870,[7] when a school program was to commemorate the last day of school. Sam Stewart, a one-armed man, who apparently disliked the Redheads, made a grand entrance into the schoolyard by riding up on horseback, with a girl behind him. Perhaps to agitate the Taylors, Stewart asked his horse how a certain person had run for president. The trained animal answered back with certain leg and body movements which infuriated the Taylors. The Redheads then pulled Stewart off his horse in an effort to start a fight. When Stewart refused to resist them, they began roughing him up. Charlie Coe recalled the details of the initial skirmish that day:

> They had a pretty big school back up Kettle Creek over there. They'd have some kind of entertainment, you know, at the end of the school.
> John Tom Patterson was sheriff of Monroe County at that time. And they asked him to come down there, since these Taylors had sent word that they was going to break

6 Babe Taylor, the other brother, was too sick to participate in the feud between the Taylors and the Coe Negroes. He died soon thereafter with tuberculosis, according to Mrs. Mattie Davidson and Charle Coe. Babe Taylor was married to Mary, daughter of Ab Short, according to Mrs. Mattie Davidson and Mrs. Etta Short on Aug. 24, 1961.

7 Tim Coe reasons that since the event happened before he was born, it probably transpired between 1865 and 1870. However, I have established the approximate date as 1880 on the basis of census data: Tommy Killman, who married Matilda Coe, born in 1864, was present at the fracas. (But he could have been several years Matilda's senior.)

it up. And so the sheriff just deputized my daddy [Benjamin Coe] to be deputy sheriff down there. The sheriff wouldn't come!

And so my daddy and my father's two nephews, they went with him. Also, a feller by the name of Tommy Killman and Bill Murley, I believe, was all in there.

Sam Stewart, a one-armed man come up on a horse. And he was asked how a certain person run for president, you know; and the horse would outrun anything that ever was. Asked him how the other'n was—I forgot who was running then—and he'd just go moping along.

These Taylors just reached up and pulled this one-armed man off the horse. That's the way they started this trouble. They got rough and got their guns out.

Tim Coe, Charlie's brother, also recounted the initial stages of the conflict: "Sam Stewart, a one-armed man, come riding up with some girl. And I suppose he had done that just in order to start something. They wouldn't try nothing; I heard my daddy say a lot of times that they wudn't trying to hurt Sam. But they pulled him off'en his horse and was a-handling him a little rough in order to start something."

With the three or four local men selected to help him, Benjamin Coe stood on the opposite bank of Kettle Creek and watched the proceedings until things began to get out of hand. He then crossed the creek and ordered the Taylors to turn Stewart loose, since Sam had done no real harm to anyone. Babe Taylor fired a shot at Coe and tore a plug from the corner of his vest. Immediately, Little Jesse Coe, a nephew, fired five times in Benjamin Coe's defense, and all five shots hit the area of Babe's heart:

> Taylor's brother-in-law told me [Tim Coe] that them five bullets didn't cover a place as big as his hand right over his heart. And Jess was a crack shot with a pistol. And course that knocked him out. And his brother-in-law told me that he hauled him home that night and that

Pictured here is the Kettle Creek school ground where opposing white factions fought it out during the 1870's.

8 Hascal Haile claimed that Killman's cylinder pin was wooden; he gave the following reason to back up this claim: Killman's mother had begged him not to go to Kettle Creek that day, and when he refused to listen, she slipped out and removed the cylinder from his pistol. Discovering the part missing, Killman whittled a wooden cylinder from a fence post.

9 Scarborough died two or three days later. The account of Scarborough's death was collated from the accounts told by Hascal Haile, Tim Coe, and Charlie Coe, and from the joint interview of Tim Coe, Mrs. Mattie Davidson, and Mrs. Etta Short.

he had a breastplate and that was what that saved him. They said he got them five battered balls out of Babe's boots—went down his britches' legs.

As soon as the school program was dismissed, the brawlers moved into an adjoining level field where "they just lined up and shot it out," taking no cover. Lint from the Taylors' clothing was flying all about them, but because of breast protectors, none of the Taylors fell. When Benjamin Coe and his men realized that the others were wearing breast protectors, they fired at the legs of the men, crippling them. "Dad," Tim Coe later addressed his father, "nobody ever accused a Taylor of being afraid. Why was it they was all on the ground and none of you fellows hurt? And he said, well, it looked to him like the Taylors were shooting at their heads all the time."

When the fracas in the field was over, Benjamin Coe started through some wooden bars which served as a gate between the field and the school grounds. By the gate stood a large sycamore tree with a great cavity at its base. A Scarborough fellow, the only one of the Taylor crew not shot up, ran up behind Benjamin Coe and started to stab him with a knife. Tommy Killman, a youngster who was accompanying Coe through the gate, had an old cap and ball pistol in his hand. Ignoring the pleas of Coe, Killman fired at the fleeing Scarborough and hit him in the back. When Killman fired, the cylinder pin broke and the cylinder flew out of his pistol. He ran down to the large sycamore tree, crawled into its trunk, and there whittled out another cylinder pin.[8] He then replaced the pistol's cylinder and walked triumphantly back into the crowd with pistol in hand.[9]

Benjamin Coe made friends with the Taylors after the schoolhouse affair quieted somewhat. But Horace Murley, Bill Murley, and Sam Smith, who also had participated in the incident, refused to be reconciled with the Redheads. One day these three were riding through the Martinsburg Gap and were at the point known as Low Gap Hill when they saw George Taylor coming up the hill from the other direction:

> All three of these men carried guns for the Taylors.[10] And they just stopped there in the road, and George Taylor rode right on up there. In fact, I've heerd one of them tell it. And [Taylor] just rode right on by them—never spoke or let on like the boys wudn't there. Just went right on by them.
>
> And one of these fellows said after he passed, said, "I'm going to shoot him right in the cross of the galluses."
>
> And this fellow's brother said there, "If you do, I'll shoot you. A man that's got nerve enough to do that, they ain't nobody going to shoot him in the back where I am." [11]

ORIGIN OF THE FEUD

Notwithstanding the instigator's role assumed by Sam Stewart, there were other and more apparent reasons for the feud which erupted between the Negroes and whites in 1888. These causes were complicated and interwoven, which made it difficult to discern the real factors involved. Among the motives for the outbreak were the desire to drive the Coe Negroes off the ridge, Cal Coe's tampering with a white man's wife, and the tortures inflicted on the Negro children by the whites. In all instances the forces of jealousy and hatred appeared paramount.

A study of the collected materials shows that all of the white participants in the feud were closely related to ex-slaveholders of the area. Furthermore, they were all descended from or married to descendants of William Short, and were closely related by birth and mar-

10 To carry a gun for someone meant that a person was prepared for a death struggle upon sight of the enemy.

11 Tim Coe. This series of incidents apparently earned the Taylors a niche in the oral history of the upper Cumberland. These events may not have had direct relations with the feud which came later, but for some reason they are known by several of the informants, black and white. If these incidents are accepted at face value only, they provide classic examples of the rowdy, unruly nature of the Redheads and their friends. These happenings may have greater significance than being simply a community fracas, however. Since the schoolhouse episode is always told as part of the history of the Coe colony, it would seem that it may have a now-forgotten significance in the Negro-white feud, which occurred some ten or fifteen years later. George Allred, a Negro informant who drifted into the Coe colony shortly after the schoolhouse incident, claimed that Sam Stewart started the feud.

Citing the older Negroes as his authority, Allred, who at one time lived with Stewart and his sister, claimed that Stewart would "carry lies to the Taylors about what the Negroes had said," and vice versa. Allred said that George Taylor came to the Bear Wallow voting house in 1892 intending to kill both Stewart and Calvin Coe. But Stewart did not show up, for evidently he was attempting to use the Coe Negroes as the channel for revenge against the Taylors.

12 William Short's children were known by both Tim and Charlie Coe, and were verified by 1850 and 1860 Monroe County census schedules.

13 According to the 1880 Cumberland County Census, Fannie was thirty years old, and John Milt was eleven. She had no husband listed on the census. John Milt died on April 15, 1898; see *Cumberland County News*, Sec. B, p. 7, for mention of his death.

14 Tim Coe, on Dec. 8, 1963, stated that Jesse Coe gave a stallion to Ike Short on the latter's twenty-first birthday.

15 Ike Short's mother was not revealed to the writer. Smith is a pseudonym used in this text to avoid any possibility of invasion of privacy.

riage to the white Coe line. In regard to the connection of William Short to the white Coe line, it is not known for certain that William Short and one Polly Short, who married a Coe, were brother and sister. Census schedules for Monroe County claim that William was born in 1818 and Polly in 1819, thus possibly indicating brother and sister. Polly Short married John Jefferson Coe, son of Master John Coe. William Short was thrice married, the second time to Malinda, daughter of Master John Coe. Troublemaking children were born to William Short by his first two marriages. His first wife bore him Beanie and Ab, while the second bore him Fannie "Tump." [12] Beanie Short was a Confederate guerrilla, celebrated in legend and song, who lived with Master Jesse Coe some of the time before the Civil War. Ab Short, William's other son, had a son, Charles, who figured in the feud, and a daughter, Mary, who married Babe Taylor, one of the Redheads. Beanie and Ab's half-sister Tump gave birth to an illegitimate son, John Milt Neely.[13] John Milt played an important role in the feud. To add further confusion to the picture, Ike Short, who later admitted guilt for starting the feud, was an illegitimate son of a close relative of Master Jesse Coe who raised him.[14] Ike's mother had another son, this time by a man named Smith.[15] A descendant of that son was Simp Smith, who became a victim of the feuding tradition in the 1920's when he was murdered on Coe Ridge.

Although the genealogy of the antagonists has been established as being closely associated with the white Coes, the question of feuding motive can only be conjectured. It appears that the relatives of Master Coe's family did not share his sentiments concerning a homogeneous Negro society in the midst of people who had once held blacks in bondage. The fact was alluded to by Mrs. Ray Anders, a great-granddaughter of Zeke and Patsy Ann Coe: "They wuz a feller told me what was the cause of this killing. They tried to run them off that piece of ground after they freed the colored folks. They give them that place, and the white people tried to run them off and take it away from them."

Calvin Coe added to the feelings of animosity when he courted the wife of one of the Redheads while the Redhead was in prison. Taylor threatened to kill Calvin, although Calvin denied the accusation by stating that he "hadn't never let that pass over his head about goin' with Mr. Taylor's wife." [16]

Almost all of the young white men surrounding Coe Ridge dipped heavily into the whiskey bottle. When they became intoxicated, their thoughts invariably turned to the Negroes on Coe Ridge. These whites, who included the Taylors, Shorts, Capps, Pruitts, Longs, and Vaughns, would run their horses through the Coe colony and often tear down the fences. One day Calvin Coe was in his house when some of the white ruffians rode through the settlement and sang out:

> Buffalo Bill,
> From Bunker Hill;
> Never was curbed,
> And never will.

Calvin, taking the song as a personal insult, grabbed for his gun and called to the other members of the colony. They armed themselves, but the white boys left the colony without incident.[17] In an episode which took place in 1879, described only in the *Chronicles* (pp. 26-28), Calvin again figures in that account as an elusive person sought by the whites.

On another occasion the feud almost erupted into open hostilities. A Dr. Hunter was a candidate for

16 Lucy Robert Coe. Calvin's relationships with a woman or women at an early date in the colony's history are hinted at but not articulated in testimonies offered by Mrs. Ray Anders, Mrs. Sarah Coe Tooley, and Judge J. W. Wells.

I found no evidence to indicate that either of the Taylor brothers served any time in the penitentiary.

17 Judge J. W. Wells. He also mentions this episode in his *History of Cumberland County,* 105-6. During the interview, Wells described the song as one that "had been handed down. They picked it up; thought it would fit their desires." When asked for whom the song was intended, Wells stated that it was "referring to the general race of colored Coes."

Calvin's fear that the song was meant to agitate him demonstrates that he most likely had previously offended the whites in some manner. Perhaps the charge was true that he had courted Taylor's wife.

18 Both Tim Coe and Charlie Coe told of "a big chestnut orchard" located on the ridge.

state representative and had campaigned among the Coes. Wright Capps and George Taylor took it upon themselves to keep the Negroes from voting. They rode onto Coe Ridge one night and went first to Bill Zeke's house. Instead of calling "Hallo" as was the custom, especially at night, they called out in a harsh voice, "Hunter men." One of Bill's small boys misunderstood, thinking the men said "Murder men." He ran and hid under the bed. Bill's wife, Mandy, pushed a table against the door, but Bill chastised her, "Take care, Mandy." He then opened the door and invited the men inside. They came into the house, but soon left without stating their business. Believing the men intended mischief, Bill sent his two sons to warn his brother Calvin that these men were on the ridge and were no doubt looking for him. Again nothing happened.

Friction between the races was intensified by some of the white boys who made it a habit to go to the ridge and freely partake of the abundant chestnut supply.[18] The Negro boys and girls, who picked up the chestnuts and sold them for cash, resented the intrusion on their personal property. On one occasion, a fight over chestnuts broke out between the races. "That's what started all that killing," claimed Tim Coe.

From that time, the whites accelerated their efforts to antagonize the settlers of Coe Ridge. One of the first incidents to be recorded was described by Mrs. Ray Anders: "Uncle Tom Wilburn, him and his wife was setting out in the yard one Sunday evening. And they's one of these Short boys out of Turkey Neck Bend, and some more girls passed there—they wuz white. And he jist pulled out his gun and just shot right over amongst Uncle Tom's little children. Said Uncle Tom didn't open his mouth."

The person just described was Ike Short, according

to Tim Coe, who had heard Short personally admit that he started the trouble which led to a loss of lives during the feud. Short and John Milt Neely resorted to cruel torture of Tom and Mary Wilburn's children, in addition to destroying books and school supplies at the Coe Ridge school taught by a white man, who was known as a "Nigger lover." Leslie Coe, Jr., remembers the story like this:

> At that time there was a lot of prejudice, like when schools would start. You know, they didn't want them to have no schooling. And the whites would go into the neighborhood and tear down the blackboard when the teacher would go off from school—go out for dinner. Split the blackboard up and carry it out in the yard and burn it; throw the kids' books away and burn up things they had.
>
> In them days they had to have white teachers 'cause the colored wasn't educated enough to teach them. And you know how it would be if you go out there doing something for those colored people; they'd call you a "Nigger lover." Quite naturally, it caused a riot.[19]

Tom Wilburn was a raftsman and was seldom home. Mary went to the houses of white neighbors to wash and iron for them, and, according to Mrs. Etta Short, often left the children at home to care for themselves. During the season of the year when gnat fires[20] were built on the ridge, the whites would come to the Wilburn home and stick the feet of the Wilburn children over the gnat fires.[21] As the children screamed and cried, the whites would stand back and laugh. On other occasions, the whites would take the smaller children and try to cram their heads through the openings between the logs of the house and would "skin their faces all up." Mrs. Cornelius Allen even claimed that while the parents were away at work, the white boys "would

19 The Cumberland County Census for 1880 records that a John Scott and family lived on the ridge. This was a white family whose oldest child was listed as mulatto. It was claimed by most of the informants that Scott taught school there at an early date.

20 During periods of gnat intensity, it was customary to build fires of chips and old rags to keep the pests away. This practice was mentioned by Mrs. Etta Short, Mrs. Mattie Davidson, Charlie Coe, and Tim Coe.

21 This manner of torture was testified to by Sarah Coe Tooley, Ruthie Coe Anders, Charlie Coe, Tim Coe, and by Mrs. Etta Short.

22 Ruthie Coe Anders and Sarah Coe Tooley both claimed that the Negro boys whipped Neely. Tim Coe, Mrs. Mattie Davidson, and Mrs. Etta Short all testified to the appearance on the ridge of Tump Neely. The *Chronicles* (p. 5) claims that Cal drove John Milt Neely off the ridge at gunpoint; on p. 38, it states that Tump declared her intended vengeance with the words, "I will have the Redheads string that ridge before Saturday night!"

23 Mrs. Etta Short. She added, "Now them Niggers tended to their own business and they didn't bother nobody if people would let them alone."

24 Concerning the date that Will Taylor went out on the ridge, Calvin Coe said, "It was sixty-eight years ago this past July 14 that our real trouble with the Taylor brothers started." Cal was two years in error, however. Sixty-eight years before his Sept. 1954 interview would have placed the year at 1886. Other accounts place the year of the event as 1888, and I prefer the latter. Ruthie Coe Anders, born in 1880, exactly fixed the date in the following manner: "But you see now, I had done got up in years, and now that's when it happened. And I know I was at home, and I know we wuz all fixing to go up on Marrowbone [Creek] to a big picnic. And I was eight years old; that was my age." Leslie Coe, Jr., also figured the date as 1888: "My dad [who was born in 1875] he was thirteen or fourteen years old."

25 For a clear description of this incident, see the *Chronicles*, 38. Ruthie Coe Anders also mentioned the incident. Both Mrs. Etta Short and Calvin Coe named Charles Short and Pat Pruitt as accomplices of Taylor.

come up there and undress themselves and walk around before the children."

The Wilburn children soon grew to the stage where they were able to defend themselves. The Wilburn boys —Charlie, Sherman, Billy, Garfield, Shirley, and Oleson —ganged up on John Milt Neely and whipped him. Enraged at the incident, Neely's mother, Tump, went to the Coe settlement and declared that she was going to send for the Redheads to come wipe out the colony.[22] Aging, but still leader of his clan, Old Zeke Coe countered Tump's threat with the prophetic warning, "Fannie Neely, when you send the Redheads out here, they will have to be hauled away." [23]

THE DEATH OF WILL TAYLOR

"Taylor had no business coming out there," commented Ruthie Coe Anders. She noted that John Jeff Webb, a white neighbor of the Coes, shook his head and warned Will Taylor, "Goodbye, I'll never see you again. You'll go out there and get among them Niggers, and go trying to fight them Niggers—them Niggers will kill you. . . . Them Niggers is full of Indian. They'll kill you shore if you go." [24]

Taylor did not heed Webb's advice. He rode to Coe Ridge to Tom Wilburn's house and asked for something to eat. He ate without getting off his horse, and then rode away. Mary Wilburn sensed that trouble was near at hand, and sent her son, Oleson, to warn her brother, Calvin Coe. Will was not alone during this visit to the ridge; he was accompanied by Pat Pruitt, Ike Short, and Charles Short.[25] After leaving the Wilburn home, they went to the home of Zeke and Patsy Ann and again requested food. Patsy Ann informed them that she had sufficient food left from lunch, but that her family had eaten all the bread. Furthermore, she had no meal left, she told them, but she would send Calvin over to Mary Wilburn's to get some.[26]

Calvin started across the hill to Mary's, with Taylor, Pruitt, and the Shorts walking behind him. Taylor pulled a bottle from his pocket: "Calvin, here, take a drink." Calvin countered, "Well, Will, I don't believe I care for any drink, but I'll run over there and get this meal for ma'am." "No," Taylor said, "that's all right. We don't need nothing." Again, he offered the bottle to Calvin, who then pretended to drink. Ruthie Coe said: "Uncle Calvin just turned the whiskey up like he was drinking it; wouldn't drink it because he was afraid it was poisoned. Because they'd do that sometime. They'd pretend to give you a drink and poison you, and, boy, you'd go down like the Titanic!" [27]

Calvin and Will Taylor went on to Mary's and got the meal. In the meantime, the Shorts and Pruitt lagged behind and hid in the fence row beside the road. On the way back home, Taylor asked Cal if he knew anyone who had some steers to sell. Cal informed him that his brother-in-law did. Taylor then jerked out a pistol and yelled, "This is the steer I have for you." [28] Calvin was then ordered to turn his pockets. "No, Mr. Taylor, I ain't going to turn my pockets." Mary Wilburn, who had been standing in her front door witnessing the affair, called to her brother, "Calvin, don't you turn your pockets for no man. Die first." [29] Will then ordered Calvin to sit down in the corner of the fence. Again Mary called out, "Calvin, don't you set down there. Don't set down there in the corner of that fence. They've killed a lot of people by doing that." [30]

Taking the advice of his sister, Calvin defied Will, "Why, hell, Will, God damn you, I'm not going to set down in no damn corner of the fence. What in the hell

26 All the informants knew this portion of the episode. Calvin Coe himself corroborated these accounts in his interview with Miss Keen.

27 The offer of whiskey was related by most of the informants.

28 Quoted by Mrs. Ray Anders. Others knowing of the steer episode include Hascal Haile and Mrs. Sarah Coe Tooley, and the *Chronicles* (p. 39) also notes it. In his personal testimony, Calvin Coe described the episode as follows:

Will Taylor, Charlie Short, and Pat Pruitt rode in on the ridge that day. Will Taylor come to our house and asked my mother to fix something for them to eat. They really didn't want anything to eat, but just said that to fool us. My mother sent me over to my sister, Mary Wilburn, to get some things to fix their dinner. As I went to my sister's house, Taylor followed me. I knowed then that he was here for trouble. He asked me if I knowed where he could buy some calves. I told him my brother-in-law had some calves. Then he asked me to take a drink of whiskey and I did. Then Taylor drawed his pistols. I told him I hadn't done anything to cause trouble. He made me walk down the road in front of him and all the time he was hitting me.

Taylor made me go to a fence. I could see that Charlie Short was hiding there so I didn't go on, but called Oleson Wilburn, my nephew. Taylor laughed at me for calling Oleson. Oleson came and my mother and father, my sister, and brother, Zeke, came, too. In a struggle with Taylor, my mother and father took one gun away from him. I thought he was going to quit, but he began fighting me again. Charlie Short ran from the fence and began to shoot. He shot Oleson Wilburn, but not seriously, and another bullet went through my mother's hair. I started after Short, but saw Taylor aim his gun at me. I grabbed him.

29 Lucy Robert Coe.

30 Ruthie Coe Anders. The *Chronicles*, 40, corroborates that portion dealing with turning the pockets.

31 All quotes were said by Ruthie Coe Anders. See the *Chronicles* (p. 39), which also corroborates this portion of the story.

32 Lucy Robert Coe.

33 The *Chronicles*, 40–41, runs at slight variance with this account. Mrs. Sarah Coe Tooley described a portion of the episode in much the same manner as Calvin himself.

do you think I am? I'm not going to do it! I'll stand right here!" Calvin then realized the seriousness of the situation and tried to reason with Will: "Now listen, Will. They ain't no sense of this, fellows. We've been boys and played together. Now why can't you behave and do like a man ought to? I don't want to do nothing to you or nobody. Ain't got nothing against you. We all played together; little play-children raised up together." [31] Acting on stubborn impulse, Taylor told Cal "to call up his crew," for he was going to wipe them all out. At Cal's call, Oleson Wilburn, Old Zeke, Patsy Ann, Mary Wilburn, and Bill Zeke all started to his rescue. While they were coming, Will "throwed his pistol down on Cal and aimed to shoot him," but one of Calvin's relatives hit the arm of Taylor and made him shoot wildly. "Uncle Calvin said run up to him and grabbed him and cut him a little around the neck and turned him loose." [32] In the words of Calvin himself:

> I thought he was going to quit, but he began fighting me again. Charlie Short ran from the fence and began to shoot. He shot Oleson Wilburn, but not seriously, and another bullet went through my mother's hair. I started for Short, but saw Taylor aim his gun at me. I grabbed him. I knowed he aimed to kill me for I turned him loose three times and he would start fighting me again. I took my knife and cut his throat.[33]

Lucy Robert Coe added more color to the death scene:

> Well, said Uncle Calvin said he run up to him and grabbed him and cut him a little around the neck and turned him loose. Said he begged to him and told him he wouldn't do it no more. And he, as he left him said a-settin' thar, and said he was out bleedin' a hog, though. And said he got a little piece from 'im, and said he jist raised up again with his pistol and gritted his teeth, cracked down on him again.
> Uncle Calvin said, "I want you to understand that

98

time when I went and got him, I throwed him down . . . ," said, "I want you to stay down."

Said he jist stuck it right in the burr of his ear, said he cut his throat from ear to ear. Said his head was jist a-swingin'.

Ike Short ran off and left the scene before the killing took place. That was typical of Short's cowardly nature, according to Mrs. Etta Short, who told about his passing her parents' house in flight:

You know, he'd get trouble up and then he was out and gone. Ike come, I never will forget it, past our house, and he had this horse that could really go.

He hollered, "Hell's up," when he passed the door. And we thought trouble was a-brewing. And then Pat [Pruitt] came along and all bloody, and told about the murder.

At another point in the same interview, Mrs. Short continued with her description of the arrival of Pruitt:

He had on one of these old-fashioned stiff, white shirts . . . and it was just bloody all over.

My pappy said, "Aw, they never killed him."

Says, "Yes, they did. I helped lay him out 'fore I left. They killed Charles, too, but I couldn't find him."

So Aunt Jane, Charles' mother, was with them when they come after Will. . . . They had a quilt over him [i. e., Will], and they turned that quilt back and let them look at him. But I didn't go up there.

Aunt Jane was a-crying and said, "Pore Charles, they can't find him."

They took Will on back that night, but Charles wudn't killed. But Aunt Mary had hit him in the back and hurt him awful bad. And he'd gone off down there and crawled off in the woods and crawled under a log. They said them Niggers come down there a-walking that log—and him a-layin' under it—telling what they wuz going to do if they found him. And, boy, he layed still! And as soon as they got away . . . he got up, and it was nearly morning before he ever got home. He went clear around by Black's Ferry and around Martinsburg and that a-way to get home.

34 George Allred. Cf. the incident concerning keeping the hogs away from the body with a similar incident which occurred during the Martin-Tolliver Feud, 1884 ff. Ben Rayburn's body "lay for three days because the citizens were afraid to pick it up; some of us children tore down a worm fence and piled up the rails about the corpse so hogs wouldn't mutilate it." See Mrs. Jeanette (Bell) Thomas, *Ballad Makin' in the Mountains of Kentucky* (New York, 1939), 10.

35 The fly-shooing episode is common knowledge among the informants, and is corroborated in the *Chronicles*, 45.

George Allred claimed that it was the two brothers who came for Will's body, while Mrs. Etta Short's testimony included the parents of Charles Short, plus an aunt and uncle, in the number who came for the corpse.

36 During the brief period of concealment, according to the *Chronicles*, 45, the adults in the colony held meetings and discussed what was best to do concerning Calvin and the law. It was decided that Cal should surrender himself.

37 George Allred related a remarkably similar recount of the sheriff's promise to defend Calvin's life with his own:

Old Man Jim Keen went out there and got Cal when he cut Will Taylor's head off—by hisself. He said they wanted him to take every man there in Burkesville. Said, "You'll be killed." He told them he didn't want nobody but Jim Keen.

And he went out there and told Cal, said, "I come after you."

Said Cal said to him, "Mr. Keen, you won't let a mob mob me 'fore we get to Burkesville, I might go with you."

Said he said to him, "Reach me your gun, you're in my hands now, Cal. If we meet a mob, I'll just reach ye your gun and we'll just swap out with 'um."

While waiting for the relatives of Will Taylor to come to get his body, Aunt Patsy Ann Coe washed the blood from Will's body, tied his head up, and then kept guard over the corpse to keep the hogs away.[34] With a branch from a peach tree, she fanned away the flies as she sang songs until midnight; then, the relatives and neighbors came for the body. They thanked Patsy for taking care of the body and assured her that they would not harm a hair on her head.[35]

Reasoning that the law would be coming to get him, Calvin went to his brother's house on Mud Camp Creek and stayed there. Calvin told this portion of the story as follows:

I knowed that I would soon be caught if I stayed on the ridge. The sheriff made a trip down here looking for me, but, of course, couldn't find me. I really wanted to give up to the law, but I was afraid white people might kill me, because many of them thought we was in the wrong.

Two days after I killed Will Taylor, I gave up to the law.[36] That was sixty-eight years ago this past July 16. I sent brother John to Burkesville to tell the sheriff, Mr. Jim Keen, that I wanted to give up, but I wanted to be protected, too. When John got to Burkesville, the sheriff had started down here on the ridge again to arrest me. He had been here the day before but I was gone. John overtook Mr. Keen and told him where I was and what I wanted.

I met Mr. Keen on his way down to Mud Camp after me. When I met him, I told him about having to kill Will Taylor and I said to him, "Mr. Keen, I want to give up, but I don't want to be killed. Will you promise not to let anyone kill me?" I'll never forget what he told me. He said, "Well, Cal, I just couldn't promise a man for certain that I would save his life, for maybe I wouldn't be able to. But I'll promise you this—I'll die with you." [37]

I knowed he would take care of me, so I wasn't afraid. I rode behind him on a horse to Burkesville and he put me in jail. There was no trouble.

I never did have a trial, for the Taylors refused to come

to court for a trial.[38] Judge Williams set three different times for them to come in, but the Taylors sent word that they didn't want me tried, for they would take their own hell out on us and settle things like they wanted to.

So Judge Williams told us to go home, load our guns, and protect our families. I carried my gun for nine years after that. We took our guns everywhere we went, for we never knowed when we would have trouble or maybe some of us would get killed.[39]

THE COES DEFEND THEIR HOMES

A few days after Calvin killed Will Taylor "a bunch down there of the Taylor gang decided they would go out there and finish wiping them out, you know."[40] Feeling that the job might not be quickly finished, the white men decided to take along an adequate supply of food for a prolonged siege of the colony.[41] They gathered up a bushel of corn meal, a side of bacon, some coffee and sugar. In the words of Leslie Coe, Jr., "They were going to cook and stay until they burned up everybody."

The timing was perfect, seemingly, for the massive surprise attack on Zeketown. Most of the adult members of the colony were away on the river tying up log rafts. Only three men and three teenage boys were left in the colony.[42] The Coes were not without white friends in the area, however. In the words of Leslie Coe, Jr., "They's always some white person who would come and tell you, you know, what's going to happen." The white savior in this instance is generally unidentified, but some felt that he was Druie Lollar. Whoever the white man was, "He shore was a friend to them getting to them in time," stated Mrs. Ray Anders. He slipped onto the ridge late one afternoon and warned the Negroes to expect an attack that evening: "They're coming a

38   There was a trial, according to the *Chronicles*, which goes into great length (pp. 51–55) in describing the court proceedings. There is no way to determine if Calvin were actually tried, for the court work was lost in 1933 when the Cumberland County courthouse was destroyed by fire.

39   Cal's recollection of the officials' names was accurate. Wells, *Cumberland County*, 110 and 116, verifies that J. R. Keen was sheriff of Cumberland County for the years 1889–93 and 1895–98; T. J. Williams was county judge for the years 1886–93.

40   Tim Coe. It appears to be common knowledge that this action was motivated by Cal's murder of Will Taylor, and two informants, Mrs. Ray Anders and George Allred, explicitly said so.

41   The informants included the following men in the group: the Taylors, Crawfords, Andersons, Shorts, Pruitts, and Williamses, and John Milt Neely.

42   Statements to this effect were made by Leslie Coe, Jr., Mrs. Sarah Coe Tooley, and George Allred, and were corroborated by the *Chronicles* (p. 47).

43 Leslie Coe, Jr. Mrs. Ray Anders testified in a similar vein.

44 Leslie Coe, Jr., and Lucy Robert Coe and their statements are corroborated in the *Chronicles*, 47.

45 George Allred, Leslie Coe, Jr., Mrs. Sarah Coe Tooley, and Mrs. Ray Anders; see also the *Chronicles*, 42.

46 Tim Coe stated, perhaps correctly, that "all the whites scattered and went into the woods."

47 Mrs. Ray Anders agreed that some of the whites were killed or soon died. Aunt Lucy specified the number killed as two or three, and that these were carried off during the night.

hundred strong tonight, going to kill every one of you. Why, they're going to burn down every house in the neighborhood. And the little ones that run out, they're going to throw them back." [43]

That evening, just before dark, the children and the old folk went to the hills to stay out of the way. They took quilts along for sleeping.[44] The six male defenders, led by Bill Raspberry, scraped up all the shotguns and pistols they could find in the colony, and then they went to a nearby store and bought all the ammunition in stock. With guns and ammunition ready, the six went down the lane a few yards away from the houses and hid behind fences and bushes.[45]

Mrs. Ray Anders described the approach of the attackers: "Along in the night, said they heerd their horses coming; talking. Said they could hear them probably a mile and a half coming over rocks and things—the horses a-walkin'. . . . Said they had oil cans tied to their horses to pour on the houses to set them afire."

Bill Raspberry instructed the other defenders to fire at his lead. Leslie Coe, Jr., described this portion of the attack and quoted Raspberry as saying,

> "Let them get up even in the lane with me—the last part of them, and I'll fire the first shot." So he fired the first shot and he let that gun talk at them! And so the rest of them started shooting. And it scared them [i.e., the whites] so bad that all of them left but about fifteen.[46] Some run into grapevines. After I was born, some of them still couldn't talk, they was marked up so.
>
> They carried the dead ones away—I don't know how many.[47]

Lucy Coe reiterated the part about the whites who were shot in the throat:

> I know they was one man that got shot in the throat. He'd speak; claimed to be sick. But they said he got shot

here in the throat and it ruined his speech. He couldn't hardly never talk plain no more. And after he got well, he stayed sick they said six or seven weeks. And when he got well, they could see where he was shot. Jist went through his swaller and windpipe and ruint his speech.

Charles Short was among those who ran when the shooting started. In the words of Tim Coe, who had heard Short describe his flight:

> Charles said they was some of the younger ones after him, and he ran down in the woods and he thought . . . they was going to catch him, and he went in a hollow log —big old hollow log.
> And two or three of these Niggers came on down there and jumped up on that log. And said that he was really afraid of them—that they'd hear his heart a-beatin'. But they finally didn't discover him. They figured he'd got away, you know.
> And Charles said when he got out of that, he didn't go back no more.[48]

Not one of the Negro men was killed but some did receive injuries. Bill Raspberry, the leader of the defenders, was shot during the fracas, but by one of his own men. Once the whites had the Negroes partially surrounded, Raspberry jumped up and started to run away, according to George Allred, who felt that the Negroes as well as the whites wanted to flee the scene of battle. Raspberry, according to Allred, "run and jumped a big high gully, and Little John was after him. Little John's gun went off and shot Raspberry in the shoulder. Uncle John said he never seen a Nigger run so fast in his life. He thought some of them white fellers had shot him."

The battle continued into the night. By morning the gunshots were no longer heard, but the few remaining whites refused to go home. During the night the Negro defenders had returned to the relative safety of their

48 Both Charlie Coe and Mrs. Sarah Coe Tooley knew of the hollow log incident, but not in such detail.

homes. They feared to go outside the next morning, however, lest a white enemy should pick them off with a rifle.

While many of the informants told a portion of this *sage,* none of the accounts approximated the length and detail of the one narrated by Leslie Coe, Jr. As an example of a storyteller's artistry, Coe's account is here presented in its entirety:

Well, my dad and his two brothers—two other older brothers—and then two brothers on my mother's side, and my grandfather on they side. Well, they went out that night—some white person slipped out there and told them, said, "They're coming a hundred strong tonight, going to kill every one of you. Why, they're going to burn down every house in the neighborhood, and the little ones that run out, they're going to throw them back." They's always some white person who would come and tell you, you know, what's going to happen.

So after they come—they went out there and waited and so they didn't have much ammunition that night. But they had a little bit, and they lined up—these six young boys and the two older men and the old school teacher was there [six is perhaps the correct number]—they lined up along the fence row.

They came a hundred strong. And they brought a bushel of corn meal and a side of bacon. Them old sides of bacon them days was that wide, you know. They brought enough to stay—I don't know how much coffee and sugar and meal they brought. They were going to cook and stay 'til they burned up everybody.

Well, when they come and warned them early in the evening that night just before dark, the kids and the old folks got out and went to the hills out of the way. But when they met 'em in that lane there—why, they was hid there. And the old school teacher he said, "Now let me fire—let them get up even in the lane with me the last part of them." And said, "I'll fire the first shot."

So he fired the first shot, and he let that gun talk; what he had he let that gun talk at them. And so then the rest of them started shooting. And it scared them so bad that all of them left but about fifteen. Some run into grapevines. After I was born, some of them still couldn't talk they was marked up so. They carried the dead ones away. I don't know how many. And so they shot this school teacher, but he managed to get away. He said he didn't want them to get hold of his dead body. So he left there. He was shot, but he got away. And my dad said that the good Lord was just with them.

The moon had just went over out of sight. It was dark so they couldn't see them hid in the fence corners and behind the bushes. And so they started a-leaving there then, they got so hot. They was about fifteen stayed. And they bullets they was coming down so hot they all left. That checked them from going to the houses and bringing the rest of them out.

They shot around the next morning quite a bit there. But they had all done gone and got out of the way. So my mother's brother, he'd got shot through the head there or something, I don't remember.

They didn't bother women folks that morning. Didn't bother my great-grandmother too much. [She'd] go out and work and so on. But my dad's brother, Sam's brother [Little John], he wanted to get out of that house so bad that morning. He was hemmed up in there; he couldn't get out of there, you know. So in the meantime, my grandfather tells me that finally he said, "If you go out of here, I'll kill you this morning." Says, "I'll kill you myself." And they was shooting all around the house— them ten or fifteen that stayed—but they was afraid to come to the house. But they wouldn't bother my grandmother—my great-grandmother. They wouldn't dare shoot her, so she'd go out in the yard and carry water, and go to the spring and get the water and everything, you know. So pretty soon they told her to come in the house. And he's so scared—my Uncle John, that; Sam's brother—he's so scared he let him go.

So he put on one of my grandmother's dresses and went on out and went up the hill. They didn't bother him; they would have killed him. He went to Mud Camp. That was about eight or ten miles away from there. He left to get out of the way. He was afraid of getting killed.[49]

49 The "dress-up" episode is also described in the *Chronicles*, 50.

It may be that Little John's escape disguised as a woman is actually a motif which is again used to describe the escape from the Indianapolis police by Jesse Coe after he had shot and killed two policemen. For details, see the last section in this chapter.

50 All the informants knew that the trouble occurred on election day. Aunt Lucy Robert Coe remembered that it was in November because she had married the previous August and moved to the ridge colony. Charlie Coe correctly claimed that Cleveland was running for President.

51 Tim Coe.

52 Tim Coe claimed it was Arch Murley; Ruthie Coe Anders stated that it was Will Murley.

THE DEATH OF GEORGE TAYLOR

After his wife died, Yaller John returned to the Coe colony in 1890 to be near his aging, widowed mother. For two additional years there was peace in the colony. On election day in November, 1892, when Cleveland was running for President, peace was again broken by the Redheads. This time it was George Taylor who lost his life by foolishly attacking the Coe Negroes.[50]

The Coes did not intend to participate in the 1892 election because "they were afraid there would be trouble."[51] But a white man, either Arch or Will Murley,[52] from the Bear Wallow community, came to the ridge on the morning of the election and begged the Negroes to go vote. With his reassurance that no harm would befall them, the Negroes agreed to go. "But," in the words of Tim Coe, "when the time come, they didn't nobody help them." Leslie Coe, Jr., described in considerable detail the politician's visit to Coe Ridge that fateful day:

> That [attack on the colony] happened in July or June. Then they had the election in August, I believe it was, the primary election in August. And they was determined to get even of them.
>
> So my grandfather, he was mixed up in that night, but they didn't know he was in it. They didn't have anything in particular against him because they didn't know he in it. So that particular morning—what tickled me, my mother had to laugh about it. She wudn't nothing but a kid about seven or eight years old, she said, at that time—and course, these politicians, they came out there that morning. They knew there was going to be trouble at the polls. It was about three-four miles from there to the polls [at Bear Wallow].
>
> So they knew they was going to have trouble out there. And they wanted to get my grandfather to vote the Democrat ticket, see. Well, grandfather wasn't going to vote the ticket. But he was a great hand—he liked his whiskey.

And they had two quarts of whiskey, and my grandfather help them drink up one quart of it, you know. After he got all he wanted of it, why, he told them he never voted the Democrat ticket and never intended to. Says, "I'm a Republican and I'm going to vote the Republican ticket." "Well, since you so smart this morning," that's what they told him, "being as you so smart, we were going to tell you something, Tom." Said, "Since you so smart, we ain't going to tell you." They knowed they was going to kill his brother-in-law—Uncle Calvin.

And so he come in the house. They left and went on. Said, "I don't care what you know. I ain't going to vote no Democrat ticket." Says, "I'm going to vote Republican." Says, "I ain't never voted Democratic and I don't never intend to."

So they left and went on. So he come in the house to my grandmother, his wife, named Mary. Said, "Mary, I don't know what them devils was up to." Said, "I'd better get on my clothes and get out there and see." So he did. He changed his clothes and walked on out there.

George Taylor had previously announced his intention to kill two white men besides three black Coes. Calvin Coe was first on the list. These killings were all to take place on election day.[53] Calvin, Yaller John, and Little John went to Bear Wallow on the morning of the election. In previous years, Calvin, and perhaps Yaller John, had earned nickels and dimes for playing the banjo on election days. Mrs. Ray Anders testified to the economic necessity for this custom: "Uncle Calvin, they was pore folks, you know, was going to pick the banjer like you would, you know. Big bunch of people around, you're goin' to have somebody to make music, you know. And they'd pitch him in money."

On the fateful day in 1892, Calvin took along his instrument as usual. During the course of voting, Calvin sat on a stump and played his banjo for the voters. Benjamin Coe was also there that day. George Taylor walked up, but evidently did not see Calvin because of

53 According to Mrs. Ray Anders and Mrs. Jesse E. Coe of Burkesville.

54 This portion of the story was related by Charlie Coe, Price Kirkpatrick, Green Graves, Hascal Haile, and Mrs. Sarah Coe Tooley.

55 Quote uttered by Leslie Coe, Jr.; see a similar statement recorded in the *Chronicles*, 72.

56 Accounts of this initial phase of the shooting were offered by Price Kirkpatrick, Tim Coe, Hascal Haile, Sarah Coe Tooley, Ruthie Coe Anders, and Mrs. Ray Anders.

57 Lucy Robert Coe. Described also by Tim Coe, Mrs. Sarah Coe Tooley, Green Graves, Hascal Haile, Ruthie Coe Anders, Price Kirkpatrick, and Mrs. Ray Anders.

58 Lucy Robert Coe. The claim that many shots went into the same hole is apparently a recurrent motif utilized to describe remarkable shooting feats. Cf. this with the incident described on page 113, this chapter, and with Motif X981, "Lie: Skillful marksman," which contains many references to tales collected from American tradition.

the voters who had surrounded him to listen to his playing. Taylor asked Ben Coe, "Is that Cal?" Taylor then walked on over and approached Calvin from the rear.[54] "Oh, yes, you yellow son-of-a-bitch," Taylor yelled out, "you killed my brother and I'm going to kill you."[55] He pointed a pistol at the back of Cal's head and pulled the trigger, but the bullet failed to penetrate the skull. Cal pitched forward to the ground on his face, perhaps faking.[56]

Yaller John and Little John were inside the voting house when they heard the gunshot. They knew immediately that someone had shot Calvin. They ran through the door and into the yard, and when George Taylor saw them coming with .38 Winchesters in hand, he began running. The people present backed out of Taylor's way, forming a lane through which he fled. The two Johns "jist went to lettin' him have it in the back."[57] George Allred claimed that "every time John 'ud pull the trigger, he'd see the dust jump out of the back of George's coat." There is disagreement as to the number of times that Taylor was shot, but it is generally conceded that both Johns emptied their guns into the back of the fleeing man. One informant claimed that the hole made by the shots was so large that a half dollar could be dropped into it.[58]

Taylor was dead, but his death was not sufficient to satisfy the angered Yaller John. In the words of Lucy Robert Coe:

> Uncle John was so mad that he went up and struck him across the head with his gun barrel and bent it.
> And there's an old man there, said, "Uncle John, don't hit him no more."
> Said he jist throwed it down on the ground and grabbed Uncle Calvin's and said, "Here's another one just as good. Do you take it up? If you do, step in his shoes. Any

man here on the ground wants to take it up, let him step in his shoes."

Said they was something workin' out of Uncle John's mouth jist as green as grass.

When Old John (Yaller John) cooled off somewhat, he went over to Calvin, who was still lying on the ground, and asked, "Are you dead, Cal?" Cal answered, "No," then asked, "did you kill the [curse words omitted by informant] man?" John replied, "Yes, we landed the son-of-a-bitch in hell." [59]

Calvin was taken back to the colony, where he was soon examined by Dr. Billy Richardson, according to Ruthie Coe Anders, who was present at the examination. " 'Well, Calvin,' the doctor said, 'yore head is as hard as a rock.' Said, 'I'll be damned, this skull's not even cracked.' "

The scene of the murder was not without its humor, which took place while Taylor was fleeing after he had shot Calvin. Lucy Robert Coe told the story this way:

Said that jist everybody give them room to shoot—and a-running and a-screaming and a-hollering. Said they was one man had a big long overcoat on—it was in November—he had a big long overcoat on, and he went to jump over a log [but] got it hung. And said thar he hung and hollered and whooped. Yeah, said he cut the masterest shine ever was. . . .

Well, finally after awhile, I believe this Old Man Anderson—I forgot his name—went and unhung him. And said he had to be took to the creek.[60]

The two Johns surrendered themselves to the police and were placed in jail to await trial. At the first trial, Little John was released, but Old John was held for trial on the charge of murder. He was sentenced to prison for two years, not for shooting Taylor, but for hitting the corpse with the stock of his gun.[61]

59 Mrs. Sarah Coe Tooley. An almost identical statement can be found in the *Chronicles*, 73.

60 "To be took to the creek" means that he dirtied in his trousers.

61 Seven informants claimed that Old John bent the barrel of the gun over Taylor's head. Five informants claimed that Old John served two years; the *Chronicles* (p. 75) states that he was sentenced for three years. In view of the total agreement that Old John did serve time, it must be assumed that he really was sentenced. Court records are unavailable for verification of the verdict.

62 Lucy Robert Coe was the only informant to call the *Rowena* by name. Mrs. Ray Anders claimed that the boat was headed downstream, while Charlie Coe and Tim Coe both stated that it was going upstream. I feel the latter position is correct because the Coe Negroes frequently rode a steamboat home from Nashville.

63 Mrs. Ray Anders and Lucy Robert Coe.

64 Tim Coe. Mrs. Anders also stated that Jess walked home after he was "banked."

JESSE COE: A MURDERER IS AMBUSHED

After George Taylor was killed, the older generation of Coes began to think about the future of the colony. They had always insisted on their rights, but they were honest people who were willing to compromise in order to have peace. They wanted the younger Coes to follow their teachings, but a large number of the boys became lax in their conduct. The younger Coes began drinking and gambling, and could not be depended on. At the same time, they developed an attitude of resentment and rebellion and were often the aggressors in personal encounters.

Jesse Coe, son of Bill Zeke Coe, was one of the younger Coes who became involved in much trouble. Jess, as he was commonly called, had an argument with the captain of the steamboat *Rowena* while en route from Nashville to Burnside, Kentucky.[62] The argument became so heated that the captain ordered Jess off the boat, some fifteen miles short of the intended destination. Two informants claimed that the captain had refused to pay Jess some money owed him for labor, and that Jess was thrown off after asking for the money.[63] Lucy Robert Coe, for example, remembered it like this: "He wuz a-ridin' on the boat and he'd give him a bill or something another to change, you know, and this pilot wouldn't give him his change back; and then made him get off—put him off and he had to walk home." Another informant, perhaps more correctly, conjectured that Jess was drinking and became so rowdy that the captain "banked him down there at Celina—below Celina a little bit—put him off the boat. He had to walk home, you know." [64]

Jess knew that the boat went upstream as far as Rowena, and would not return until the next day, ac-

110

The Cumberland River flows peacefully between Black's Ferry and Martinsburg, a course which is synonymous with the drama of Coe Ridge.

65   Details of the shooting vary in considerable detail. Mrs. Ray Anders stated that one
shot went through the captain's hat. Lucy
Robert Coe said one bullet "scaped him across
the face." Again, Lucy Robert Coe noted that
when the shooting started, the captain just
turned the wheel loose, and when the boat
passed through Celina, it "was going ever
which-a-way." Mrs. Anders, on the authority
of her mother's word, stated that the boat ran
aground.
66   Oral tradition dated the event in the mid-
1890's. The *Chronicles* (p. 91) specifically stated 1896, and the Clay County, Tenn., Circuit
Court Record Book G, p. 220, verifies the year
as 1896. Wilburn's name is mentioned in the
Chronicles (p. 80), but oral sources fail to record his name. Clay County records verify that
Wilburn was one of the three.

cording to Tim Coe, who described the subsequent incident in this manner:

> So Jess got his Winchester and come down and placed
> himself on the river bluff right above Martinsburg. And
> when the boat got about even with him, he began (you
> see, them old Winchester rifles they shot sixteen times)
> and he began shooting through the engine room, and
> through the pilot house and the cabin. Them fine splin-
> ters, they said, wuz a-flyin' everywhere. And, well, he
> happen not to hit anybody. The pilot he knew that them
> was bullets coming through there and he laid down right
> flat on the floor on his stomach.
> And he could hold onto the pilot wheel and watch the
> top of the river bluff along there to guide the boat by.
> Boy, when them bullets begin coming through there, he
> called to the engineer to get him all the steam he had.
> And he just opened that thing wide open, and when he
> passed through Martinsburg down there, the bow of the
> boat wuz runnin' under the water some.[65]

Later that same year Jess Coe, Robert Coe, and Shirley Wilburn[66] went to Celina, Tennessee, to seek employment as raftsmen. They proceeded to a general
store located on the banks of the Cumberland River,
where prospective employees gathered. While these Negroes were standing on the high front porch of the
store, Milt Williams, a white man, shoved Jess off the
porch and sent him sprawling to the ground below.
The motive for the shove is not agreed upon by the informants, nor are the events which immediately preceded the incident. Hascal Haile felt that Williams was
a friend of the Taylors, and possibly distantly related
to them. Mrs. Ray Anders claimed that Williams was
the captain of the boat shot at by Jess. At the store,
Williams approached Jess and asked, "Wuz you the
man . . . shot me through the hat?" Jess replied, "Yes."
Williams then pushed him off the porch. Still another
informant holds that Williams simply slipped up be-

hind Jess and kicked him off the high porch.[67] In any event, all informants agree that the defensive action taken by Jess was justified.

Jess mounted the steps to the store after regaining his composure, only to be faced by a gun held by Williams. "Well, I'd love to know what I've done to anybody," Jess pleaded, "that would make them want to mistreat me like that?"[68] Williams apparently answered Jess by firing at him. One shot hit Jess,[69] but he managed to take the gun from his assailant, who then turned and fled from the porch. In the hands of Jess Coe, a gun was expertly put to use. Mrs. Ray Anders described Jess's marksmanship: "They said he was the shootinest man that ever had hold of a pistol. Said he could start a flour barrel down the hill and shoot every stave in it before it got to the bottom of the hill. Said he could throw up a pin and shoot the head off it."[70]

Mrs. Anders described Williams' death in all its gruesome detail:

> Shot him twice, and he run a-loose there. He got loose from [Jess] and run out into the street and grabbed a-hold of a post, they said, and swung there to it 'til he died—and turned loose.
>
> They's one man said there, said he tried his best to get behind a tree. And said every time he tried to get behind that tree, said he'd look and said he's standin' there jist as clear as anything where everybody could see him. Said he's tryin' to get behind the tree all the time, but everytime he'd look, said he'd be out where you could see him jist as plain as anything.

Hascal Haile, quoting the words of an eyewitness to the shooting, related his recollections of the shooting:

> Well, I'll tell you, Old Man Faye Bailey has told me about it. Said he was over to the Cullum Hotel and heard

67 Ray Anders. Official records of the Clay County Circuit Court make no reference to the motive.

68 Mrs. Ray Anders.

69 Mrs. Ray Anders; see also *Chronicles*, 81.

70 This account of Jess's shooting ability is definitely related to Motif X981, "Lie: Skillful marksman"—especially to X981(ch), "Man rolls barrel downhill, putting pistol bullet through bunghole each time it comes around." This tradition has been reported once from Texas tradition in 1931.

71 The *Chronicles* (pp. 81–85) holds that Jess was placed in jail pending trial, but oral tradition is apparently correct, for bond was set by the Clay County Circuit Court.

this big fuss, you know, out there, and he stopped eatin' his dinner. He'd stopped there with a raft on his way to Nashville, you know.

He said that when he went out there, why, this feller Milt Williams and one of them Coes—I don't remember what his name was, this Coe feller that did the killin'. But anyway, Milt Williams jerked a pistol on him and tried to shoot him, and he [Jess] wrung it out of his hands and emptied the other five bullets in his back. . . .

I'll tell you who arrested the colored feller then. The sheriff was out of town. Old Uncle Captain Jim Davis and Jim Dick Tome went out and took two big sticks and arrested him.

They wudn't any law officer there, see, and they were dist citizens of the town and they arrested him. They were pretty nervy men, you know.

And Old Uncle Wild Bill [Williams] rode up pretty soon after that. Wild Bill was a little bit older than Milt. Wild Bill was a brother of Milt's, don't you see. And he come up with a double-barreled shotgun and kicked him [Jess] from Old Town up to New Town and put him in jail, trying to get him to do something, going to kill him, you know. Yessir!

Jess was able to post bond and return to Coe Ridge with his associates.[71] When the day arrived for his trial, Jess was not there. A posse formed with the intention of going to Coe Ridge to get him. Hascal Haile told that the posse, formed mainly in the Tinsley Bottom area south of Celina and composed partly of Williamses, came by the store of his father and ate lunch. There were about one hundred men in the posse. After crossing the Kentucky line, the posse proceeded to the home of Benjamin Coe, son of Master Jesse Coe. They requested Coe to accompany them to Coe Ridge, knowing his position of neutrality in any incident in which the Negroes were involved. "You fellers go on back home," Coe told them; "I'll go up there and get Jess." After they left, he rode horseback to the ridge. Not long afterwards, "He came back down the creek, Jess riding behind him."[72]

The officers at Celina felt that the associates of Jess should also stand trial as accomplices. Sheriff Joe Parker sent two deputies to bring them in. All three stood trial[73] for the murder of Milt Williams, but only Jess Coe was sentenced to serve time in the state penitentiary at Nashville.[74] Jess, upon his release from prison in 1898, returned to the Coe colony embittered toward life. In the words of Samuel Coe, he acted "like a wild Indian"; he would yell out as loudly as he could, "Can't you hear me, old home, I am back again!" The members of the colony were disturbed by Jess's attitude; it meant trouble not only for him but also for them all because they would not forsake him in that time of trouble. "The people of the community knew the circumstances, sympathized with the foolish fellow, and avoided any trouble with him."[75]

Jess Coe left the colony in 1901 and went to Indianapolis. His attitude there was the same as it had been when he first returned home from prison. Because he felt that the Indianapolis policemen were lax and unfair in the execution of their duties, Jess started carrying a pistol as a means of protecting himself.[76]

Jess and a friend, George Williams, along with a group of boys loitering on an Indianapolis street, were told by officers to "move on." Jess remarked under his breath that he had done nothing wrong and that if any officer should interfere with him he would "burn him up." The other boys, knowing Jess's temper and unreasonableness, persuaded him to leave. They knew that all their lives were in danger when he was in that frame of mind.[77]

At ten o'clock that night, September 30, 1906, the officers approached Jess to ask him where the other

72 Charlie Coe.

73 The *Chronicles*, 89, claims they were tried in Livingston, Tenn., located in the adjoining county. Hascal Haile said they were tried in Celina. Actually, both traditions are correct. The trial was begun at Celina, but feelings were running so high against the Coes that the trial was transferred to Livingston. See Clay County, Tenn., Circuit Court Minute Book G, pp. 281–82. The trial was held in Livingston, during the February term of the Circuit Court, according to Overton County, Tenn., Circuit Court Minute Book J, p. 220.

74 Overton County Circuit Court Minute Book J, p. 220, records that Jess was sentenced for two years at hard labor in the state penitentiary, and that Shirley Wilburn and Robert Coe were set free.

75 *Chronicles*, 91.

76 The *Chronicles*, 103–5, articulates Jess's hostile feelings toward the Indianapolis policemen: "In this very city of Indianapolis in 1902, the writer was attacked by what is known as the 'Bungalow Gang,' and a policeman could have stopped it with a word [but stood] there with his hands behind him as if he were a member of the gang enjoying watching them at their lawless work. . . . Jesse knew of [this injustice] and he became more bitter against the policemen of that city."

77 *Ibid.*, 106–7.

78   The *Indianapolis News* carried front page articles from Oct. 1 to Oct. 14, 1906. According to the newspaper and most informants, two policemen were killed. Jesse Coe supposedly killed Charles J. Russell, while George Williams shot Edward J. Petricord, who died on Oct. 2, 1906.

79   *Chronicles*, 108.

80   Tim Coe told the same tale of Jesse's hiding in the corn shock, but claimed that the corn was grown by Sephus in a garden located to the rear of the house.

81   Others who claimed that Jesse dressed as a woman were Mrs. Kit Crabtree, Mrs. Ray Anders, Charlie Coe, and Tim Coe.

82   The *Indianapolis News*, Oct. 2, 1906, p. 1, stated, "Had the earth opened up and swallowed Coe he could not have disappeared more effectively."

boys were. Jess quickly ran his hand into his shirt, and thereupon the officers, taking no precautions, walked near him and asked him what he had. Jess did not reply but shot and killed the two policemen, then disappeared into the night.[78] Along with Jess, George Williams, whose revolver had been fired, was also charged with murder. Williams was later tried, convicted, and hanged in Michigan City, Indiana.[79] Jess, however, as soon as he killed the two policemen, quickly fled to the home of Sephus Coe, a first cousin. George Allred told of the fugitive in hiding:

> Said he went to Sephus's house and scared Sephus's wife to death. She kept carryin' on. And Jess crawled back under the floor. There was a kinda low place under the floor; and they made Sephus hold a light and they looked under the floor but couldn't see Jess.
>
> Said Jess said he got scared there and come out— went out in a man's cornfield, pulled a shock of corn apart and got in there and pulled the corn back up around him and stayed in there all night.[80]

The following morning, Jess managed to walk out of Indianapolis in some sort of disguise, despite a group of onlooking policemen. It is commonly claimed that Jess disguised himself as a woman by donning a dress, apron, and bonnet and by carrying a shopping basket on his arm. Mrs. Ray Anders described the escape as follows: "They got to huntin' fer him and he slipped and got out of Indianapolis. He put him on an old dress and bonnet and he got out of Indianapolis. Jess walked right out of Indianapolis with a basket on his arm and an old Mother Hubbard dress on and a bonnet. And nobody didn't know who he was." [81]

George Allred claimed that Jess was able to pass through the police lines by pretending to be a laborer, with a pick, shovel, and dinner basket in his hands.[82]

When Jess neared home he began to relax his vigilance. "He come out in the open when he got to Tompkinsville. And he had that basket full of cartridge shells." [83] Jess knew that the chase was not over, however; it would be sometime before he could be free to roam the countryside. With that thought in mind, the fugitive slipped into the barn of Bob Murley, a white man who lived on Judio Creek not far from the Coe colony. While Jess was hiding in Murley's barn, word entered Monroe and Cumberland counties that Indianapolis had offered a substantial reward for his return dead or alive.[84] Furthermore, Mrs. Ray Anders recalled, "They said when he died, that all they wanted was the tip of his finger and a teaspoonful of his brain. Said he was the smartest man that ever got out of Indianapolis."

Tom Jones, sheriff of Cumberland County at that time, made the statement, "I know where Jess is, but I'd give up my office before I'd kill a man. That's what I'd have to do. I wouldn't kill a man for that reward." J. E. Bryant, the sheriff of neighboring Monroe County, did not feel that way, however, and set out to obtain the reward money; he was joined by Johnny P. Jenkins and two Conkin brothers, Granger and Lowry.[85] They searched the Kettle Creek and Judio areas, and, on different occasions, almost discovered Jess in Murley's barn. Finally, Murley began to fear for his part in shielding the criminal; he had already lied to the law in denying that he knew anything of the Negro's whereabouts. Therefore, Murley told the fugitive, "Now, Jess, they has been here one or two trips offering me all kinds of money to tell if I knowed where you was. I'd druther you'd leave this barn." [86]

Jess left the barn and went to Coe Ridge, where he hid in a cave for many months. The Monroe County

83 Charlie Coe. Tim Coe claimed that Jess also carried a gun in the basket. As described by oral tradition, Jess's escape has been garbed with motifs taken from a migratory legend. A story found in Dorson's *Negro Folktales in Michigan*, 98–99, contains motifs about a man who disguised himself as a woman and carried guns concealed in a basket. For additional occurrences of the same legend, see Dorson's note 63, p. 218.

84 Informants agreed that a reward was offered, but could not agree on the amount specified. Green Graves and Price Kirkpatrick simply stated that a reward was offered. Charlie Coe, Mrs. Sarah Coe Tooley, and Bill Poindexter said that the amount was $500, but Mrs. Ray Anders stated that $900 was offered. The only mention of the reward found in the *Indianapolis News*, Oct. 2, 1906, p. 1, noted only that the amount had already reached $300.

85 The names of those in the posse were offered by Green Graves, Mrs. Ray Anders, Charlie Coe, and Price Kirkpatrick.

86 George Allred.

87 Mrs. Ray Anders related this portion of the story in an unrecorded interview, June 11, 1963.

88 Mrs. Sarah Coe Tooley.

89 The names of Wilburn and Old John (Yaller John) were contributed by George Allred and Tim Coe.

posse and other bounty hunters came very close many times to finding the cave. Jess told Little John and Cal, who would slip to him every night with something to eat, that he could see dirt fall across the entrance to the cave when the pursuers rode above him. However, it took Claude Anders, a person whom Jess considered as his best friend, to betray him and provide the means for his murder.[87]

Claude Anders was more commonly called Monkey Anders. Very little was said of the relationship of these two before Jess left the colony for Indianapolis; it may be that their friendship developed during the period of Jess's hiding on the ridge. At any rate, Jess, considering Anders to be a good friend, occasionally ventured out of concealment long enough to shoot a few squirrels or to drink moonshine whiskey with him. Other members of the Coe colony watched the relationship of these two closely, aware that Monkey could not be trusted. "Don't you fool with him, Jess," warned Calvin Coe.[88] Tom Wilburn and Old John[89] even went so far as to advise Jess to kill Monkey Anders, claiming he was the worst enemy Jess had. Jess could not see the value of their advice. According to Mrs. Sarah Coe Tooley, his usual rebuttal was, "Aw, he wouldn't betray me."

Claude Anders was paid by the posse from Monroe County to betray Jess Coe. At a prearranged spot and time, Anders was to point out his friend, step aside, and then watch Jess fall before the crossfire of the Monroe County posse. Tim Coe told of the gruesome details:

> About 25 or 30 feet to where they [the posse] were in the path, why, they was a scaly-bark hickory tree stood there—and Anders had been going out squirrel hunting lots with Jess. And that's the way it was all made up and understood that Anders he would pretend that he saw a squirrel in the top of that tree in order to get Jess's attention in the other direction. . . . And Monkey said,

"There's a squirrel in the top of that tree, Jess." Well, of course, Jess's eyes were on the top of that tree. He told him, says, "You stand right there, now, and I'll walk around above that tree and turn the squirrel for you." And that was in order to give Monkey a chance to get out of the range of the guns, you see. And as soon as he got out of the range of the guns, they let him have it.[90]

No one knows for sure who shot Jess. From all indications, only one person fired the death shot. Tim Coe surveyed the scene of the murder at a later date, and formed the conclusion that the men in the posse "was awful bad shots, or awful scared, or didn't want to hurt anybody, one or the two." Coe based his conclusions on the distribution and location of some shots which were purposely fired wildly:

> They was a stump . . . twelve feet out of the path that Jess was in. And I stopped and got down and looked around there. I soon saw that they was somebody in that bunch that was an awful bad shot or awful scared. . . . Well, in four inches of the ground on the lower side of that big stump—them fellers in the posse was all back here below that big stump, you see—waiting for Anders to bring Jess around there—and they was a whole load of shots that didn't cover a spot bigger than a half dollar, that was right almost in the roots of that stump. And then they was twigs shot off at least six feet over his head.

The posse took the body to Squire John Williams' place in Turkey Neck Bend, where they had previously left their horses. From Williams, the posse obtained a buggy in which to haul the body to Glasgow, about forty miles away, where it would be shipped to Indianapolis by rail. From Williams' place, the procession went to McMillan's Landing, crossed the river, and headed for Big Sulphur Creek. Green Graves saw the corpse at that point:

> It wasn't very long until my little boy he come on to

90 Similar accounts of the murder were told by Price Kirkpatrick, Mrs. Ray Anders, Mrs. Sarah Coe Tooley, and George Allred.

91 This account given by George Allred.

the house and says, "Pappy, they've got a dead man in that buggy." Said, "I seed his feet a-hanging out the back end of the buggy." I said, "You never, Dave." "Yes, I did. I knowed it was a man, fer 'is feet 'uz sticking out the hind end of the buggy." Well, it wasn't but a few minutes till there's a bunch of men come down the—workin' the road—come on down the road and they told us about them takin' Jess Coe up and havin' him in the hind end of the buggy.

Calvin, John, Robert, and some of the other male members of the Coe colony were in the area of Biggerstaff Bar on the river getting some logs when they were told by a young white boy that Jess had been betrayed and murdered. "They made for home, grabbed their guns, and they got way out here towards Tompkinsville when they met a feller who told them they jist as well go on home—they had done passed through town with him." [91] More precisely, it was at McMillan's Landing that the Coe pursuers were told to abandon chase. Martin Williams, operator of the store there, told the Negroes that the posse was half way to Tompkinsville, or farther. In truth, the sheriff's posse had just crossed the river and was "just out of sight," according to Green Graves.

Another version of the chase, related by Mrs. Ray Anders, gives credit to the women of the Coe colony as the group who tried to catch the posse:

All the women—most of the women on Coe Ridge—put on pants, got their Winchesters, jist like they was going to catch them. They'd been war with 'um if they'd caught 'um. . . . I guess they wuz 40 or 50 Winchesters. They liked jist a little catching them. They had crossed the river, gone out of sight. And some of them begged them not to go no further. They liked that much catching them. They was going to kill 'um.

Monkey Anders made a fast disappearance from Coe

Ridge after Jess was killed. He went to Glasgow, where he was seen not long afterwards at a local fair. At that time, he was described as the "finest dressed man of any colored feller had ever been in Glasgow." [92] When would-be avengers got too close in pursuit, Anders moved to Chicago, where he still lives. Now nearing the century mark, Anders never returned to Coe Ridge after the death of Jess, perhaps because of the vows of Yaller John Coe. Old John was later asked to join the church, but even then vowed not to do so "until he got that feller that killed Cousin Jess." [93] Even in his old days, John cried every time he thought about Jess getting killed. "Said he never would die satisfied until he got to kill the man who killed Jess." [94]

Like Old John, the other members of the colony were enraged at the man who had professed to be a friend, but who had betrayed their kinsman, a member of the colony. This betrayal caused the Coes to wonder if all people whom they had trusted would become enemies rather than remain friends. It seemed as though the whole colony might be wiped out as a result of this attitude toward others. Just at that time, however, when everything seemed very dark for the colony's future, their attitude was changed greatly by the teaching and preaching of Cassie Raspberry Wagner, daughter of Bill Coe and granddaughter of Zeke and Patsy Ann. Mother Wagner, as she was called, returned from Indianapolis and, being a very religious woman, influenced the colony to become calm and peaceful.[95]

92 *Ibid.*
93 Mrs. Sarah Coe Tooley.
94 George Allred.
95 *Chronicles,* 74.

5 *The White Gals*

White women came to live among the Coe Negroes from 1885 to 1920, the turbulent middle years of the colony's history. Their presence coincides roughly with the days of feuding, and with the early years of moonshining and bootlegging when murder and violence gripped the colony and produced the genesis of the colony's internal sickness and ultimate extinction. These white girls were young and pretty, so it is said, and under normal circumstances could have easily found suitable mates in their own society. But certain personal factors drove the girls away from the white man's society and into the realm of the legendary Negro colony on Coe Ridge.

The backgrounds of these young women were not identical by any means. Virginia Warren and Julie Newton came from the finest homes and had well-respected parents. The girls "went bad," however, and were driven from home by their own people. Two other girls, Sue Ann Barton and Patricia Smith, originated from a poor white background where society apparently cared little about moral standards—as a matter of fact, Sue Ann and Patricia were introduced by their parents to life in the Coe colony.[1]

The white people who had homes surrounding the Coe colony were apparently apathetic toward the presence of white women in Zeketown. The white oral traditions collected on this situation contained very few derogatory comments about the habits of these white women, and no words of condonation. The few comments that were offered never pointed the finger of guilt at the Negroes, but always pointed at the white women, whom the white informants considered one rung lower than the Negroes on the social ladder. Even the Negro informants displayed a languid attitude about their ancestral relations with the white women in the Coe colony. It is apparent that these informants accepted the days of cohabitation in Zeketown as a once common thing, perhaps deriving justification for the practice from earlier times when the slave masters used the Negro girls as they saw fit.

MOLLY AND NAN

During their visits to the homes of Yaller John and Joe Coe,[2] in the late 1880's, Calvin and Little John met and courted two white girls from the Mud Camp community. Cal's sweetheart was Molly Ballard, a daughter of Vince Ballard, and Little John's girl was Nan Anderson, daughter of Walter Anderson. Barely in their teens, both girls lived at the mouth of Mud Camp Creek, near Cloyd's Landing in Cumberland County.[3] Cal and John became acquainted with Molly and Nan while working in the woods in the vicinity of the girls' houses; the men may have occasionally boarded at one or

1 Virginia Warren, Julie Newton, Sue Ann Barton, and Patricia Smith are pseudonyms, used in this text to avoid any possibility of invasion of privacy.

2 Shortly after 1880, Old John and his brother, Joe, married Tennessee and Tilda Black, sisters from the Mud Camp community of Cumberland County, according to Mrs. Cornelius Allen, Jan. 24, 1964.

3 The Ballards lived at what was then called the Hunter Place, now owned by Jim Butler, according to Bart Ballard, the brother of Molly, on Oct. 12, 1963.

4 Mrs. Susie Taylor Moore claimed: "They jist said they wuz talkin' to two white girls. They was a-boardin' there at that place, and they got to talking to them two white girls."

5 The kitchen episode was described in an unrecorded interview by Cornelius V. Allen, Oct. 12, 1963, and by Bart Ballard, on that same date.

6 Statement made on Oct. 12, 1963. Little John was nine years old in 1880, according to the 1880 Cumberland County Census. Mrs. Allen was three years in error about her father's age, for he was nineteen when the attempted elopement occurred in 1889. This discrepancy in dates is explained when Barren County Court records are cited later in this chapter.

7 Mrs. Etta Short. The *Chronicles*, 63, corroborates this testimony by stating that the four had spent the previous night in Glasgow.

both of the homes.[4] Soon thereafter, Molly and Nan would slip away from their homes to meet Cal and Little John at the home of Sam Smith, a white neighbor whose wife, Bell, perpetuated the whole affair by letting the four rendezvous in her kitchen any time they desired.[5]

Although Calvin was a grown man, about twenty-five years old, Little John was no more than sixteen. In the words of Mrs. Cornelius Allen (Little John's daughter), "His Uncle Cal led him astray. You know how a boy will worship his uncle. Well, that's the way it was with my father and Calvin." [6] After a few weeks of these secret meetings in the Smith home, the four decided to elope to Indiana where they could be married. It is generally felt that they were going to Indianapolis, but Little John's daughter emphatically clarified the matter: "Now let me set you straight on something! They were not going to Indianapolis! They were going to Jeffersonville; just far enough into Indiana to get married."

The whole plan of flight backfired at Glasgow, the nearest train station some forty-five miles from Zeketown. The four lovers went to the home of a Negro friend in Glasgow and there spent the night. The next morning they were apprehended at the railroad station. A white informant recalled their arrest:

> And they got on the train there in Glasgow. But they'd stayed all night, you know—no travel, no way of traveling much then, and they had to go to Glasgow and stay all night and catch a train out.
>
> So the next morning, why, the girls they wore veils over their faces to keep anybody from knowing they'uz white, you know. But this colored (they stayed in a colored man's house, and of course they had to let him know everything). And they went up to the depot then to get on the train, why, he went out and got the officers, and they went and got them.[7]

Most of the informants did not agree that the police were notified by the Negro host. Tim Coe, for example, placed the entire blame on a tiny bee, which got behind the veil over one of the girls' faces. In fright, she knocked the veil from her face and revealed white flesh. George Allred, quoting Calvin Coe himself, related the incident in this manner: "They said they'd got away with them women . . . but them women had on veils. One of them kindly raised up the veil to scratch her face, and this colored feller saw her and he went and told the law that them colored fellers wuz running off with them white women, and they arrested Calvin and John."

The wind is blamed in the account given by Mrs. Susie Taylor Moore: "And they bought black veils, and them girls put them on, and they got on the train to leave. And it happened the wind blowed up one of the girls' veils and they seen they was white, and they arrested them right there and brought the girls back home." [8]

The four were taken to the Glasgow jail. Molly and Nan were sent home on the next stage, according to Tim Coe, and Cal and John were released on bail put up by Boles and Botts, two Glasgow attorneys. The *Chronicles* claims, however, that the two stood trial and were freed after John paid a fifty-dollar fine for drawing a gun on an officer. Barren County official records for 1889 give an account of the whole event. The Glasgow city attorney brought charges on July 20, 1889, against John Coe, Calvin Coe, and John Coe, the latter (Yaller John) being completely neglected by oral tradition. Their charge was for unlawfully assembling "themselves together for the purpose of causing the marriage of a white woman to a Negro man." Bail was set at $200 each. That same day they went before the county judge for trial. Their sentence was affixed at a fine of

[8] The *Chronicles*, 64, claims that one of the girls took off her gloves while eating, thus revealing white skin.

The scene at the Glasgow train station has proved to be quite elastic. Certain accepted "historical truths" associated with the event are nothing more than a series of motifs which serve to give that portion of the legend its cohesiveness. It is not known whether one of the girls' gloves fell down to reveal a white arm, a bee got under her veil, the wind blew the veil up, or if she raised her veil to scratch her face. The folk who relate this portion of the legend apparently call upon such motifs to give the story its elasticity. Historians and folklorists need to be aware of the possibility that the folk may improvise history in order to preserve its core of veracity.

9   The trial is described in the *Chronicles*, 64. The official record, found in Commonwealth Order Book 4, p. 79, contains no mention of Boles and Botts, or of John drawing a gun on an officer.

10   The Glasgow episode dissolved the courtship of Molly and Cal, and Nan and Little John. Nan never married. She went to Bowling Green soon thereafter to live. She died a few years later in Cumberland County, according to Bart Ballard, Oct. 12, 1963. Mr. Ballard told that his sister Molly eventually married Wes Spears and raised a large family on Marrowbone Creek. I accompanied Bart Ballard to the cemetery in Marrowbone, where Wes and Molly are buried. Their grave markers are inscribed "Tillman Wesley Spears, 3-7-1865, 4-20-1948"; "Mary Ann Spears, 11-11-1873, _____." Her death date has not been affixed on the stone.

11   Oral narratives accompanied the spread of the ballad, and the affair between the Negro boys and the white girls soon won a niche in storytelling situations. The courtship assumed the proportions of a regional saga, and has remained extremely tenacious despite the passing of seventy-five years since the event transpired.

$150 each and fifty days each in the Barren County jail. They were released from jail in September, 1889.[9]

Shortly after the attempt to elope was foiled,[10] a ballad was composed to describe the incident. It is said that Little John and Cal wrote the ballad. The song quickly entered oral tradition and was diffused over a fairly large geographical area.[11] George Allred stated that the song was known in the coal mining camps of Fentress and Overton counties, Tennessee, some sixty miles from Zeketown: "I heard that old song, 'Molly and Nan,' before I ever heard tell of Zeke Ridge. Them darkies used to sing that in the coal mines over about Livingston."

The banjo-picking Cal himself was the instrument by which the song became widely known. Practically every informant could testify, "I've heard Cal pick it on the banjo and sing it lots of times." Little John, too, was heard to pick the banjo and sing the account of their Glasgow episode. In the words of Bill Poindexter: "John and Cal would pick that on the banjer and sing that on themselves. I've heerd them pick that and sing it thar at Black's Ferry. They'd come to the store and fellers would have them to pick it. Carried the banjo with them. They'd pick and sing anything anybody'd ask them to."

Lucy Robert Coe claimed that Cal earned money by singing "Molly and Nan": "Uncle Calvin used to go out to the election. Why, they'd have him, I'll bet you, pick that song who-e-e-e-e, I couldn't tell you at the times. He'd make money out there—six and seven dollars every time he'd go to the election. They'd just throw him in half a-dollars and quarters, and jist first one and another, you know, jist to hear him sing that song."

It appears next to impossible to reconstruct the parent form of the ballad, "Molly and Nan." The form is different in virtually every variant gathered, for blues ballads usually celebrate and comment on an event instead of presenting a straightforward, circumstantial account. Where one variant, for example, may contain the words, "All off the train, boys," another may state, "Gettin' off the train, boys." Thus one form is versed as though there is a command from the law officers to get off the train. The other form indicates that John and Cal took the initiative in leaving the train. Such inconsistencies appear throughout the fragmented verses, and are characteristic of blues ballads, which are generally variable, subjective, lyrical, and yet dramatic in narrative content. Printed below are the incomplete versions as sung or recited by the various contributors. In its entirety, the ballad relates that John and Cal loved Nan and Molly, that they went to Glasgow, got on the train, were arrested and placed in jail, and were released at different times and placed on the stage bound for Cumberland County.[12]

A. VARIANTS

Sung by Mrs. Cornelius Allen:

All in the train girls
All in the train
Don't you see those blue-eyed girls
Getting on the train

All in the train girls
All in the train
Don't you see those blue-eyed girls
Getting on the train

All of you Glasgow boys
You live all in vain
Don't you see those blue-eyed girls
Getting on the train

All on the train boys
All on the train

12 By knowing the story to a fair degree of accuracy, one can see that the song gives the full story. It would be virtually impossible, however, to take the song fragments and figure out the sequence of events without knowing the oral narrative traditions which accompany the ballad.

13 After the words "John and Cal," the singer paused briefly and apparently improvised the next line.

Don't you see John and Cal
Getting on the train

All off the train boys
All off the train
Don't you see John and Cal
Getting off the train

All off the train girls
All off the train
Don't you see those blue-eyed girls
Getting off the train

Railroad, railroad
Troubles any man
Don't you see John and Cal[13]
Walking around the town

Walk down to jail boys
Walk down to jail
Don't you see John and Cal
Going down to jail

All on the stage girls
All on the stage
Don't you see those blue-eyed girls
Getting on the stage

Railroad, railroad, railroad
Do you trouble any man
Don't you see John and Cal
Walking around in jail

Walk down the stairs boys
Walk down the stairs
Don't you see old John and Cal
Old Sam Bowles getting them out of jail

Sung by Mrs. Susie Taylor Moore:

Getting on the train, boys
Getting on the train, boys
See old John and Cal, boys
Getting on the train

Sung by Mrs. Green Graves:

You oughta seen them blue-eyed girls
Gettin' offa that train

Recited by Mrs. Etta Short:

Get on that stage
Get on that stage, boys
Can't you see Miss Molly and Nan
Gettin' on that stage

Peep through the keys, boys
Peep through the keys
Can't you see Miss Molly and Nan
Gettin' on that stage? [*chuckles at this point*]

Walk down to jail, boys
Walk down to jail
Can't you see old John and Cal
Walking down to jail?

Recited by Mrs. Mattie Davidson:

All out of jail, boys
All out of jail
Can't you see old Sam Bowles
Gettin' us out of jail?

Back in the land, boys
Back in the land
Can't you see old John and Cal
Getting back in the land?

Recited by Bill Poindexter:

Can't you see old John and Cal gettin' up them
    steps, boys
Gettin' up them steps
Don't you see old Molly and Nan

Recited by Lucy Robert Coe:

Can't you see Molly and Nan a-follerin' John and
    Cal
And can't you see John and Cal follerin' Molly
    and Nan?

Get off this train, boys
Get off this train
Don't you see John and Cal gettin' off this train?

All down to jail, boys
All down to jail

Can't you see old John and Cal goin' down to
    jail?

Sung by Sarah Coe Tooley:
    You oughta seed old Molly and Nan
    A-gettin' in that, on that
    Gettin' on that train

    All on that train, boys
    All on the train
    Can't you see old Molly and Nan
    Gettin' on the train

    Walk down to jail, boys
    Walk down to jail
    You oughta seed old John and Cal
    Gettin' in that jail

    You oughta seed old John and Cal
    Gettin' on the train
    All on the train, boys
    All on the train

    Can't you see old Molly and Nan
    Gettin' off that train

    Walk down the jail, boys
    Walk down the jail
    You oughta seed old John and Cal
    Gettin' offa that train

Sung by George Allred:
    Get off the train, boys
    Get off the train
    Don't you see old John and Cal
    Crawlin' off the train?

    Walk up in jail boys
    Walk up in jail
    Don't you see Cal and John
    Gettin' up that jail?

    All on the stage, girls
    All on the stage
    Don't you see them blue-eyed girls
    Gettin' on the stage?

130

Back in the land girls
Back in the land
Don't you see Miss Molly and Nan
Gettin' back in the land?

Walk out of jail, boys
Walk out of jail
Don't you see old Cal and John
Walkin' out of jail?

Pick up your guns, boys
Pick up your guns
You ought to see Cal and John
Pickin' up their guns

Sung by Mrs. Ray Anders:

On the train boys
All on the train
Don't you see old John and Cal
Gettin' on that train

Railroad, railroad trouble in the land
Don't you see old John and Cal
Love Molly and Nan?

Railroad, railroad trouble in the land
Don't you see old Molly and Nan
Love John and Cal?

Get on the train boys
Get on the train
Don't you see old John and Cal
Gettin' on that train?

Oleson Wilburn Is Killed in Cal Coe's Stead. The elope-ment attempt with the two white girls ended in trag-edy. Oleson, the oldest son of Tom and Mary Wilburn and the grandson of Zeke and Patsy Ann, was the first of the Coe clan to be killed by the whites in payment for the breach of community mores.[14] After the Glas-gow episode, public sentiment was stirred against the Coe Negroes in general and against Calvin and Little John Coe in particular. Vince Ballard was offered help

14 The exact date of Oleson's murder could not be established by oral informants, although they all claimed that it occurred about 1890. The *Chronicles* (p. 65) dates the event in Aug. 1889, but at that precise time Calvin and John were still in jail.

131

15 Most of the information in this paragraph was furnished by Bart Ballard, Oct. 12, 1963.

16 *Chronicles*, 65–66, et passim. Mrs. Sarah Coe Tooley claimed his body was found "in a brushpile."

17 Only Mrs. Ray Anders told of the buzzards.

18 Mrs. Etta Short noted that they "never did get nobody up for it or nothing."

19 Two people stated frankly that the killer was unknown. Twice during the interview with Mrs. Etta Short, she stated that "they never did know who it was." The *Chronicles* (p. 66) also admits that the murder remained undetected.

should he decide to kill Calvin Coe in retaliation for the offense against his daughter. Included among those who offered help were Bill Irvin, a rabble-rouser who had recently arrived in the community after a hitch with a circus, and all residents of the Cloyd's Landing community in Cumberland County. Another local resident, Jim Glass, offered to lend them his musket for their dirty work.[15]

Unaware of the conspiracy to kill his Uncle Calvin Coe, Oleson Wilburn left Coe Ridge with his grandfather and started to Mud Camp to visit a relative. When Oleson and his grandfather came to a forks of the road, Oleson went in one direction, Zeke in the other. Oleson, however, never reached the home of his uncle. He was found three weeks later in the woods, a good distance from the road, buried in a shallow grave[16] already discovered by encircling buzzards.[17]

Most of the informants claim that the assassin was never brought to trial,[18] and they only hazard guesses as to the identity of the killer.[19] "They think Bill Irvin done that," offered Charlie Coe; Ray Anders did not agree, and instead blamed the Redheads for Oleson's murder. Neither Bill Irvin nor the Redheads did the killing, according to Bart Ballard, who stated bluntly, "My father killed him."

Although Tim Coe and Cornelius Allen had mentioned the possibility that Ballard killed Oleson, the writer was taken aback with this statement from the son of Vince Ballard. Bart Ballard was visited by me in hopes of obtaining information which would help to date the murder, nothing else. After he began to talk, Ballard, then eighty-three, lay on a couch in his Marrowbone home and related the whole incident in all its gruesome detail. He told how his father, along with Irvin, Goodhue, and Welch, were in Tally Hollow, near Bluff

Landing, when they spotted Oleson and mistook him for Calvin Coe.[20] They hid and waited for the figure to come closer. When Oleson got within firing range, Vince Ballard shot him, hitting him in the left side of the throat; Ballard then emerged from hiding and ran to his fallen victim, who was still groaning. Realizing that the victim was not Calvin Coe, Ballard, nevertheless, picked up a large rock and beat Oleson over the head "until he quit hollering." [21] A few days later, the body of Oleson was discovered by Mary, daughter of Alec Goodhue. The girl became so frightened at the ghastly sight that she fell down upon her knees, then in kindness removed her apron and covered the face of Oleson.[22]

Bart Ballard stated that his father, along with Bill Irvin, was jailed in Burkesville and stood trial for the murder of Oleson Wilburn. The case did not come to trial for about nine months, with both men remaining in jail during this period. At the trial both men were cleared, but in the meantime public opinion had turned against them while they were in prison. Immediately after the trial, Bill Irvin, Porter Welch, and Vince Ballard left the country, never to return. Ballard stated that his father probably went to Tennessee and, with a tone of bitterness in his voice, added, "He left my mother and a houseful of children to root hog or die."

Joe Coe Dies from Bullet Intended for Little John. After the murder of Oleson Wilburn, Joe Coe, a son of Zeke and Patsy Ann, was the next of the Coe clan to be killed. During the 1880's Joe had married and moved to Mud Camp Creek.[23] He left his family at home one Saturday afternoon and went to Coe Ridge to spend the night with his parents, possibly to persuade them to move away. Just before daybreak the following day, Joe started from his father's house toward the barn to feed the

20 Mrs. Short had heard that the killer thought he was shooting Calvin Coe.
21 Bart Ballard, Oct. 12, 1963.
22 *Ibid.*
23 It is common knowledge that Joe Coe lived at that time on Mud Camp Creek.

24 Many of the informants knew of the shooting, but Tim Coe was most conversant on the topic.

25 Ruthie Coe Anders also placed the guilt on "them Taylors."

26 Mrs. Etta Short agreed that Irvin and Ballard did the shooting.

27 Bart Ballard, Oct. 12, 1963. (Ballard's father seemingly could not have shot Joe because he was either in jail at the time, or in Tennessee; see p. 133)

horses. Before he reached the barn, a shot from the darkness cut him down.[24]

The family never learned who killed Joe. Some placed the blame on the Redheads. In the words of Calvin Coe, "We never knowed who killed him, but we always thought it was one of the Taylors."[25] The white people of the area say that the Ballards were responsible for Joe's death. "I sorta think Bill Irvin killed him," testified Price Kirkpatrick.[26] Bart Ballard stated that his father, Vince, and Bill Irvin shot Joe thinking he was Little John, just as they had mistakenly killed Oleson instead of Calvin.[27]

Joe Coe's death is the last charged against Bill Irvin. Irvin nurtured a hatred for Calvin Coe for several years, but was content to leave Calvin alone as long as the latter stayed away from the Mud Camp area, according to the following testimony offered by Price Kirkpatrick:

> [Cal] was on Mud Camp one time. (They moved to Mud Camp Creek in Cumberland County, logging over there.) And Bill went over there, and Cal was coming along the road one day. (He always carried his Winchester over his, slinging over his back, you know.)
>
> Well, Irvin was the kind of man that you couldn't, you didn't know when he was going to bob up. But all at once he bobbed up in front of him with his big knife, you know, and made him lay that gun down. And he told him, "Get out of here and leave Mud Camp Creek." And he left Mud Camp Creek, too! Got away from there. He never tried to kill him, he just made him leave.

VIRGINIA AND CLARA WARREN

Old John lost his wife, Tennessee, about 1890 and returned to Zeketown from the Mud Camp community to be near his aging, recently widowed mother, Patsy Ann. On the ridge, John built a small cabin which soon became a bachelor's quarters for himself, Calvin, and Little John. The three lived there for a few months, carousing around the neighborhood in search of fun as well as occasional work. One day, perhaps in 1891, they were down on the river at Black's Ferry tying up a raft.

While the three Negroes worked, a steamboat docked at the landing. From the steamboat emerged a young, pretty white woman, carrying a newborn babe in her arms.[28] She was Virginia Warren, who had been ostracized by her prominent family and friends at Carthage, Tennessee, when she became pregnant and gave birth to a daughter, Clara.[29] In the words of Mrs. Ray Anders: "Used to, back in those days when a woman would . . . have a child or something 'fore she was married they'd jist run her off."

Virginia packed her belongings in a bag, and with her babe in arms boarded the first steamboat leaving Carthage. That boat happened to be northbound for Burnside, Kentucky. Virginia had only enough money to purchase passage as far as Black's Ferry, located in Monroe County about one mile from Coe Ridge.[30]

The Coe Negroes at work at the Black's Ferry landing watched the young mother for several hours as she loitered around the store there, apparently with no place to go. Later in the day, the Negro boys began talking to her and learned of her plight. According to Mrs. Anders, it was not the nature of the Coes in Zeketown to neglect a person in distress:

> They would take care of people. You, a stranger, it didn't make any difference who went there and wanted to put up with ye for a night or two. As long as they could put up with it, they'd take care of you, and wouldn't let nobody bother you. Feed you, do the best they can with ye, give ye a place to sleep. I've seen people right

28 Although the date of Virginia Warren's arrival at Black's Ferry is not known, it is commonly accepted that she came from Carthage by steamboat. Statements to this effect were made by Mr. and Mrs. Ray Anders, Mrs. Myrtle Kerr, Bill Poindexter, and George Allred.

29 Clara Warren is a pseudonym, used in this text to avoid any possibility of invasion of privacy.

30 Statements based primarily on comments offered by Mrs. Myrtle Kerr.

31 Brief comments about the death of Virginia and her son were offered by Mrs. Etta Short, Mrs. Mattie Davidson, Mr. and Mrs. Ray Anders, and Mrs. Myrtle Kerr. Willie's name was supplied by Mrs. Cornelius Allen, whose mother raised Clara Warren.

32 Statement by Mrs. Cornelius V. Allen, Jan. 23, 1964.

out, I mean different people that come thar too, maybe strangers that they wouldn't know nothing about. They'd jist say they was on they way somewhere, trying to get somewhere.

When the Coes returned to Zeketown at the day's end, they took along the strange young mother and her child. Old John, who had recently lost his own wife, carried Virginia's young baby in his arms. When the procession arrived in the colony, John took Virginia and Clara to his cabin. It is community knowledge that the new arrivals never left the shelter of his cabin home. Bill Poindexter remembered: "Old Uncle John's woman, her name was [Warren]. He got her a-way up here up the river somewhere where he was a-logging. She went to the camps with two of them and dist took up with him—and come home with him. She lived with him 'til she died." Yaller John and Virginia lived together just a little over a year, for she contracted tuberculosis and died. Before her death, however, she bore John a son, Willie, who soon followed his mother in death from the same disease.[31]

With the death of her mother, Clara went to live with Little John Coe and his family. Clara was then just a mere child, with a crop of lice in her hair. Mary Ellen, Little John's wife, made up a mixture of tobacco stems and papaw bark and applied it to Clara's head to remove the lice. Through the years, Clara developed into a shapely lass with sandy hair and blue eyes, and was considered by both whites and Negroes to be a very beautiful young lady. When she turned twenty-one about 1910, Clara was advised by Little John and Mary Ellen to leave the colony to seek a place among her own race. She pleaded to stay in the colony: "I won't feel right with white people. I've lived here all my life and want to live the rest of it here." [32]

136

Her wish was granted, and she remained an adopted member of the Negro race. About a year later, or when she was twenty-two, Clara took up with Vern Baxter, who was "as black a man as they was out there." [33] Vern had a sister in Zeketown but was not a resident when he first courted Clara. But with their "marriage" arrangement, he moved into the colony, where they built a home and "had a bunch of kids." [34] They are light yellow in skin color, and have often been referred to as quite handsome. The grandchildren of Clara and Vern assumed various colors, from light yellow to black. White blood in that family line has not resulted in a feeling of shame on the part of the descendants. Clara was good to her children and they loved her. To them, that was all that mattered.

JULIE NEWT

Another white woman to enter Zeketown was never accepted by the colony's inhabitants. She was Julie Newton, commonly called Julie Newt, an outcast local girl of good parentage.

About 1900 Julie became the community prostitute. Prior to that time she had strayed up and down the countryside, and her parents, who were of the very finest stock in the area, were shocked and saddened by her aberrant actions. Finally they refused to let Julie remain at home to disgrace the family name any longer. "She was dist bad. And her folks run her off, and she went to the darkies," testified a white lady. Julie wandered into the Coe colony and took advantage of Zeketown hospitality. She went from one house to another, spending a little time at each place. Eventually she took up with Ross Williams, a black man who had drifted into the Coe colony during that same period. Calvin Coe

33 Statement by Mrs. Myrtle Kerr. Mrs. Etta Short described Baxter as "the blackest Nigger you ever saw." Vern Baxter is a pseudonym, used in this text to avoid any possibility of invasion of privacy.

34 Statement by Mrs. Myrtle Kerr. One of these children claimed that he had three brothers and two sisters.

35 Sue Ann's daughter stated that her mother died on Oct. 19, 1920. By utilizing the comments made by Bill Poindexter, I was able to establish 1895 as the approximate date that Sue Ann went to the Coe colony.

36 Mrs. Edith Williams stated that Sue Ann even claimed to be part black.

37 Black Jim Barton is a pseudonym, used in this text to avoid any possibility of invasion of privacy.

built a small cabin behind his own for Ross and Julie. They lived there a few months, but eventually drifted off to Indiana.

Julie refused to live with Ross very long after they got to Indiana; she left him and came back to the Coe colony asking to be accepted as one of them. They refused to have anything to do with Julie this time. Ostracized from the black man's society, she finally wandered off and disappeared completely. About twenty years later, a skeleton was found in a cave in Glasgow, near where the jail now stands. Certain identification marks on the skeleton pointed to Julie Newton. There is no reason to believe that either the Coes or Ross Williams had anything to do with her death. Julie died apparently all alone, rejected by both races.

SUE ANN BARTON

Sue Ann Barton, another white girl, made a more lasting impression on the Zeketown inhabitants and their white neighbors. She lived with Calvin Coe for approximately twenty-five years, from 1895 to 1920,[35] and bore him eight children.

Sue Ann was allegedly part Negro herself. Price Kirkpatrick, a recent president of the Peoples Bank in Tompkinsville, who went to school with Sue Ann and her brother, described her as a person who "passed as white," but "had something in her besides white blood." George Allred, Negro, hinted strongly at Negro blood in her when he said, "They *claimed* they were white." [36] At any rate, Black Jim Barton's family was economically deprived, and for this and other reasons the children were avoided by the other youngsters at school.[37]

Mrs. Susie Taylor Moore recalled when Sue Ann left home:

> She was pretty. I seen her when she left home before she went to Zeketown. I was dist a little child at my grandmother Short's. (See, after my daddy died, I was jist about a year and six months old when he died. Well, after he died, my mother took me back there, you know, moved back to her daddy's.)
> And I was up right smart little girl. I can remember when she left home. She lived over yander in Dogtown across the Cumberland. And she was up behind a white boy when they come thar. And they come in. I don't know how come them to come in. I don't remember now whether she was trying to get a place to stay, or what.
> And then the next thing we heerd of her, she was in Zeketown staying. And she died out there—she stayed there 'til she died.

Black Jim Barton taught in the Coe Ridge school. It was due to his teaching there that Sue Ann actually made the acquaintance of Calvin Coe. George Allred claimed: "He come there and taught school, and brought this girl. She went to school there and took up with Cal. They went to housekeeping." The legal authorities at Burkesville could not readily break up the affair, because both poor roads and lack of courage deterred any attempt to invade the legendary Coe colony. Eventually Calvin and Sue Ann were arrested, but not until after they had brought eight children into the world. Calvin was sent to prison for one thousand days in an effort to break up Cal and Sue Ann's relationship. The law then told him he would be turned loose if he would agree to leave the country. But "he told them he wasn't going nowheres—going back home when he got out." [38] Calvin fulfilled his warning to return to the ridge, but he was then returned to jail for another one thousand days' confinement.[39]

38 George Allred.
39 Hascal Haile.

40 Although there may have been no custom involved, the fact that Calvin took a banjo to jail may be significant. Sellers, *Slavery in Alabama*, 278, notes that "when slaves having musical talent were jailed, their melodies no doubt partially relieved the monotony of prison life for themselves and the others."

The informant was probably correct in naming Garner as jailor. Wells, *Cumberland County*, 111, does not give dates of jailors' terms, but lists W. T. Garner as jailor during that period.

41 Much of the information contained in this paragraph was related by Ray Anders.

The following story, told by Ray Anders, points up the determination and grit of Calvin while in the Burkesville jail:

He was doin' time down here in jail. That Garner wuz jailor. He had his banjer kept in thar, and picked the banjer. Probably the jailor would go back there and pick, you know, everybody'd come in jail there and want him to pick. Thought it might have 'sturbed 'um downstairs, so the jailor told him to quit pickin' the banjer, and he did. Se he set down and wrote to Frankfort about would he have a right to pick a banjer in jail? They wrote back and told him to go ahead about his pickin' his banjer if he wudn't a-pickin' no, singin' and pickin' nothin' that, I mean songs that he wudn't due to. So this jailor come up and he told him, said, "Here's a letter I got from the governor." And so the jailor took the letter and looked at it, and throwed it back down. Old Man Cal jist went ahead about his banjer pickin'. And he come up one night and told him he told him to quit playin' the banjer, and he come out with his pistol and was aimin' to shoot 'im. And did fire on him! Uncle Cal made, made fer him and did get to him in time. The pistol it fired and went through jist kindly grazed burned his arm there. Uncle Cal took the pistol away from him and gonna kill 'im; some of 'um grabbed Uncle Cal and kept him from it. Done had the pistol! [40]

When the Zeketown residents got word that Cal was being mistreated in jail, they formed a mob to march against the jail in Burkesville to demand the release of Cal. The law officials heard of the move and formed a posse to wait in ambush along the road from Zeketown to Burkesville. The Coes were able to get into Burkesville unmolested, however, because, anticipating trouble, they went by another road. By the time the posse arrived back in Burkesville, Cal had persuaded his kinsmen that he had no intention of leaving with them. The sheriff subsequently agreed never again to molest Cal while he played his banjo.[41]

Sometime during Cal's imprisonment, Sue Ann, too, had been placed in confinement at Burkesville. She died in jail, suffering from tuberculosis. Uncle George Allred summed up the Calvin-Sue Ann affair in terms of Negro attitudes: "I talked to Cal about it. But they wouldn't last no time in Tennessee where I come from, trying to live with them white women. That's where people done wrong here. They let them stay [i.e., together] 'til they raised a big family. They had children by them colored men. They ought to broke it up there on the start, if they'd been aim to break it up."

'TRICIA SMITH

The chief actor in the next Negro-white girl drama in Zeketown was Leslie Coe, commonly called "Big Les," a son of Chester and Ora Coe, and grandson of Yaller John Coe. As a young man, Big Les began to practice the evil habits of his older kinsmen. Then, in 1920, he brought grief and sorrow to the Coe colony, when, along with Little John, he murdered Simp Smith, a white man. Like the trouble with Calvin, Big Les's sorrow was caused by his interest in a woman—a white woman, by the name of Patricia Smith.

Patricia was one of five children of Tommy and Martha Smith, a family that lived on the upper reaches of Kettle Creek.[42] Tommy Smith died, leaving Martha to care for their four surviving small children. About 1909 she married Black Morgan, of the poor white class, and they went to Zeketown and pleaded with the Negroes to give them a home there. Robert Coe had a little house in the Toot Field, but it was surrounded by young, green corn. "You'll tromp down every bit of my corn if I let you move in out there," Robert argued. "No, no, we won't," countered Black Morgan; "we won't touch nary

42 Tommy and Martha Smith are pseudonyms, used in this text to avoid any possibility of invasion of privacy.

43   All the comments in this paragraph are based on the interview with Mrs. Cornelius Allen, Jan. 23, 1964. George Allred also knew that the Morgans lived in the storehouse belonging to Old John Coe.

44   Comments based on the interview with Mrs. Cornelius Allen, Jan. 23, 1964.

45   It is common knowledge that Patricia was Garfield's "woman."

46   Mrs. Cornelius Allen, Jan. 23, 1964. The incident is alluded to in the *Chronicles*, 115. Again on page 121, the *Chronicles* notes that Big Les was shot in the arm, leaving it almost paralyzed.

47   Betty Smith and Dee Wade are pseudonyms, used in this text to avoid any possibility of invasion of privacy.

stalk." But Robert prevailed in the argument and sent them away from his house. Black led his family of "rough folks" to the premises of Yaller John Coe, and begged him for a place to stay. Old John finally agreed that they could move into an old run-down log building located at the edge of the colony and then used for the storage of field crops. The Morgans lived there for a few years, during which time Martha's children became young men and women.[43]

When she came of age, Patricia went to a community near Tompkinsville and found employment as a maid and cook in some white home. While there, she became pregnant and had to return to her mother's cabin near Zeketown.[44] A few months later, she took up with Garfield Wilburn, a son of Tom and Mary Wilburn, and lived with him until he died a premature death not long afterwards.[45]

'Tricia became a prostitute after the death of Garfield, and was available to all comers, black or white. Her house was constantly occupied by the men of the neighborhood, so say the folk, especially by Big Les Coe. He never officially lived with her, but spent most of his time in her company. Big Les's frequenting her cabin almost cost him his life at the hand of an assassin's bullet; someone took a shot at him when he was returning home from Black's Ferry after delivering a load of moonshine whiskey. The shot pierced the glass jars carried in a grass sack over his shoulder, but a metal jar rim caused the bullet to career away, resulting only in a flesh wound.[46] The chain of events which followed would indicate that the shooting was committed either by Patricia's brother, Simp Smith, or by Dee Wade, who had recently lost his wife, Betty, a sister of Patricia and Simp.[47] It is commonly felt that the shot was fired by Wade, for he wanted Big Les out of the way so that he could persuade Patricia to come live with him and raise his children. Finally, Patricia did leave the ridge settlement to live with her brother-in-law as his wife. In the words of a white informant, Wade "took her away from this Nigger."

The story did not end there, however, for Big Les was not willing to give up 'Tricia that easily. When Wade was taken to Bowling Green to appear on the federal docket to answer to a charge of bootlegging and moonshining, Big Les took 'Tricia back to Zeketown, this time to his home. After a series of incidents, Simp Smith, accompanied by some other white men, went to the ridge settlement to get his sister, but he never returned. Simp was shot to death during the night in a wild gun brawl, and the guilt was placed on Big Les and Little John. Mrs. Susie Taylor Moore summarized the whole sordid affair:

> [Simp Smith] was married and had a wife and two children when they killed him. But people thought—I jist as well be plain with ye—people thought that they killed him because he went there and got his sister. His sister ['Tricia Smith] had went there and was staying with them darkies. And he went and got her.
> And she was living with her brother-in-law [Dee Wade]. Her sister had died. She was living with her brother-in-law and the children—taking care of the children.
> And then he went back out there, they killed him. And people thought that was what it was about, 'cause he went and got her away. She was out there living with one of them.

George Allred told the story with a slightly different slant:

> [Dee's] wife died, and he wanted that woman to come live with him and help him raise his children, you know. And she went down there. He come and got her and

[Dee] went off up there then and they got him up about some whiskey—had to go to Bowling Green.

While he was gone, they slipped down there and brought her back on the ridge. Well, he'd get after her every time he was out there to try to make her leave the ridge and go and live with [Dee]. And he was out there one day and started to leave the ridge, and they run across and headed him off and killed him.

They said the bullet just fitted Les's gun, and they had shot him through the head after he fell.

'Tricia Smith Wade was given an opportunity on May 17, 1969, to relate her recollections of the events which led to the death of her brother. A reconstruction of her comments is as follows:

My mother and father were born in Cumberland County, Kentucky. He was [Tommy Smith]; she was [Martha], the daughter of Mr. Capps. During the first months of their marriage, they moved to Casey County where four children were born. One of these children died in infancy—a daughter. My mother and father brought me and my sister [Betty] and my brother [Simp] back to Cumberland County, where one more child was born in our family. My father died while I was little.

Next, my mother married Black Morgan, who came from some place in Tennessee. All of us moved to a little storehouse at the foot of Coe Ridge on a place that was probably owned by Benjamin Coe, a white man. My mother and step-father didn't live there long until they moved to Pea Ridge about three miles away.

About the time we moved to the storehouse at the foot of the ridge, I went to Shattersburg, between McMillan's Landing and Tompkinsville, and moved in with a family and worked for them. It wasn't long until I went back to my mother near Coe Ridge, and spent the next few weeks with them before we all moved from there to Pea Ridge. My mother died a few years later.

My brother [Simp] had married and moved to Kettle Creek. My sister [Betty] died during the big flu epidemic. I helped [Betty's] husband [Dee Wade] take care of their children. Later on [Dee] and I got married.

The reason that [Simp] got killed was because these two white girls were going across Coe Ridge with two white men. [Simp] and a Blythe man went after the girls to get them from these men, but [Simp] was killed as they crossed the ridge. They always told me that it was John Coe who killed him.

We didn't get word that [Simp] was dead until the next morning.

Big Les and Little John were placed in jail at Burkesville, and were tried for the murder of Simp Smith. Little John had nothing to do with the murder, according to Mrs. Allen, but he would not turn state's evidence against Big Les, who was not man enough to take the blame. As a result of the verdict at the trial, both men were sentenced to the penitentiary for fifteen years.[48] After serving slightly less than half the sentence, Big Les came down with the "scarflo" [scrofula] and died. Just before he died, he confessed that he alone was guilty for the murder of Smith. When Little John was released, about 1928, he returned to Zeketown only to discover that his wife, Mary Ellen, had taken their children and had moved to Indianapolis in 1923. He went to them, but was soon hit and killed by a train in that city.[49]

The murder of Smith provides some valuable insights into both Negro and white beliefs concerning spirits of the dead and the manner in which the guilty party can be identified. It was reported that a ghost man and dog were seen walking at the spot where Simp Smith died. In the words of Mrs. Sarah Coe Tooley, who did not see the creatures but gave credence to the possibility, "They said that they was a dog and a man—you could see a dog and man a-walking. But I don't believe it, 'cause I've traveled that too much. I never did see nothing."[50]

Although Big Les finally admitted killing Simp

48 Ray Anders claimed that Leslie got a twenty-year sentence and Little John fifteen. The *Chronicles*, 122, states that both were sentenced for fifteen years.

49 George Allred related the train episode. Mrs. Cornelius Allen did not mention how her dad was killed; she stated only that he died soon after arriving in Indianapolis.

50 One informant remarked about any murder, "I believes in ghostes. Anytime a person is killed or dies unnaturally, his spirit is gwine a-hover at the spot where he died." The joint appearance of a ghost man and dog is apparently unreported previously. A ghostly dog complex, however, is known all over northern Europe and is generally identified under Motif E423.1.1, "Revenant as dog." The ghost of the man probably comes under Motif E231, "Return from dead to reveal murder," or Motif E334.2.2, "Ghost of person killed in accident seen at death spot." J. Mason Brewer's *Dog Ghosts and Other Texas Negro Folktales* (Austin, 1958) contains several oral accounts of dog ghosts.

51 Richard M. Dorson, *American Folklore*, 30–33, records instances of Motif D1318.5.2, "The corpse bleeds when murderer touches it." The Simp Smith incident is identical, however, to the belief that "wounds of a murdered man bleed in the presence of the murderer," recorded with additional references in *The Frank C. Brown Collection of North Carolina Folklore* (Durham, 1952–64), VI, 490, item number 3695.

52 Mrs. Tooley also related an account of blood streaming from the body of a young Negro boy, murdered by another Coe Negro who was seeking revenge on the lad's father. That episode is withheld from discussion in this study because it occurred within recent years and is too controversial for print at this early date.

Smith, the inhabitants of Zeketown and their white neighbors knew at the time exactly who had killed Smith. Blood oozed from the corpse when Big Les walked up and looked at it. Lucy Robert Coe told the story this way:

Well, now I heerd 'um say like if you killed a man and this man was still laying here, and if you went a-near him, why, you'd appear in this man's eyes; or else if you killed him, hit him or knocked him or bruised him anywhere, said he would bleed. And I reckon that is shore so. You know, Big Les, Little John and them killed [Simp Smith]. Well, they killed him like last night. And then this morning Big Les went over on Judio—started over there, and Moop Dodson said he just wanted to see if it was so. Said he set right by him—he was shot up here in the head, said, "I'm gonna set here and see every man that comes up, and see if he does go to bleeding."

Said he sot there and watched. Said they's I bet you was a hundred people (they found him dead, you know, up in the aige of the woods, out of the road) and I guess they was a hundred people they said thar. They said just to see the body, you know, before they held the inquest over him. But they'd been so many there to see him. And said he watched to see if every man come up who he if he bled. And said Big Les come up standing thar talking about him; said he the blood just commenced oozin' out of his head and runnin' down. . . .

And he said when he come up was standin' thar, the blood jist commenced streamin' down out of where he was shot up thar. Said it jist streamed down, just run out big jist down his cheek.[51]

Sarah Coe Tooley claimed she actually saw the blood flow from the corpse: "He was dead there and they was going down there to a dinner. And so when [Simp] 'er when Leslie come by uh blood did flow! I seen it! I saw the [blood]. That's no doubt about that!"[52]

6 *Woods and River*

Coe Ridge was a wilderness when the Coe Negroes moved there in 1866. At that time the entire course of the upper Cumberland between Celina and Burkesville was lined with stands of virgin timber—some of the finest cedar, oak, ash, poplar, beech, walnut, and hickory in the United States were found in that area. Prior to the Civil War very little of this timber had made its way to market; sometime between 1865 and 1870, however, many lumbermen in the area began to cut the virgin hardwood timber near the banks of the Cumberland River and to raft it down to Nashville or to saw the logs into rough lumber to transport by packet. By 1880 the lumber business had increased to a point which is barely comprehendible today.[1]

LOGGING IN THE FORESTS OF COE RIDGE

The virgin forests on Coe Ridge were utilized by the

1   Douglas' *Steamboatin' on the Cumberland*, 233–34, et passim, contains statistics of the lumber volume from the upper Cumberland. At the close of 1882, for example, it was estimated that the Nashville mills had handled lumber from this area valued at $3,372,000.

2 The intent to use log and lumber money for purchasing additional land was mentioned in the statements made by Mr. and Mrs. Ray Anders, and by Ruthie Coe Anders, who claimed that the Coes received between five and six hundred dollars for a raft of logs.

Coes in the construction of cabins and log barns, but the Negroes soon proposed to begin commercial logging activities in response to their need of cash. The money was to be used to purchase additional land for the Coe clan.[2] The first markets for the Coe timber were the local sawmills, which utilized the wood in making crossties, ax handles and staves; the sawmills also used the timber as rough lumber for export to Nashville. Pea Ridge was an early milling center specializing in ax handles, and Martinsburg became a rather important local shipping center, having a warehouse built especially for storing ax handles made in the Pea Ridge community of Red Bank. Tim Coe related the following narrative describing an episode centering on a Coe Ridge Negro and the first mate of a steamboat:

The *Joe Horton Falls* had landed here at Martinsburg, and at that time they was a handle factory out here at Red Banks on Pea Ridge. And all those handles that was made—ax handles, pick handles and so on—was hauled to Martinsburg and shipped down the river on boat. And they had a big warehouse stacked full. And this boat stopped there to pick them up. And, course, these lower river boats they, I guess they had as many as thirty deck hands. But on a job like that, they'd hire just anybody they could hire to get the boat loaded. And so they'd hired a whole bunch of extras there at Martinsburg, and Tom [Wilburn] showed up directly, and they hired him, too. Well, Tom was a slow-motion man. I don't guess he'd a-got in a hurry if the house had a-been on fire.

And old Catty Martin, the mate, he placed hisself between the boat and warehouse—the road they wuz a-travelin' here made a bend right up here jist before they got to the warehouse—well, Catty he got up on the bank, on top the bank where he could see to the boat and to the warehouse. And he actually had 'um a-trottin'. And old Tom he come along—they hired him—and Tom was takin' his time. And old Catty bawled out at him, "Hurry up!" And Tom didn't pay him any mind. And Catty reached

148

down and got him a rock. Said, "I said fer you to trot." Tom said, "Si, by God, I don't trot. I don't trot for myself or nobody else." And old Catty told him to throw that rock down. He told him, said, "You throw yours down or I'll kill ye." Instead of passin' on by him, Tom was goin' toward him all the time. And Catty dropped his rock. And they all quit trottin' then after Tom settled Catty. Old Catty, he was a cat, too!

Coe Ridge logging activities were clearly divided into two chronological periods. From 1866 to 1885, the ridge economy was geared almost solely to sawmill products;[3] from 1886 to 1910, when the upper Cumberland reached its zenith as a logging area, the Coes turned to the river and rafting for their economic lifeblood.

Two factors sent Zeke and the male members of the Coe settlement scurrying into the forests during the initial phase. First, because cleared land on the ridge was at a premium at that time, they were interested in clearing the trees from the land so that the small patches of "new-ground" could be plowed and cultivated the next spring. There was much need for fields on which to grow a subsistence corn crop, plus fields to grow seed peas which could be sold for cash. Second, the hardwood trees, once they were cut into logs, provided a major source of cash income for the needy Negroes. Cash was essential, for they had borrowed money and charged groceries on the promise to pay with future log sales. Their logging activities were necessarily relegated to late fall and winter; the crude customs of agricultural production dictated that the Coe Negroes spend the growing season plowing and chopping weeds from the crop rows.[4]

Stands of hardwood timber on the upper Cumberland declined rapidly after 1910. For many years after that date a few logs were annually floated down the Cum-

3 The sawmilling period contains a cycle of narratives revolving around Bill Zeke, Old Zeke and Patsy Ann's son, who had returned from bondage in Texas to live with his people in the Coe Ridge settlement. The Coe Ridge logging stories, in extolling Bill's tremendous physical strength, single out the giant trees, the loaded log wagons, and the sawmills. Never once is the rafting industry mentioned in them; evidently at that time the Coes had not turned to the river as a means of transportation.

4 Statements to this effect were made by Mrs. Edith Williams and Ray Anders.

5 This rafting period of the Coe logging era is rich in tradition when compared to the period from 1866 to 1885. Depicted in the narratives are such seemingly unimportant aspects of the Coe economy as raft construction, yet the accounts rose to a point of excellence when vivid descriptions were offered of life aboard a raft or of the untimely deaths of the Wilburn brothers in the river. Rafting was a life unto itself, but it suited the independent spirit and courage of the Coe Negroes, a people who became identified with the timber and rafting industry on the upper Cumberland. The Coes made river history, and that history turned into tenacious legend that was perpetuated by white neighbors as well as by the Zeketown people.

6 This episode is not recovered from oral tradition; it is found only in the *Chronicles*, 21–22.

berland to Nashville, but revenue from the sale of the logs was never an important factor in the economy of the upper Cumberland. Rafting on the Cumberland, as far as the Coes were concerned, had become the prime occupation in the area. The rafting era began with Calvin Coe, Yaller or Old John Coe, Little John Coe, and the sons of Tom and Mary Wilburn. After these Zeke Negroes began this dominant economic activity in 1886, such an imprint was made on the minds of their people that it is even possible at this late date to get an accurate description of rafting activities on the upper Cumberland.[5]

Legends from the Woods. Zeke did not have oxen or horses during the first years of the Coe colony; therefore, before he could get his logs to the mill, it was necessary to hire someone to snake or haul his logs from the woods to the sawmill. In his initial business dealings following freedom, Zeke learned that all white men were not fair and honest like his former master. Zeke was surprised and shocked to learn that his more fortunate white neighbors were quick to take advantage of him, and the first of Zeke's revealing experiences of his neighbors' dishonesty came when he made a verbal contract with a white man to haul some logs for him. It was understood that Zeke would cut his own trees, then section them into logs measuring twelve to fourteen feet in length. After Zeke had fulfilled his task, the white man refused to honor his part of the bargain, and the logs were left in the woods.[6]

Fortunately for the ex-slave and his sons, they were still able to get the logs to market within the year. At the market, however, Zeke was again wronged by a white man, and this time the result was disastrous. Unable to read or write, Zeke trusted the word of the log buyer who gave him one dollar bills in the place of one hundred dollar bills. Zeke sued the log dealer when he learned of the deceit, but he lost the case in a trial rigged by the white man's friends. Zeke was then forced to pay the court costs.[7]

The early logging years on the ridge were dominated, according to tradition, by the exploits of Bill Zeke Coe, an extremely strong man. Bill was a master at cutting logs, specializing in the use of the broad ax and the pole ax. But he also split rails, built houses, made stocks for plows, and sharpened and set cross-cut saws.[8]

During the early years of the Coe Ridge colony when he was helping to clear new ground, Bill's prodigious strength was demonstrated, showing up at the same time some white men who were present:

> It was reported that two white men had boasted that they could carry more logs than Bill and Tom, Bill's brother. Bill laughed and said, "I ain't trying to beat nobody, but this race will get more logs moved than any other way." So he and Tom accepted the challenge and the contest was on.
>
> Bill and Tom would take the stick on one side of a log, and two white men on the other side and, in that way, they carried many logs of different weights and lengths. They did not finish and it was agreed to return the next day and complete the work.
>
> On the second day the work began with the same arrangements as on the previous one. In the afternoon it was noticed that one of the white men had begun to weaken, while Bill and Tom were as strong as ever and carrying their loads without faltering.
>
> According to Bill's story, it was the custom to have at least a gallon of whiskey at the logrolling. This they had on the first day, and Bill said when he'd drink whiskey he felt like he could move a mountain; so they drank the entire gallon on the first day and had to get another for the second day.
>
> Beginning as usual they would place their hand-sticks

7 *Ibid.*, 22–23. With the two incidents just described, Zeke passed from mention in the traditions associated with the ridge's logging adventures.

8 *Ibid.*, 31.

9 *Ibid.*, 32. Stories of superhuman strength are as old as history itself. In America, legends of this sort took roots in the lumber camps in the boreal forest areas. This story about Bill is related to Motif X940(a), "Remarkable lifter," and more precisely to Motif X940(am), "Strong man lifts a tree ten men have failed to budge," reported only from Cornish tradition.

10 *Chronicles*, 33. This story is related to Motif X942(bp), "Strong man carries sixteen-foot log from 300-year-old tree," reported only from Michigan lumberjack tradition.

11 *Chronicles*, 33. Both of these stories fall under Motif X940(a), "Remarkable lifter," and Motif F624.3, "Strong man lifts cart."

12 *Chronicles*, 33.

13 *Ibid.*

14 *Ibid.*, 34. See note 11 for parallel references.

under the log and walk away with it at the time mentioned. When the word was given, this white man failed to raised his end of the stick. Bill laughed at him and said, "Move, all of you, and I'll carry it all by myself!" Nobody believed that he could or even that he would try, but while they looked on in amazement, this giant raised one end of the log and carried it and dropped it on the wagon.[9]

It is reported also that Bill once carried a log sixty feet long and eighteen inches in diameter.[10] Again, when a wheel on a log wagon broke, Bill held up the side of the partially loaded wagon while the others made necessary repairs. On one occasion, "a white man who saw Bill holding up the end of the log circulated the report that he had seen him holding up two trees at the same time." [11] Another white man reported that he was going "to whip Old Bill Coe" the first time he saw him, but changed his mind after he heard the report about Bill lifting two trees.[12] One white man did try to whip Bill. Bill "caught the man's finger in his mouth; caught him around the waist and hit him three times in the side; and soon he found him limp in his arms. . . . He soon revived, and when he was able to speak, he said, 'I'm through; I won't ever try to fight Bill Coe again.' " [13] Once Bill picked up a wagon: "Calvin Coe told how his brother Bill carried a wagon around on his shoulders. Several young men had failed to lift it when Old Bill said as usual, 'Move away, boys,' then catching hold of the coupling-pole, put the whole thing on his shoulders and danced around, singing a song." [14]

Bill was in a class to himself when it came to rail splitting:

Old Bill used to laugh and tell an experience in rail splitting with his brother-in-law, Thomas Wilburn. They had a joint contract to finish a large number of rails.

They cut down trees, cut the logs and hauled them to a handy place to work.

Bill said, "Well, Tom, if you can make as many rails as I can, we will finish this job Monday."

Tom's reply was, "I can make as many rails as you can or any other damn man can."

"Let's go," was Bill's challenge.

Bill started off, working rapidly, and forgot about Tom. When he did come to himself and looked around to see what his helper was doing, he discovered that Tom was standing there looking at him. When asked for an explanation, Tom said, "Why, Bill, I thought I could make rails, but since I see you at it, I concluded that you are in a class by yourself, and I got no business in the woods with you." [15]

Bill could outlift mill workers:

At a sawmill, some men were trying to put a huge log on a carriage but could not succeed. Bill and his brother Tom observed the futile efforts, and the former asked, "Can I help you, boys?" And the foreman readily consented.

This modern Sampson [sic] picked up the hook used to lift logs, clapped it around the log, and braced himself for the effort. His brother Tom called, "Look out, Bill, don't break that pole." The young men laughed! One sneered and said, "You can't do it when four or five of us couldn't." But Bill said, "If this pole don't break, I'll put it on." But the pole broke and splinters flew everywhere.

Laughing, Bill said, "Get me a handstick that won't break and I'll show you what I'll do." They got him another stick; he squatted, raised up and the log tumbled over on the carriage; then Bill and Tom went on their way.[16]

Bill's logging adventures were not accomplished without accidents detrimental to his health. While he was driving a log wagon, his hand was caught in a pulley and two fingers were broken off. He became an invalid at forty-five, after exhausting his great physical strength

15 *Ibid.*, 33–34.
16 *Ibid.*, 30. This story is related to Motif X940 (am), "Strong man lifts a tree ten men have failed to budge." See note 9 for mention of similar occurrences.

17 There are indications from the introductory comments in the foregoing Bill narratives that the stories passed into oral tradition and that Bill personally perpetuated them. It can be deduced, therefore, that these logging experiences were told and retold in family and community circles. Two recent stories were collected that show a striking resemblance to the Bill cycle. One told by Charlie Coe seems actually to be the same story, with only the chief actor replaced (see text indicated by note 19). It appears safe to say that the motif pattern in the Bill narratives was utilized by the Coes to epitomize the more recent generations who went into the woods.

18 Tim Coe. Ray Anders told the same story in almost identical detail.

in the woods. Bill Zeke died in 1903 at the age of fifty-eight, being cared for during the last thirteen years of his life by his wife and children.[17]

Like Bill Zeke Coe, Tom Wilburn was a very powerful man who had extremely large arms and hands. Wilburn was so extraordinarily large and strong that Tim Coe was prone to comment, "You might as well have had hold of a grizzly bear." Again he stated, "You could look at his foot, and, golly, it was about sixteen inches of his leg turned up. I never seen such a foot on a man." People knew Wilburn also for his exorbitant bragging and stubbornness:

> Oh, he's stout! I laughed at one of his boys a-telling a tale—a joke on Old Tom. They didn't call him daddy, pappy, or nothing. They called him Tom. And back at that time they had lots of good timber. All roofing was made from boards—white oak boards. And Tom and a couple of his boys was going to saw some board timber. It was on a steep hillside, and Tom was sawing on the lower side. And Charlie, one of his boys, laughed and told me about it.
>
> Told him, "Tom, you'd better be careful down there. The board cut will roll over you."
>
> Old Tom says, "Si, no board cut don't roll over Tom."
>
> "Well, now," he said, "this hill is awful steep, and that's big and heavy and it will get you down."
>
> And they went on and sawed it off. And when they sawed it off, Old Tom grabbed it, was going to hold it, and it did get him down! And it rolled right slap over Old Tom's head. And after they saw it didn't kill him, they got to laughing to him about it. And this boy told me, said, "Well, Tom, thought you said no board cut couldn't get you down."
>
> "Well," he said, "it didn't! Why," he said, "it rolled over my head, but it didn't roll over me."
>
> Now that's the way that old Nigger argued it—it didn't roll over him.[18]

Tom Wilburn's son, Charlie, saved the life of a little

154

white Coe boy by lifting up a wagon to allow the wheel to pass over the child without touching its body:

> He was a-driving a log team for my brother—oldest brother, up on Galloway Creek. And he had a little boy, my brother did, four, five, six years old. They thought lots of Charlie. And he was a-riding on this wagon—log wagon, or somewheres close by. You know, if you ever saw a big old log wagon they're heavy. And they, he saw it was a-going to run over him. And it had steers [hitched] to it. He just reached and grabbed that wagon by the hub that way and held it up and walked with that 'til it went over this kid.[19]

RAFTING ON THE RIVER

The timber was gone from Coe Ridge after 1885, but there was still much left near the river in Monroe, Cumberland, and Clay counties. The Coe Negroes then geared their economy to the presence of this abundant growth in those counties: first, by occasionally purchasing a boundary of trees, which they would cut and market;[20] second, by cutting a white man's timber "on the shares"; and third, by hiring out as raftsmen and raft pilots on the hundreds of rafts that went down river to Nashville. They worked for the Kyles of Celina, Bill Murley, Ed Scott, and other local log dealers.[21]

After the logs were cut in the woods, they were snaked along trails or hauled in log wagons to areas on the river bank known as tie-up yards. These yards were located at two places—either at the river landings or at low-bank points. Most of the rafts on the upper Cumberland were constructed in accordance with the number of board feet desired by the purchaser. No logs were cut less than ten feet in length, with the longest being fourteen to sixteen feet. An average raft con-

19 Charlie Coe. Cf. with the narrative (indicated by note 11) that mentions that Bill held up one side of a partially loaded log wagon while the wheel was repaired.

20 Tim Coe, Dec. 23, 1963, stated that Yaller John, Calvin, and Little John Coe occasionally purchased a tract of timber on Mud Camp Creek, then cut the timber into logs which were rafted to Nashville.

21 According to the testimonies of Mrs. Edith Williams, Mrs. Ray Anders, and Lucy Robert Coe.

22 Judge J. W. Wells. Mrs. Ray Anders claimed that the rafts would be from two hundred to three hundred feet long. Lucy Robert Coe estimated the length of some rafts as between two hundred and three hundred yards.

23 Judge J. W. Wells claimed that he had seen poplar logs with butt ends that were eight feet across. The *Chronicles*, 20, states that some were nine feet, and I personally saw some rotted stumps on Coe Ridge that were in excess of six feet in diameter.

24 For a description of raft construction, see Douglas, *Steamboatin' on the Cumberland*, 236. In the mechanical construction of a raft, according to Mrs. Edith Williams and Tim Coe, it was necessary to have on hand a supply of hand-sharpened wooden pins made from seasoned hickory. Stacked up on the river bank was a pile of whaling, which is made from hickory saplings about four inches in diameter and in varying lengths up to several feet. Through 5/8-inch auger holes drilled through the whaling, wooden pins were driven into each log, thus anchoring each log in position.

25 The pilot and raftsmen, also called helmsmen, received different salaries, depending on the period of history in which they labored and the economy of the time. "Old time helmsmen were paid fifty cents a day and upkeep. An expert pilot received $1.50 per day and food," according to Douglas, *Steamboatin' on the Cumberland*, 236. None of the oral accounts placed the figure that low, however, because they were mainly concerned with the years after the turn of the century. Even the oral traditions varied considerably, due perhaps to the different years represented. Some claimed that the pilots were paid between $15.00 and $20.00, while their helpers received about $12.00 for the trip. Still others said the helpers received $25.00, while the pilot received between $40.00 and $50.00.

26 Judge J. W. Wells and Mrs. Edith Williams.

27 Douglas, *Steamboatin' on the Cumberland*, 237.

tained from fifty to 150 logs in a single tier.[22] Sizes determined the number of logs in a given raft, for many of the logs were between eight and nine feet in diameter at the butt ends.[23] In the event the rafts contained more than one tier of logs, the logs were fastened together by letting the longer logs from each tier protrude under the whaling of the others.[24] As a rule, the average raft was manned by a crew of five men and a pilot.[25] Large oars were fastened on the front and back of each raft; each oar required the services of only one man, except during periods of extremely high tides or other dangers. The pilot was totally responsible for the raft and any mishaps.[26] He "knew the turns and eddies," according to Mrs. Edith Williams, and had to anticipate the hazards well in advance in order to tell the others how and when to paddle in order to keep the raft in the main channel. Orders to the helmsmen had to be accurate and instantaneously obeyed. Taking a big raft down the Cumberland on high tide was no easy matter; it took great physical strength to manipulate the sweeping oars and courage to hold onto them in wind and storm. In the words of an eyewitness, "It is one thing to watch with awe and admiration a big raft gracefully swing around the sharp bend of the river, but still another to steer and pilot one on its tortuous course."[27]

Calvin Coe took over one hundred rafts down to Nashville during his lifetime, making his last run after he was over seventy years old. Mrs. Sarah Coe Tooley gave an idea of what he experienced while on the river:

He had it all to a "T." He told everyone [how many] he had took down there, and about all the hard trials and tribulations they'd get into, you know.

One time they done without food and they didn't have no money, you know, and nothing to eat. And so they went out where the old cows eat these punkins, and they got that and cooked it up. And some feller wouldn't eat punkin, but he eat some of that [*chuckles*].

It took seven days to run a raft on good tide from Burkesville to Nashville, six days from Martinsburg, and five from Celina. In early days the rafts were tied up at night, but later on the more adventurous raftsmen ran straight through, provided the water was at a safe level. Rafting at night was a dangerous business, however, and often resulted in accidents and shake-ups, not to mention verbal combats with the packet captains, who were guilty, according to the raftsmen, of "hogging the channel." Calvin Coe told of the times when he and other pilots fired rifle shots above the packet cabins to make the boat captains share the channel.[28]

Life on a raft was a world unto itself. The shanty[29] was the center of social life on the trip. There the hardy Coe raftsmen slept on straw and ate their meals which were usually well prepared even though cooked on a small rock grate above a hearth of mud and clay. Lucy Robert Coe described one incident which depicts the life on a raft:

> [They'd] have a little shack they'd call, a little place fixed up—put straw in thar. They'd crawl back up in thar and have a quilt there to pull over them.
>
> And said one night they wuz goin' down the river and they run over a big old snag—the river had rose and they didn't know it was there. The pilot (Uncle Calvin used to be what they called a pilot to run these rafts and guide 'um, you know) run over there and scattered that straw, said, all from under 'um. Said talk about pullin' and gettin' out of there!
>
> They finally got up, though, got it back together; went on down somewhere else to someone's straw stack and got 'um some more straw the next day and fixed their shack back.[30]

With sympathy in her voice, Mrs. Edith Williams de-

28   Tim Coe, Dec. 8, 1963. Douglas, *Steamboatin' on the Cumberland*, 236, offers very similar comments. Additional comments concerning points covered in this paragraph were offered by Lucy Robert Coe and Mrs. Edith Williams.

29   The term "shanty" was used by Judge J. W. Wells and by Mrs. Edith Williams to denote the raft cabin.

30   The description of the rock grate was provided by Mrs. Coe, Aug. 14, 1963.

31 Mrs. Sarah Coe Tooley also stated that the rafts were pulled into a river landing in the event of bad weather.

32 Mrs. Sarah Coe Tooley.

33 Lucy Robert Coe.

scribed how the Coes faced the elements: "They had shanties and slickers. And just mostly took it if you want to know, just mostly took the rain. My husband used to have a store at this place. And they'd pull in here and, you know, be at the store and warm and dry and stay here." [31]

Mrs. Susie Taylor Moore further described living conditions on the rafts, and gave a pathetic account of a death back home that could not be imparted to the kin on the river:

> They had scaffolds built up over them. They just built scaffolds on them rafts and had it big enough that they could lay down in there and sleep, you know, when they tied up. And had it big enough that they cooked in there and everything. They'd take cooking vessels, and they meat and everything to cook, with them.
>
> And if one died while they's gone, they wudn't getting them no word a-tall, you know; they'd be on the river. They wouldn't know nothing about it 'til they come back home.
>
> One of my aunt's little boys died while her husband was gone on a raft to Nashville, and she dist had to bury the little thing. They wudn't no gettin' him no word, you know.

The Coe Negroes earned a reputation of honesty and fair play from their white employers and the people who lived along the river banks. It is claimed that Calvin Coe was able at anytime to borrow a canoe down river on the merit of his reputation, although the lender did not personally know Cal.[32] The lumbermen trusted their personal credit at the various stores en route to Nashville to the Coe clansmen who were in their employ. The Negroes were instructed simply to obtain a receipt for the purchases.[33] The following humorous story was told about the purchase of a big fat hen by some of the Coe raftsmen:

They said they'd go out sometimes and buy 'um hens and pick 'um, clean 'um, maybe put them on [to cook] at night. Some of them would lay down. And while they's asleep, some would slip up and eat the chicken left, you know [chuckle].

Said they would have a lot of fun like that when one would get up, he'd done be full, you know, and done gone to bed and be sound asleep or let on like he was. Somebody would get up to see about the chicken—the chicken would be all gone [laughter].

. . . Robert said one night they went out and bought a great fat hen and picked her and put her on to cook. They was all aimin' to set up, you know, and watch her to keep ones [i.e., each other] from gettin' it.

Robert said he went on to bed like he wouldn't aimin' to bother the chicken. Said he went on to bed, and they got this chicken done. Said they eased up, him and Jesse Coe, eased up and went and got forks. Said they got that chicken out and they eat the chicken. Eat it all but this old saddle piece, you know, left it in the pot [laughter]. And crawled back in bed.

Said one of them got up and said, "By God, somebody has eat all this chicken up." "By God, Robert, that 'uz you." "Jess, it was you."

Said they all just snored like they's asleep. "By God, you ain't asleep. You all jist ate that chicken up [laughter]." Kept going on; kept cussin' around.

[Robert] waked up and stretched. Said, "What are you talking about? Are you all a-eatin' that chicken?"

"By God, some of you all done eat that chicken."

Said, "We haven't . . . we've been asleep."

Said, "I went to bed 'fore you all did. You all dist slipped that chicken and eat it up."

[Robert] said him and Jess eat the chicken. Oh, the rest of them rared and scoffed about the chicken. Said, "By God, the next chicken we get, I'm gonna set up—see if it's eat—to help eat it."

Well, said they went on down again a little piece somewheres, and they went out again and bought them another big hen.[34]

Once the rafts were delivered to the Nashville saw-

35   Mrs. Sarah Coe Tooley and Lucy Robert Coe.

36   Mrs. Edith Williams and Lucy Robert Coe.

37   Sparse details of the drowning were related by Mrs. Etta Short and Mrs. Ray Anders. The *Chronicles*, 99, states that Billy drowned in 1896.

mills, the Coes were faced with the problem of returning to Coe Ridge. Sometimes, when they did not want to spend their hard-earned money for steamboat fare, they walked, arriving home footsore and weary after three days on the road and two nights of sleeping in cornfields. The usual route was via Gallatin, Tennessee, and Scottsville and Tompkinsville, Kentucky. Occasionally, the Coes took a train from Nashville to Bowling Green, Kentucky, and walked home from there via Glasgow and Tompkinsville.[35] For the most part, however, the Negroes rode a steamboat up the river to Martinsburg. The cost varied from one to three dollars for deck passage, and cabin passage started at five dollars.[36] Most of the homebound raftsmen preferred the former since steamboat fare would take most of their earnings.

DEATH ON THE RIVER

Billy Wilburn Drowns. Billy Wilburn, in his mid-twenties, was the first of the Coe clan to die on the river. With some other men from Coe Ridge, Billy was assembling a raft up river at the Biggerstaff Bar, located just above the mouth of Mud Camp Creek. Billy was in a skiff occupied with his work when he was suddenly seized with some kind of spell, probably epileptic. He pitched backwards into the river and drowned before his kinsmen could rescue him.[37]

Sherman Wilburn Is Shot to Death. Sherman Wilburn was a very unruly member of the younger generation of Coes. Once he tried to kill his teacher after being corrected for misbehavior at school. He then ran away from home when his father severely punished him for his actions. A decade or so later, in 1900, hot-headed

Sherman was killed in a gun fight at Martinsburg Landing.[38]

As the story goes, Sherman consented to take a raft to Nashville for Ed Scott, a local timber dealer, but before the trip began, Scott sold the raft to another local dealer, Vince Vaughn. With this negotiation, Sherman's services were no longer needed, for in the words of Tim Coe, "Usually a man that follows running a raft, buying logs . . . has his own pilot, don't you see. And so that knocked Sherman out of piloting that raft to Nashville." Vaughn had nothing personal against Sherman, nor did he doubt the latter's ability as a raft pilot, but Sherman still took the loss of the job as a personal insult.[39] A few days later Vaughn sent word to Sherman that the pilot's job was his after all. Half-drunk, Sherman went to Martinsburg and stood on a bluff where he could see Vaughn at work below on a raft tied up at the landing. Price Kirkpatrick, who placed all the blame on Sherman, claimed that Sherman commenced cursing and abusing Vaughn verbally and then shot him in the shoulder. Vaughn then fired at Sherman, who "pitched over towards the water, a dead Nigger." [40] Hascal Haile, whose father witnessed the shooting, told the story this way:

> Vince Vaughn was rigging up a raft to go to Nashville, you know. And this colored feller had gone a time or two before with him. And they couldn't agree about a pipe or something, and they got in a big fuss at the store. My daddy happened to be there to see it. And he said that the colored feller was up on top of the bluff and Mr. Vaughn was down on the raft. They began cursing one another and abused one another, and finally the Coe Nigger got so mad that he took his pistol out and shot at him. And I guess all that saved Mr. Vaughn's life is that he was shooting a .45 pistol, and he had a .44 cartridge in it. He had paper wrapped around it and it didn't fit the rifle,

38   There is little doubt among the informants that the only shooting occurred at Martinsburg, Monroe County. The only dissension was expressed by Tim Coe who specified Vernon, located across the river from Martinsburg, as the scene of the murder. The *Chronicles*, 93, states specifically that Sherman was killed in 1900. Two oral informants, Price Kirkpatrick and Charlie Coe, figure that the event took place in 1900 or close thereto.

39   Tim Coe.

40   Mr. Kirkpatrick personally listened to Vaughn describe the incident: Vaughn "went on down to Nashville [after the shooting]. And I was going on a raft to Nashville at that time myself, and I met up with him in Nashville. And he told me about how it come around. And I've heard the other fellows tell it, too."

41 Charlie Coe also testified that the bullet in Sherman's gun was of improper size. Bill Poindexter claimed that it was a .38 pistol with a .32 bullet.

42 Charlie Coe and Lucy Robert Coe also claimed that one of the bullets is still in the wood by the fireplace.

43 Bill Poindexter claimed that Wilburn died the same night he was shot.

44 The *Chronicles*, 94, states that Vaughn was tried, but found not guilty. Both Lucy Robert Coe and Price Kirkpatrick stated that Vaughn never came to trial for the crime. Monroe County court records for the years 1888 to 1904 make no mention of Vince Vaughn. Sherman Wilburn was tried once during this same period for a misdemeanor not worthy of mention in this connection.

you know, too good. So he shot him in the shoulder—broke a collar bone and knocked the old man down. And daddy said he thought he never was going to get his pistol out—you know it was a big .44.[41] And he got it out and shot him twice right through the breast and it went through this house where old man Johnny Coe lived there. Aunt Hun, Johnny's wife, was a-settin' before the fireplace, and one of the bullets went right by her. It's in the wall down there today.[42] It's in there today. You can see it.

Sherman lived for two days. After the shooting, he was taken to the home of Aunt Nellie Halsell, who lived in the log cabin once occupied by Aunt Mime Coe on the old Coe plantation. It was there that Sherman died.[43] When asked how the onlookers reacted to the shooting, Bill Poindexter, himself an eyewitness, replied: "Never done nothing—only dist stood thar—and looked at it. One of [Wilburn's] brothers was thar—Garfield—and some of them asked him, 'Don't you aim to do nothing?' He says, 'What can I do?' He says, 'If I was to do anything, he'd kill me.' And he says, 'Thar ain't nothing I can do about it.' "

Vaughn had killed Sherman in self-defense, but fearing the vengeance of the Coes, he left the community. In their usual Coe colony custom, the Negroes held council and considered the facts of the case. The Negroes were convinced that Vaughn had shot Sherman in self-defense and that they would have done the same thing under such circumstances. After the decision of the Coes, Vaughn came out of hiding and returned to his home without ever being molested.[44]

Shirley Wilburn Drowns in the Swirling Eddies. Shirley, another of the Wilburn brothers, fully intended to kill Vince Vaughn but could never come upon him at an opportune time. Shirley, still carrying a gun for

Vaughn, met his death two years later in the spring of 1902 when some of the Coes were taking a raft down river to Nashville. One night two skiffs were tied to the raft; one skiff was in good condition and the other, which had been neglected, was dry and unsafe for use. After the Coes had secured the raft for the night and were preparing for bed, for some unexplained reason the good skiff came loose from the raft and floated on down the river.

Realizing that they most likely would need the good skiff, Calvin Coe, the pilot, ordered the lines cut and the raft was again launched. As they approached an eddy in the river,[45] the skiff was again sighted. Shirley grabbed the old leaky skiff and yelled for someone to get in with him. Robert Coe flatly refused, and even Calvin cautioned everyone not to be so foolhardy. Yet, George Williams was persuaded by Shirley, so the two got into the old skiff and headed toward the good one which was now dangerously near the swirling eddies. They did not get far until their boat was swamped by the eddies and began to sink. Williams was able to swim back to the raft. In the words of Lucy Coe, wife of Robert:

> George swum, and they said it was the coldest time ever was—George swum to the bank. And somebody held a pole or something another out and he got hold of it and they pulled him out. But he like to have froze to death. They took him to some spring and wrapped him in yarn blankets and wallered him in the spring I don't know how long and thawed him up.

Shirley was a good swimmer, but he must have been overcome by cramps in the icy water. In addition, his body was burdened by the .45 caliber pistol that he carried, plus an extremely heavy overcoat which pulled

45 The *Chronicles*, 98, claims it was called King's Eddies; Bill Poindexter called it White's Eddies; and Tim Coe referred to it as Cane's Eddies.

163

46   The account of Shirley's drowning was given in remarkably similar details by Lucy Robert Coe, Tim Coe, Mrs. Mattie Davidson, and Mrs. Etta Short. Their accounts are corroborated by the *Chronicles*, 98–102.

47   Lucy Robert Coe. The *Chronicles*, 101–2, claims that Thomas E. Coe and Garfield Wilburn, who was the youngest son of Tom and Mary Wilburn, went to search for the body. There is no recorded parallel in folk belief which claims that the body will surface at the end of the ninth day, but Mrs. Janet Simpson reported in 1967 that in Lewis County, Ky., this belief has been reiterated by the Ohio River valley residents. In Harry M. Hyatt, *Folk-Lore from Adams County, Illinois* (New York, 1935), item 10282, p. 589, it is stated that if a person's bladder bursts, the cadaver will surface.

him under after it became thoroughly soaked.[46] His body was never recovered:

> Never did find him. They searched about nine days for his body, but they never did find it. And his mother hired somebody to sit on the bank for nine days, and I just forgot now what she paid them, though, for sittin' thar. You know they say at sunup the ninth morning they'll rise. The gall will bust and they will float up. But they won't stay up long. And she had him a-watchin' on the bank there; him and some of his boys watched on that bank fer him fer nine days and nine mornings . . . .[47]

This final blow was more than Mary Wilburn could endure. For years she had bravely stood the sorrows that life had brought, but she died soon after the death of her fourth son.

7 *The Decline of the Coe Colony: 1911–1958*

Farming and logging activities contributed much to the early economic welfare of the Coe Colony, but the most lucrative activity, the one providing the most cash income was moonshining and its partner in crime, bootlegging. These illicit practices came last in the colony's history and were the major factors in the extinction of the colony. One cannot help sympathizing with the Coes in their moonshining activities, for this was their last resort to adjust nature to their needs. Their economic situation had deteriorated as the timber, the one great natural resource, was cut. And the land grew less productive as the years went by; moreover, large gullies caused by sheet erosion threatened to engulf the colony even further within the confines of its already rugged terrain. The remaining thin and meager lands were hard put even to grow corn, a crop which was difficult to move out over non-existent roads and which brought very little money at Burkesville or Tompkinsville. Converted to whiskey, however, the corn found a ready market in any of the nearby towns and communities. The same mule that had difficulty in moving ten bushels of corn to market could readily transport ten gallons of whiskey.

An extensive knowledge of the geography of Coe Ridge is needed to understand fully the recollections recorded in this chapter. In the true sense of the word, the Coes were a people apart. They lived in virtual isolation from the surrounding communities. Royce Cary, a Negro informant from Mud Camp, pointed this out when he told of the times he went back to the ridge to "get a little drink":

> Sometimes you would go down there and couldn't get back unless you walked three or four miles, because they wudn't no road back there to get in there with nothing but a wagon and a mule. Couldn't drive your car back there; had to walk out and in.
>
> Later on, after time passed, they finally got to where they could get cars. But they never did get a road in there 'til just a few years ago—about two years ago.

The Negroes seldom had casual visitors. Whenever a person went to Zeketown, he was looking for whiskey or was hiding from the law. Even if he were not drunk when he entered the colony, such was the case when he emerged. Many times the visitor became involved in a drunken brawl or a crap game and was never heard from again. The 1920's witnessed so many crimes on Coe Ridge that former Judge J. W. Wells was led to comment that "more murders were committed in that part of the county than all the rest combined."

Mother Wagner (Cassie Coe Raspberry, a daughter of Bill Zeke and Mandy), who had returned home from Indianapolis to preach peace and coexistence in the early 1900's, was able to hold her people in check for a

166

few years, but when the internal troubles commenced in the 1920's, she, along with many others, left the colony for good. From that time until the 1950's there was a steady flow of migration from the colony. This was especially true during the 1930's after the building of roads nullified the area's inaccessibility. Some did **not** leave to avoid trouble, however; they left to evade the law after committing a murder, after breaking into a white person's home, or stealing articles from one of the local grocery stores. Still others were forced to leave the county and state when, after several offenses, they were probated by the federal court.

The events recorded in this chapter constitute recent history. For this reason the Negro informants were not too willing to talk about their own people who, for the first time in the colony's history, were to blame for the events which occurred. Only after much deliberation would they identify the ones who were involved in drunken brawls and murders, and rarely were descriptions of the crimes offered. Even the white informants were hesitant to talk about the occurrences in the Coe colony after 1920 because, frankly, they were afraid to. They had been witness to the development of what a revenue man described as "a legend within a legend." To quote that source:

> It was rumored that the Coe people were half wild, mean and dangerous. Occasionally, drifting out from the heavy forest, came tales of killings and of the disappearance of people into the woods, people who never returned, or burials at night without benefit of clergy. Generally these tales were improved with each telling. Mystery made monsters of a little-known people.[1]

The whites who lived near the Coe colony remained afraid of what might happen to them should they divulge information about the recent Zeketown Negroes.

1 Quinn Pearl, "Legendary Coe Ridge," *Louisville Courier-Journal Magazine,* Dec. 12, 1954.

2 In addition to the humor emanating from their recollections of fleeing from the revenue men, the Coes found something funny about the various times they appeared in federal court at Bowling Green. This period of the colony's history has given rise to what appears to be a cycle of folk narratives destined to be perpetuated orally. Almost all of these tales are humorous and contain what may be called a motif: man swims river and then walks seventy-five miles in time for his trial at Bowling Green; man to be tried in court gets out of sickbed and goes to Bowling Green where he crawls into the courtroom; boy outraces automobile and warns the colony that revenue men are coming; and so on. On occasion, a known folktale does creep into this group of narratives, thus indicating that all of the moonshiner stories may have oral parallels not yet recorded.

On the other hand, there is nothing really incongruous in these tales of Coe moonshining days. It may very well be that the details embodied in them actually occurred. At least the character personifications in them are excellent, and the geography is always consistent with that of the upper Cumberland and Coe Ridge.

After a recording session, one informant followed the writer to the car, cautioning all the while, "You know what to do with that tape recorder stuff so that there won't be any trouble come up between us and them Coes. We have to live here, you know." Still another white man described a murder committed by one of the Coes, but would not call any names. When asked to identify the parties, he laughed nervously and said, "I'm sorta 'fraid to tell that 'cause he's still living pretty close to me."

Moonshining, however, was a topic that was freely discussed by both Negroes and whites. Virtually every ridge occupant took part in this practice and did not consider it morally wrong; to them, moonshining was an economic necessity. In addition, the Negro informants looked back with delight on the times they were chased by the revenue men, for the Negroes were usually the winner. This is the only period in the colony's history at which its former members find reason for laughter.[2]

CASSIE COE WAGNER PREACHES TO HER PEOPLE

Mother Wagner returned from Indianapolis shortly after 1900 and preached a doctrine of peace to her people. Hascal Haile noted that "one of them got religion and come back and she began to enlighten some of the rest of them." Religious services were held in the homes of the ridge occupants and in the schoolhouse. Cassie was able to hold sway over her people through spiritualistic rituals which involved dancing, shouting, and fire-eating. George Allred described their religious singing in a tone which verged on jest: "Well, sir, now I never did hear them sing very much. Let's see, I forgot what kind of songs they did sing in church. But they'd go jist like they had a meeting, now. They'd go jist like a hard groan, and they'd go like, 'Ah, cha, cha, cha, ah, cha, cha, cha.' Then they'd go, 'Woo, woo, woo, woo, woo, woo.' [*Chuckles.*] And they'd dance around in the church and carry on."

Frank Murley, a white man from Ellington's Landing, told about an attempt made by Cassie's group to convert Uncle Tom Wilburn:

I used to as a boy go back on the ridge with my father to church. He said he wanted me to see how they worshipped. Now, they's some carrying on back there when I was a kid!

One time when Tom was way up in years, they couldn't get him in church. Said they was all praying for his conversion. Well, Tom always liked my grandfather; always called him Massa Lollar. He would do anything my grandfather told him. So they fixed to pretend my grandfather's spirit was a-coming back to talk to Tom. Some Nigger crawled under the floor and was a-going to talk like my grandfather, when Tom talked to him.

They finally got Tom in the notion of going to church one night. When Tom got there, they told him that he could talk to Massa Lollar, and asked him what he wanted to ask him. So Tom said, "Massa Lollar, do you mean to tell me that you went through dem pearly gates after the way you hit me with that sledge hammer that time?" This Nigger under the floor grunted that he did. Then some of the other Niggers said, "Ain't you ready to be converted now, Tom? What do you think about hearing Massa Lollar's voice?"

Old Tom said, "By dern, I say that there's a Nigger under the corner of the floor."

And, you know, after that they never could get Old Tom back inside the church.

Cassie won fame throughout the countryside as a healer, a person who could eat fire, and as a chief priest who spent much time fasting and praying. Mrs. Edith Williams stated: "Cassie . . . was chief priest out there. Taught some. I've seen her a few times. She's always, well, she was nice and polite, and she wanted to talk to you about religion and things like that. But there was nothing objectionable about her that I ever saw. If you were nice to them, they were nice to you." A fire-eating incident was described by Mrs. Myrtle Kerr, who personally witnessed the episode:

> She was the one they claimed had all that healing power. Had all that power to do out there. Fasted and prayed, you know, and eat fire.
>
> I'll tell you what I know about this, now. They kept on having that meetin' out thar, and one of these miracles that that old woman could do. And me and my sister and that boy of mine, and I guess ten or fifteen girls and boys around all made it up that we'd go out there one night and see. Well, we went out there and found seats over on the side. It was in the wintertime. And, well, they had a big fire in the stove, and lit a lamp setting on a table over there.
>
> Well, they shouted and did everything in the world. Well, one thing was that Old Aunt Cass she danced over to the little table and turned—you've seen a-many a-lamp, I guess, with a globe on it—well, she taken that globe off and set it down on the table, and took the wick, the thing that the blaze goes to—now, I'm telling you what I seen! She reached and got that lamp in her hand and she danced all over that old log schoolhouse [with her hand over the blaze], and come back and set that lamp down so unconcerned . . . . Then she went over to that stove and got a little splinter of a piece [about three inches long] and put it back in behind her teeth and danced all over.

Despite what outsiders said about Cassie and her carryings-on, she commanded the utmost respect from her own race. In the words of George Allred, "They's carrying their guns 'til she come in here preaching, and she got after them and they laid their guns down." As stated by the Coe chronicler, her presence in the colony was even more profound as a stabilizing influence on her people:

> She came from Indianapolis, professing and preaching sanctification; with the Bible in her hands and prayer on her lips. And she even claimed to be able to hold communion with the dead. She preached and prayed until she almost lost her voice; and she urged the members to live in peace; not to kill or revenge but to go and leave it all with the Lord who would in his own time set all things right. This preaching and pleading had great effect on the Coe colony; they became calm; they decided not to take revenge, as had been decided previously.[3]

EARLY MOONSHINING ACTIVITIES ON COE RIDGE

Judge J. W. Wells was among the first county law officials to confront the inhabitants of the ridge colony with the consequences of a life of crime. Whiskey, he felt, was the root of all the Coes' problems:

> Being county judge of this county in 1934 to 1938, I had quite a bit of experience in litigation with the Coe family. The Coe family reaching way back has always been noted for being outlaws and moonshiners. But I'm proud to say and thankful to say, today they are a different family.
>
> They embraced Christianity, many of the old ones died out, new ones grew up, and the state has built roads through that country. They have nicer homes, have better schools, and it's not the way it used to be.
>
> But during my period of court work, I'll say that at least a third of my docket originated on Coe Ridge. It was still handed down in the younger generation, but it's nearly died out now. The courts never came but what they had someone from Coe Ridge.
>
> When I made the race in the campaign for county judge in 1933, I met up with a man on the road (we was both on horseback, of course). He wanted to ride with me and tell me a little history of that part of the country. Well, we came along and directly we came to a big stump on the side of the road. He says, "Right there was where

3 The *Chronicles*, 110. The subsequent sections of this chapter reveal that while Cassie was able to cause her people to put down their guns, her preaching was not sufficient to stop their moonshining, bootlegging, and thievery.

4 Mrs. Short was born in 1879, thus placing the origin of Coe moonshining in the early 1890's.

5 At another point in the narration, Poindexter claimed that Calvin had the whiskey in his saddle bags. The price paid was $1.00. No attempts were made to establish the selling prices of Coe whiskey, but occasional comments give some indication: during the 1920's and 1930's whiskey sold from $2.00 to $3.00 per gallon; during the 1950's a gallon brought $5.00 on the ridge and $12.00 if delivered.

6 Poindexter dated this hog drive in 1904, specifically stating that he was twenty-two at the time.

so and so was killed." And on another 100 yards or so, there was another tree a-standing: "Right there's the tree that marks the place where another so and so was killed." And he went on the whole journey showing where murders had been committed, all on the account of liquor, the love of liquor.

Judge Wells did not fix the precise date when moonshining activities on the ridge commenced, but he felt that the practice came with the pioneer Coes when they migrated to Kentucky. Furthermore, he noted, "the original Coes thought they couldn't make a living without it come from the bottle." Mrs. Etta Short did not agree with such an early beginning of the moonshine industry on the ridge. She defended the early generations from the guilt of making whiskey: "I remember when they started that up. I guess I was almost a young lady. I was fourteen, anyway." [4]

The Coes had definitely established their reputation as moonshiners by 1904. During that year, Bill Poindexter bought a pint of whiskey from Calvin Coe:

I used to go through thar and buy whiskey from them back when I was young. I'd go through thar and buy whiskey from them. Me and Oss Coffey was coming from Arat, up from Leslie, with a drove of hogs the first time I ever bought any whiskey from them. And it was a-pouring down the rain on us.

And I seen Old Uncle Cal a-coming. I told Oss, "If he's got any whiskey, I'll get me a pint of whiskey from him." He rode up and I asked him, and he said, "Yessir, I've got it." [5]

Well, that hope us up. [Chuckles.] [6]

Whiskey-making on Coe Ridge on a large scale can be traced to the decline of rafting employment. A few of the Negroes had found work with the local white farmers, according to Leslie Coe, Jr., but such labor was seasonal and paid practically nothing for wages.

Most of the Coes turned to commercial moonshining as a last resort. "It's like Uncle Robert [Coe] said," recalled Mrs. Edith Williams; " 'You need things, and when you've got a family, they need things.' " In a sympathetic voice and at the point of tears, Mrs. Williams continued, "And the land was awful poor out there." She then described the barren landscape on the ridge:

There was no fence that I ever knowed anything about. Jist out in the woods little places around their homes .... Just have little places cleared for little gardens or something of that kind. But they was no fences, I don't think. Now you couldn't find a poorer, more desolate looking country—poor little scrubby bushes and things like that, and sassafras and sawbriars and things like that.

About this Robert, he worked for me more than any of the rest of them—for my husband. I used to tell him, "Robert, if I was you, I'd get my sack and get all I could." But, now, Robert didn't bother what you had.[7]

During the 1920's and 1930's the Coes peddled their moonshine throughout the countryside. Royce Cary also described this aspect of the Coe enterprise:

Some of them used to tell how they got by the law. They'd leave before daylight every morning. Leave at 2 o'clock and get in Burkesville around about 3. Everybody'd be asleep. And they'd have the car plumb loaded down with whiskey—all they could carry. They'd come on out of there, and lot of times they'd come out of Salt Lick Bend.

Now that's back in the time when they'd pack the whiskey out. They didn't have no cars then. I ought to remember 'cause I helped drink a lot of it. They'd come across that river at that ferry down there—they had a boat, and they didn't have no motor to it. They'd paddle that skiff all the way across that river. And they'd come across that river down there and they come up through the Noah Hollow.

And they'd sell a load to the Noah Hollow, and then

7 Others in the colony turned to stealing and breaking into stores in desperate attempts to provide food and clothing for their families. These episodes did not occur in the main until the 1940's and 1950's, however, and are considered in another section of this chapter.

8 Judge Wells told about the fear experienced by law officers who went to Coe Ridge during those years. The sheriff usually went alone to Coe Ridge, for when a murder had been committed, the Coes would turn the offender over to the law if guilt had been definitely established.

9 The names of those who were killed during the 1920's and 1930's are perhaps ascertainable, but were not sought. Even those names known will not be printed here since the informants are quite touchy on this subject. The years in question were the darkest in the colony's history, excepting the period of trouble with the Taylors. Unlike the Taylor feud which gave rise to numerous tenacious legends, the latter troubles are not voiced about, especially into tape recorders. The remaining Coes, now scattered throughout Cumberland and Monroe counties and in several Northern industrial centers, do not want to talk about this latter phase of their history. For one reason, such gruesome happenings still occur. About two weeks after I talked with a former member of the Coe colony, he blew out the intestines of his "wife" with a shotgun.

they'd come on to Leslie. And they'd sell all they had there at Leslie, and then they'd go back and get more whiskey. During that time they never did get much farther than Marrowbone and Waterview and Leslie. That's as fur as they usually got with it. That was about as far as they could get 'cause they didn't have any transportation. That's the only way they could make it.

Some of the early moonshine whiskey was substituted for cash at the local grocery stores where proprietors were willing to exchange sugar and groceries for the Coe whiskey. Anytime the Negroes from the ridge delivered their liquor, they had to be constantly on the alert for law officials who lay in wait for them all along the way. It is common knowledge that at that early date the authorities were afraid to enter the legendary community itself, and further the area was still isolated due to the lack of passable roads.[8]

SIGNS OF INTERNAL SICKNESS

Rumors spread during the 1920's and 1930's that the Coes were fighting among themselves and killing members of their own race. It was further rumored that certain individuals who went to the ridge settlement never came out alive. They were victims of the razor and shotgun, lethal weapons called upon to settle disputes arising from lovers' quarrels and dice games.[9] It was also told that the law would occasionally go into the wilds of Coe Ridge only to be chased away by the occupants. During this decade of uncertainty in the Coe colony, the rough element of the younger generation made it virtually impossible for the older occupants to conduct religious services and to live normal lives. There was a mass exodus from the ridge to such places as Indianapolis, Chicago, and Kansas City, Kansas.

Most of those who left never returned. Only seven families remained in Zeketown by 1938–39 when the first county road was completed across the ridge. The heads of these families were E Coe, Calvin Coe, Joe Coe, Robert Coe, Charlie Wilburn, Otley Coe (son of Thomas Ezekiel and Lucy Coe), Ray Anders, and a bachelor, Everett Anders.

The period of despair which gripped the colony during the 1920's was brought about by financial insecurity. The Coes were driven deeper into the depths of poverty during the depression years. They pursued moonshining and bootlegging to the point that even women and children were actively engaged in these nefarious activities. It is commonly claimed that a Negro woman was the clan leader during these last days, and that she took a cut from every whiskey sale made by anyone in the colony.[10] Even children were taught to make whiskey, and taught at a very early age. That facet of Coe history is humorously illustrated in the following widespread story:

> One time when Judge Wells was running for judge, he was campaigning on the ridge for the Nigger vote. He went back to the school, and before he walked in the school he could hear E Coe saying, "Now, yesterday we studied the making of the mash, and tomorrow we will study how to run off a batch."
>
> Old Man E Coe seen that Judge Wells saw the diagram on the board and had overheard. So E knew that he better help Wells out. Every Nigger on the ridge voted for Wells due to E Coe's influence.[11]

THE COMING OF THE REVENUE AGENTS

Frequent raids were made against the Coe moonshiners after 1940. The initiative was taken by the Cumberland County sheriff's department, aided in force by

10 This statement was made by J. B. Groce.

11 Frank Murley told this story in the general store at Ellington's Landing, Cumberland County, in the presence of five others. All laughed and said that they had heard the tale many times. This same story was related by Jack McClendon of Tompkinsville, and is also found in "Coe Ridge Gained Fame," *Cumberland County News*, Aug. 16, 1960. Royce Cary told the tale in more authentic tones; in his account, it was claimed that Old Man E had a model still in the schoolhouse, and that he would constantly write the whiskey-making recipe on the blackboard until the children could recite it from memory.

12 "Coe Ridge Gained Fame," *ibid*. I heard the same story as a high school student in Tompkinsville, and recently it was told by my brother-in-law.

federal agents from Louisville, Campbellsville, and Bowling Green. In the accounts told about raids on Coe Ridge, certain names among the revenue agents stand out, such as Isom Williams, Big Six Henderson, Charles Summers, and Quinn Pearl. In praise of Williams especially, Sheriff Groce stated: "Williams was a hard man to beat as a revenue man. I'll tell you what he could do. He could go down through there [i.e., Coe Ridge] and find out more than any man I ever seen. And could walk up on you and you a-looking at him! He would jist walk as steady over them rough roads and things as he was dist walkin' on level ground."

William Henderson, always called Big Six, is the epitome of the "revenooer," however. Any mention of raiding stills on Coe Ridge always brings to memory this man whom every Negro on the ridge feared, yet greatly respected. The following story presents a typical picture of Big Six in action:

Once Henderson allowed himself to be covered over with leaves not more than ten feet from the still pot. He lay there most of the night. About 8 A.M. three men appeared, built a fire under the pot and began to work.

"Man alive," one of the men joked to the others as they ran off the first batch, "wouldn't ole Big-Six Henderson like to see me now." The man almost died of fright when, no sooner than he had gotten the words out of his mouth, Henderson grabbed him by the ankles.[12]

When the officers started raiding the ridge regularly, the Coe Negroes developed a warning system as a means of notifying each other when the law was at hand. The first of the moonshiners to see an officer would throw back his head and yell, "Fi-i-i-re in the hole." The yell was strangely like a yodel in which the long vowels were accented. The last syllable was long and was held on a high note. Like an echo, the yell was repeated by another still farther along the ridge, then another, and so on until the call had reached the deepest ravine occupied by a moonshine still.[13]

The Coes' warning system was not restricted to one cry. Royce Cary described another often used by them:

> They used to have a noise they'd make 'fore the revenue'd get there. They'd have a man, have one of them kids spotted up on one of them trees out there. He'd be way up in one of them trees, you know. When he'd see the revenue, why, he'd make a noise through his mouth er blow through his hands—make a noise. That'd give the others time to get back the stuff out of the way before he'd [i.e., revenue man] get there.

Some of the Coe moonshiners would pretend to call pigs if the lawmen were spotted. "Pig o-o-o-o-ey, pig o-o-o-o-ey," issued from the lips of the last moonshiner on Coe Ridge, was heard many times by Sheriff J. B. Groce.[14] Because of the lookouts who were posted, the federal agents had to take extreme caution in getting into the ridge settlement; they would park their cars and walk miles across country to slip in unnoticed. If the Negroes had reason to suspect a forthcoming raid, due to timely tips from certain white neighbors, they took precautions to set warning devices near the stills which could not be detected by the unsuspecting lawmen. Should the officers plan to lie in hiding near the stills, they would invariably spring the trap. One such warning device, according to J. B. Groce, was a black thread which was strung ankle high around the still area.

The Coe Negroes were known to have shot at outsiders who came snooping about, but they always played it safe with the law. Since there was no shooting, a raid often resolved itself into a footrace between the moonshiner and the lawman. The Coes feared the revenue men more than the local lawmen. The following story related by Groce and Rowe illustrates this point:

13 This call was mimicked by **W. T. Rowe**, who described an actual situation in which the call was used. It is also mentioned in Quinn Pearl, "Legendary Coe Ridge," *Louisville Courier-Journal Magazine*, Dec. 12, 1954, and in "Coe Ridge Gained Fame," *Cumberland County News*, Aug. 16, 1960. Richard Glass and Emmit Cain discussed the yell, and Ray Anders told me personally of the times that the call had been employed as a warning device. J. B. Groce claimed that the timber men in early Cumberland County often yelled "Fire in the hole" when felling a tree. The yell was also employed by miners and by demolition teams during World War II.

14 Hog and cow calling as signals was mentioned also by Richard Glass and Emmit Cain.

J. B. Groce: Charlie Keen was sheriff [1950-54] and me and Charlie Summers went down there one day. You wudn't with us, were you, Bill? The time we got that little Nigger down in the holler a-burning brush and had a lard can still and iron worm. Wuz you with us? Do you remember about puttin' Charlie up there behind that tree?

W. T. Rowe: [*Chuckles.*] Yeah.

Groce: Well, we left him on the path so that if the man run along he could stop him, you know, and talk with him. And we got after this little Nigger, and he had a big dog. He was a-jumping at Summers, and Summers back at the Nigger across the hollow. And he come right up over that bluff, and I jumped at him. And he jumped at me, and the dog right after me right up the hollow.

Charlie Keen was a-standin' up there behind a big beech tree and he stepped out and said, "St-o-o-op, b-o-o-oy." [*Heavy laughter.*]

This little Nigger said, "I thought you wuz a revenue man, Mr. Keen. If I knowed it would have been you, I wouldn't stopped."

"You better stop now." [*Informant is speaking very slowly.*] He was too lazy and too slow to catch any.

Sheriff Groce was always in the middle of a chase, and usually got his man. Emmit Cain tells how he outran one of the moonshiners:

They run this colored boy out thar one time. And they wuz a big fence up and they's a hog hole under the fence. Man Groce wuz with Big Six. And the boy said he knowed Man Groce wuz a-going to catch him. Said he run him full blast down hill. And said he fell, and said he hit that hog hole just a-center. Said Man Groce wuz on the other side of the fence and ready to grab hold of him. [*Chuckles.*]

On occasion, the lawmen were not able to catch the moonshiners in action. When such was the case, the officers followed the men to their homes and managed to persuade them to admit guilt and surrender themselves. Groce and his ex-deputy, W. T. Rowe, teamed up to describe such a situation:

Rowe: About the most fun of airy raid we had was the time when we went down there to this house just before dinner, you know. Me and you and Charles Summers and Quinn Pearl, and they said they was going to catch him.

We heard them holler for dinner. And they left and got back to the top of the hill. And we looked and seen the still down there. And they said, "Now we'll get down to the mouth of the hollow, and we'll catch them." They'd done run over you and Charlie.

Groce: Run them over me and Charlie, Bill and Stanley had.

Rowe: And I said, "Now we'll catch the sons-of-bucks when they come out." So Man got over on the hill next to where they went up and got under a brush pile. And I got just across the hollow from the still under a big brush there.

Man said, "Now get down there and go to work. We'll run over them sons-of-bucks. We'll see if they catch them." Said, "They'll be asleep."

Groce: Yep, they'd [i.e., the revenue men] been up all night before a-fishing, see, down on Dale Hollow—Quinn Pearl and Charles Summers.

Well, this big Negro man come down the path right by me. And he jumped down there and he was taking these rocks off from around the still—was going to put some new rock around it. After while here come one of them right down by me and had a big rock under his arm—big limestone rock, you know. Come right on down, went on down and laid it down and looked at this still. And he said, "Will it do to run tomorrow?"

"Nope."

"Well, it'll have to. Tomorrow is Friday."

"Nope."

And we had raised up this tin on there. (He had it covered over with a lard stand tin, you know.) Rock a-laying on it. We'd moved that, some of us had.

He said, "Them god damn son-of-bitches from Indiana has been down here again. This is their last god damn time."

This one here took the still off the furnace, walked across and set it down on the bank of the branch. When he raised up, he looked me right in the eye. I was looking right over on him. He went, "Whoop, eeyoow, that's Man Groce!" They got down to the mouth of the hollow there. We heard them [i.e., revenue agents] holler, "Halt, halt." Directly a gun fired. And they quieted down awhile. And directly the Nigger had got away from Quinn Pearl and was going up the ridge. When he got up on that ridge he hollered, "Fi-i-i-i-re in the ho-o-o-l-l-e. Fire in the hole!"

They had three strands of barbed wire down here over this road in the holler. They'd hit the ground jist like that and scooted under the fence. And this one hit a big rock right there and tore his clothes in two and split his britches leg plumb up to here. And he got up to the house and had his shoes off, right up them stairs he went.

He come in the back. And that big tall one was in there behind the cupboard. And I said, "Come out from behind there."

"I, I, I ain't done nothing." I said, "No, you just run off from a still down yonder was all."

Quinn Pearl started upstairs, and there was a whole bunch of them little Niggers there. Said, "You ain't got no suuch warrant. You ain't got no suuch warrant."

I said, "You get back out of the way, we don't have to have no search warrant. This man run off from a still. We come up here after him."

Quinn Pearl started upstairs. Here come that Nigger down like a lizard on a hot rock. "What is this, Mr. Groce, a holdup?"

I said, "No, it ain't no holdup. You run off from that still and we come up here after you, and they ain't no argument coming." And got him out of the house. He put on some more clothes.

One of the most effective methods of apprehending the Coes was to catch them away from the ridge with whiskey in their possession:

I went down here to Neely's Ferry one Christmas eve morning by myself. Told my wife here, "It's about time they was crossin' the river with a load of liquor now." I went down there and parked in the driveway off the side of the road. I heerd the motorboat start up. Got on this side, I heerd the old Chevrolet they got off Mayor Starns (old four-cylinder job, I believe it was) come up the bank. And I dist backed my car out right square across the road and stepped out.

Both doors of their car flew open just like that! I never seen as many Niggers in my life climbing the river bank and going down through them fields and a-right after them. I caught (they went across this slough, a big log across there—they all went across it, next to the last one he went under and come out and went down through the field just as wet as a rat). And I caught this big one. They had twenty-eight gallon of moonshine liquor.

I told him (I brought his liquor and car on to town), I said, "I want to tell you something. You can bring them others in here in the morning, them other three, and you all can be tried here in this court and serve your time here in this jail, or I'll call the federal men right now."

He says, "Don't do that. I'll bring them in here."

The next morning he come in and says, "Here them boys is."

Well, they give them a hundred dollars and, I think, thirty days in jail.[15]

15   J. B. Groce.

Every raid against the Coe moonshiners was not successful. Sometimes the Negroes were able to outrun the lawmen. And on numerous occasions the approach of the officers was broadcast before the raid materialized. The next five stories depict these aspects of Coe moonshining. In the first, State Patrolman Stanley Butler loses his race with a Coe:

Groce: We had been going down on the ridge and gettin' after them Niggers down there and they would run off and leave their stills. Stanley Butler said, "Now, I'll catch them."

I said, "I'll take you along today and see if you can catch them."

We went down there and got after them. Charles Summers and a bunch of them—we got after a bunch of them down there at a still. We run one of them all even-

16 J. B. Groce and W. T. Rowe. "Track coaches brag about the four-minute mile," according to Big Six Henderson, "but in the old days, there were a dozen men on Coe Ridge who could break it." Henderson is quoted in "Coe Ridge Gained Fame," *Cumberland County News*, Aug. 16, 1960.

17 Emmit Cain.

ing. We run him up the hill and down the hill. And Stanley run him up the hill and started back and caught him by the hand and caught a bush. Well, Stanley Butler had to turn that bush loose. He was about to pull him in two.

Rowe: Yeah, that Nigger jumped over that bluff about ten foot high and Butler had to turn him loose, you see.

Groce: That evening after we got started back, I said [to Butler], "What did you say?"

"Ah, hell," he said, "a greyhound couldn't catch one of them." [16]

When Big Six Henderson got after an Anders, the pursued threw down his crutches and outran the lawman: "Anders had his leg cut off nearly. And he was jist a-flying; run off and left his crutches. And Henderson found his crutches. He took them up and throwed them down in his brother's yard and told him to give Anders his crutches when he come in." [17]

The white people who lived near Coe Ridge were good neighbors to the Coe Negroes. Most of them would aid the Coes whenever they could, even at the risk of being arrested as accomplices. If the revenue men were in the area of Coe Ridge, the whites always attempted to get word to the moonshiners, even if it meant a special trip back on the ridge. Marion Smith's son was arrested by the officers, who were foiled by his quick trip to warn the Negroes that the lawmen were on their way:

They's one guy went out thar—Marion Smith's boy went out thar. See, they [i.e., revenue men] come down here and left their car. The road's so bad he couldn't get out thar in a car. Well, this [Smith] boy jumped on a horse, you see, and they seen him leave there at this store.

Well, when they got in Zeketown he was there. And they'd saw him down there at the store, you see, when they drove up thar. He got there that quick, you see. He beat them out there. Well, he saved them all from being caught that time.

A typical hillcountry patriarch harvests a patch of burley tobacco in the tradition of his people—a people who knew, and, in the main, befriended the Coe Ridge Negroes.

18 This account given by Emmit Cain.

Well, they didn't do a thing only bring him back, and they just put him in the car and made him go home and change clothes. They took him with them.[18]

The proprietor of a general store near Coe Ridge, Emmit Cain credited his good relationship with the Negroes to his willingness to warn them of approaching revenue men. The account below relates how he kept several of the moonshiners from being caught about 1948:

I was running a store right down below them. And the revenuers came. Isom Williams wuz with them at that time. They wuz six of them—Man Groce in the bunch. And they come over by my place, and I had a little tobacco barn across the creek. And they went on through and parked this car in the shed and had the doors shut. It was so tight you couldn't see through cracks.

This colored boy come down to the store. He didn't [see them]; they had dodged him. And he had his rifle, and he'd walked down the hollow to the store. And, of course, these revenue men had dodged this boy and went up the point.

Well, I seen he's walkin' awful slow and I knowed he didn't know about them being here. And, of course, I was there at the store and he come on down. And I'd always try to be a friend to 'um because, you know, I'd hate to see them get took away from their family—get all messed up. And they'd a-died 'fore they'd give anything away on me . . . .

I told him, I said, "Hey, did you see the law there?"

"Why," he said, "no."

I said, "You mean you didn't see 'um?"

He said, "No, I didn't see 'um."

"Well," I said, "they're about six of them. They're gone yonder way."

Well, they wuz running in five different places over there, he told me, that day. Well, he turned and looked ever which-a-way. And about that time I saw a little Nigger comin' down the hill on a mule. And I motioned fer him to come on. And you can motion fer one of 'em, I mean, he gets there! Knowed they're something another wrong.

Well, he whooped his mule and come on down the hill—down to the store. And I told this colored guy, I said, "You jump on that mule and you go around, you can beat them around to the main ridge." And I said, "You'll save part of them from gettin' caught."

And that colored boy he got on this mule and I mean he moved him out, too! He went on around, but they'd done got so close to one place that they run off all but one. They got one of them boys, and the rest of them got away. And they tore this place up and brought this boy on down to the store.

And so this other boy—this guy that got on the mule, he got to these other places, see, and got the word by that whistle they had .... And these other places, they jist walked off and left the whole works thar runnin' jist like it runs, you know. They wuz so bad scared; 'fraid they were so close on 'um.

They come on back to the store after it was all over. They [i.e., revenue men] brought the little boy down and asked him several questions. He kindly winked at me when they put him in the car. And I said, "Watch yourself, son," just like that. He jist winked at me and said, "I always know what to do." Course that little feller had it cut and dried in his mind, you know. He wouldn't tell them nothing. They never could get him to tell on them that run off. He told them he didn't know none of them. Said, "You all dist caught me," said, "I don't know none of the rest of 'um. You'll jist have to hunt 'um up."

Moonshining and bootlegging were continued on the ridge through the early 1950's despite determined efforts of the lawmen to stamp them out. The agents would stage a raid, make arrests, and the Negroes would be sentenced in federal court. Once the Coes served their time, however, they would return and start making whiskey again. Some were repeatedly arrested. One ridge occupant who was hauled into court on a whiskey charge was asked: "What kind of a record do

19 An identical version of this tale is found in "Coe Ridge Gained Fame," *Cumberland County News*, Aug. 16, 1960, and another version related by J. B. Groce. It is my belief that the oral account stems from the written one.

20 W. T. Rowe.

21 According to W. T. Rowe and J. B. Groce, those in the party included themselves, State Patrolman Speck, Big Six Henderson, Quinn Pearl, Charles Summers, all revenue agents, and the local sheriff, Charlie Keen.

22 W. T. Rowe and J. B. Groce.

23 The prison sentences are mentioned in "Coe Ridge Gained Fame," *Cumberland County News*, Aug. 16, 1960, but no names are mentioned.

24 This robbery was described by Mr. and Mrs. Tim Coe.

you have?" "Judge," he replied, "my record is puffect—I've been in court nine times and sent to the pen nine times." [19]

Slowly the law began to take its toll. It became increasingly difficult for the Coes to raise the $150 to $200 needed to get a still back in operation once it was destroyed. During the years 1951–54, when Charlie Keen was sheriff and W. T. Rowe was deputy, seventy-two stills were confiscated from Zeketown moonshiners.[20] The most massive raid ever staged on Coe Ridge occurred on January 27, 1954. It all started, according to W. T. Rowe, when a revenue agent "went out there like he was going to fish. He bought whiskey off all of them. He dist had a party with all them. He bought whiskey from all of them and then he got a search warrant for all of them." In the raiding party were seven cars which carried revenue agents, local officials, and state policemen.[21] It was prearranged that the lead car would stop at the first Negro house, the second car at the second house, and so on until all seven houses on the ridge were entered and searched.[22] Seven arrests were made. Three offenders were sent to prison, while the other four were placed on probation on their promises to leave Kentucky.[23]

THE FINAL CURTAIN FOR THE COE COLONY

About 1940, stealing was added to the list of criminal offenses committed by the Coes. Several of the younger Coe boys began breaking into the houses and stores in the nearby communities, and occasionally included a post office as an object of plunder. The first known robbery committed by the Coes occurred in 1918 when a store at Blythe in Monroe County was entered.[24] That incident was exceptional, however, until the period of

World War II, when break-ins became the rule of the day for the occupants of the Coe colony. J. B. Groce volunteered several accounts of Coe thievery, and most of them are surprisingly humorous. The following[25] describes an attempted arrest about 1950, after a private home had been looted by a Negro from Zeketown:

Back when Charlie Keen was sheriff, he summoned [the woman leader of the colony when one of the younger boys] had stole some tires off them Roaches—Howard Roach and them. And she didn't come. And they issued an attachment, and I wudn't no officer or nothing at that time. I wudn't no sheriff. I'd done went out as sheriff. Charlie Keen wanted to know if I'd drive Hobart Spears, the Constable, down there to serve the attachment on her. "Oh, yes," I said, "I ain't doing nothing else."

I drove his car out there. We got out to this lane where you go down to her house, about 200-300 yards down there to the house.

Well, she could see us coming. She seed us coming, and she went and tied one of them old black-looking rags around her head and jumped on a little old bed of a thing —laying over there, her head was dist a-killing her.

Me and this constable went in, you know. And he looked at her. "Well," he said, "what would you do?" "Well," I said, "You can't make her go and her sick." I said, "You see her head's tied up here and everything." [*Laughter.*]

Said, "We'll jist have to leave her then." [We] started back up towards the car. (They was a hog head laying there on the hearth, I guess it was that long—hadn't been half cleaned.) And I said, "What kind of return are you going to make on your attachment, Mr. Spears?"

"I don't know. What would you do?"

I said, "They ain't but one thing you can do."

"What's that?"

I said, "Put it 'Full of hog head and sicker'n hell and couldn't go.'" [*Laughter.*] (That hog head was that long and it was turned up at the nose, you know.)

Thievery played a major role in the litigations in which

25 In addition to this text, J. B. Groce told also how two of the Coes robbed Bill Thrasher, and how these and other Coe Negroes broke into the store at Black's Ferry on various occasions. From the post office there, they took checks, money, and packages. The robbery of Bill Thrasher was also described by Mr. and Mrs. Tim Coe. I made no attempt to collect accounts of thievery from the Negroes themselves.

the Coe Negroes were involved, and ranks along with moonshining and bootlegging as a cause for the death of the colony. "What would you say actually closed the colony?" the writer asked J. B. Groce. He replied, "Catching them [moonshining], and they got to breaking into people's stores and stealing." W. T. Rowe added a comment that might be considered strange coming from a lawman: "They dist didn't have nothing to go on. They had to live." Groce then came back with the following story which perfectly illustrates the state of affairs during the last years of the Coe settlement:

One of the Negro families had a big bunch of stout boys. I told them down there one day, I said, "Boys, I'm going to tell you something. You're laying down here on this old ridge making this old bad liquor that ain't fit to drink." And I said, "You're naked, and your old car is all to pieces and you are starving to death." I says, "Why don't you get out of here, you boys, and get you some work somewhereas? You can do it if you will."

Well, one of these boys got killed between Chicago and Milwaukee about a year or two years ago. And I had been up there to the old post office. And they was two big cars full of them setting there—biggest cars they put out. And I passed along and one of them hollered, "Hullo, Mr. Groce."

And I said, "Hello, hell, I don't know you."

"You mean as many times as you've arrested us, you don't know who Ise is?"

"Well," I said, "I shore don't." And it was them! And they said, "Now, you are the only man that ever give any 'vice." (They didn't say advice; said 'vice.) They said, "You told us to get out from there. Look at our cars and our clothes now. Look at 'um."

I said, "I told you." I said, "Your old car was all to pieces, and you're naked and you're starved to death, and stealing everything you can get a-hold of." I said, "Now you've got a job, and you've got a car and you've got clothes."

"We shore do."

Some of the Coes who left the colony grew bored with city life and returned to the ridge where they again resumed their illegal pursuits. The law was strict on such offenders. Local and federal officials despaired of sending the Negroes to the penitentiary only to see them released to resume their old practices. The only course left for the law was to probation the criminals. They were set free from any charge provided they would leave the state by a certain date, never to return. Such is the present status of many of the former occupants of Zeketown. Their probations caused them to join relatives who were already living north of the Ohio River, especially in Indianapolis and Chicago.

Those in Indianapolis live in a cluster between West 32nd and 34th streets. Their clannishness still prevails to the extent permitted by the urban environment. They frequently visit each other and talk over old times on Coe Ridge. Whenever a death occurs, the body is returned to Zeketown for burial, especially if it is an older person whose roots were deep in the colony's soil.

Only three houses remain today on Coe Ridge, those belonging to Ray Anders, Everett Anders, and the heirs of Lucy Robert Coe. There were five occupied houses on the ridge in 1955. That year Lucy Robert lived alone, except when some of her grandchildren spent the night with her. One of her sons, Joe, lived there on the ridge with his wife and fourteen children, all of whom were named for movie stars. Actually, Joe himself was not there, for he was finishing a five-year prison term for selling moonshine whiskey. Ruie Coe, his wife, received from the State Department of Welfare $111 monthly toward support of her children. Lucy Robert received $31.00 monthly for old age assistance. Ray and Fannie Anders had their large family on the ridge at that time, and Otley Coe and Everett Anders lived

26 Statistical information in this paragraph was supplied to Miss Mary Ann Keen by Mrs. Jimmie Mann, supervisor of the Public Assistance Program.

as bachelors in separate houses. The total amount of taxes paid in 1955 by the ridge occupants was $51.18. This figure included those people who paid taxes on property no longer occupied.[26]

In 1958, when the writer first visited Coe Ridge, two of the five houses had been deserted. Lucy Robert Coe had moved to Fountain Run in Monroe County, and Ruie Coe and children were in Burkesville, Cumberland County. Her husband, Joe, had been released from prison, but he had left his family on Coe Ridge and was living in Chicago. Just after my visit, the Ray Anders family moved to Burkesville so that the children could enroll in the recently integrated school system there. The departure of the Anders family left only the two bachelors on the ridge. (The houses belonging to Joe Coe and Otley Coe were destroyed by fires of unknown origin in 1967.)

One of the younger former members of the colony despaired of life in Chicago and returned to the ridge in August, 1961. The reason for his return, stated below by one who knew him well, is typical of the way most of the former occupants feel toward their new urban surroundings:

> He moved back last week. I was down there this morning. He'uz helping the white folks down there in a tobacco crop. He went to Chicago and stayed four or five years —said he thought he was through with that city life for awhile. "Too much like being inside," he said; "Jist get up and go to work, come back and lay down, get up and go to work." Said, "That was all there was to it." Then he said he wasn't saving anything after that. Thought he'd come back home and try it back there awhile.

The return of the Negro boy ended on what might be considered a pathetic note. His young wife, who had rapidly become acclimated to an urban society, left Coe

Ridge and returned to Chicago. Her farewell message to him was, "If you want me, you'll have to go back to Chicago to live." He followed her a few months later.

Zeketown has passed into history and will never be revived. Coe Ridge is rapidly being reclaimed by nature, and within a few years every sign of the Coe civilization will be erased from the landscape. Even now, weeds higher than one's head are growing rank everywhere on the ridge. What few buildings remain are being engulfed by this secondary growth. The legend-makers are all gone, but it will be many decades before the legend of Coe Ridge itself will be removed from the lips of local storytellers.

Epilogue: The Contribution of Oral Tradition to the History of the Coe Colony

The central purpose of this study has been to demonstrate the usefulness of oral tradition in the reconstruction of local history. To test this thesis, I selected a small Negro colony located in an area of southern Kentucky where written records were at a premium. Available printed source material was utilized throughout this work as footnote data, the purpose being both to show the interrelationships of oral and printed history, and to indicate the extent to which oral tradition adheres to reality.

Because of its unique history, which is bound up in the geography of the upper Cumberland, the Coe settlement was an important factor in the life of neighboring white people. In order to keep racial bias from weighing too heavily in this study, I collected accounts of the colony's history from members of both races when possible. Folk attitudes invariably crept into the traditions, but, surprisingly enough, even white informants admitted that the Negroes were consistently wronged. Thus, the white recollections served mainly to reinforce those related by the Negroes.

By collecting the colony's history from local people, I was able to set down in print an account that could never be written by most historians who are accustomed to doing research solely in libraries and archives. Such a stand does not assume that all oral traditions are historical truths. Personal recollections *are* history, however, from the viewpoint of the folk who perpetuate them. The validity of folk history does not receive a central position in this study, although three factors can be enumerated which attest to the historicity of the spoken word: First, if a tradition has persisted in the same geographical area; second, if it exists in more than one racial group; and third, if it attests to a local occurrence of a widespread phenomenon recorded in regional historical literature. If any of these factors are present, then most likely the tradition is grounded in fact. Oral recollections associated with the Coe colony fit all three categories in most instances: The geography of the surrounding area has been especially favorable to perpetuation of local historical legends; most accounts of the colony's history were gathered from both Negroes and whites; and oral accounts that describe local antebellum plantation conditions reflect identical situations as those in other parts of the South commonly portrayed in regional literature.

Materials collected for this study cast some light on certain basic questions regarding oral history, such as the forms it assumes and the selective processes at work in its transmittance. Five cardinal tenets may be stated as follows:

(1) *Informants are truthful.* The folk do not con-

sciously falsify information when discussing a historical event. Their statements may not be true in the strict sense of the word, but they are uttered for truth by the informants. Prejudice may slightly alter an interpretation of a basic event because the occurrence usually has personal meaning to the narrator. On occasion, informants refuse to discuss certain episodes, but, when information is offered, the contribution is consistent with parallel accounts gathered from other narrators and corroborative printed sources.

(2) *The folk may improvise details of an event in order to preserve the core of veracity.* Oral tradition frequently confuses places and details, but seldom varies concerning the actual event and chief actors. By gathering a sufficient number of accounts which describe an event, the historian is able to determine precisely what happened. In other words, nine separate narrations about the same incident cannot be accepted as accurate depiction of history, but the nine can be collated to discern the basic historicity involved. For the sections of the story where there is total agreement among the informants, the folk historian can, without too much hesitancy, accept these as factual history. For example, if all accounts told about a murder mention the same assailant and victim, then that portion of the legend can be accepted as fact. Incidental details must be evaluated with extreme caution. The folk will often give a sensational flavoring to an incident to make it acceptable in storytelling situations. Such improvisations do not take away the core of veracity, however, because the embellishments are concerned only with insignificant details. It is during the process of coloration that universal folklore motifs and floating legends are sometimes utilized to produce a good story. The folklorist with his tools of research can detect what ex-

terior forces are at work in the formation and perpetuation of oral history.

(3) *It is necessary to collect as many accounts of an event as possible and collate the data into an archetype in order to obtain a complete story.* Rarely does an individual informant know all there is to be learned about specific historical occurrences. It is necessary to query several people and collate their traditions before the complete picture can be seen. Varying descriptions are usually not incompatible. Each account represents an articulation of the event as recalled by the individual informant. For example, Bill Poindexter claimed that only his father was willing to go to Coe Ridge to get the body of Will Taylor. Other accounts stated that Taylor's own family members went for the corpse. These traditions seem to contradict each other. What actually occurred was that when Will's family made preparations to go for the body, they called upon neighbors to accompany them, and only Poindexter responded to the request.

(4) *Events are dated through association with another incident which occurred just before or after the one under consideration.* Never were the informants able to identify the precise year of the occurrence in question. Dates are fixed in human memory in accordance with other events of a personal, local, or national level, which happened during the same period. Ruthie Coe remembered that Calvin Coe killed Will Taylor about the time she went as a girl of eight years to a dance at Marrowbone. By obtaining the year of her birth, which was 1880, it could be seen that her testimony placed the murder in 1888, the year it actually did occur. Richard Glass recalled that John Coe murdered George Taylor on election day when Cleveland was running for President, yet he could not name the year. Cor-

roborative evidence verified that 1892 was indeed the year when Taylor was killed.

(5) *Major historical episodes may receive primary attention in storytelling situations of a closely knit group.* Coe traditions associated with the plantation culture of slavery times have assumed a position of secondary importance to the period of racial turbulence experienced during the colony's middle years. On the surface, there is nothing about the second generation of Coes for the descendants to be proud of, yet the Negro informants cling to that portion of their history and offer narrations about it at the slightest opportunity. Plantation tales commonly found among Southern Negro groups are virtually non-existent among the Coe Negroes. Apparently, this absence can be explained in light of the nature of the colony's subsequent history which saw the Coes in a continuous struggle for survival. The Negro informants were all queried as to the nature of the tales narrated by the colony's storytellers. Invariably the reply was, "They always talked about the troubles they had with the Taylors and the other white people." Some people might argue that folk groups down through the ages have experienced survival situations similar to those known by the Coe Negroes. If historical occurrences thus drive out vestiges of universal folktales, then today's oral tradition would consist only of historical narratives. This is sound logic, but the Coe story stands as mute testimony to what can happen to older forms of folklore in crisis situations.

What has this study in local history contributed to the field of historical research? I feel that it has opened up a totally untapped reservoir of American history. Throughout the United States there are numberless folk groups like those of Coe Ridge whose history will remain unwritten unless more historians become willing to turn to the spoken word. This type of study has been avoided in the past by those who are living under the erroneous assumption that "old people's recollections are notoriously fallible," and that oral history springs up "whenever trustworthy records are not available."[1] This treatise in the folk history of Coe Ridge proves that the first statement is much too strong, and that the second should be modified to read, "In the absence of written records, the historian should gather and analyze historical traditions of the local people."

[1] Hockett, *The Critical Method in Historical Research and Writing*, 49, 51.

Appendix A: Sketches of the Informants

NEGROES

ALEXANDER, Chester, b. ca. 1925 in Burkesville, Cumberland County. Chester is a polished musician and is in great demand in local circles. I met him one evening in August, 1961, at the home of Ray Anders, when he wandered in with Bully Wilburn. Their appearance interrupted a narrative session with the Anders family, and the rest of the evening was spent recording folksongs and Negro spirituals.

ALLRED, George, b. June 1, 1873, in the coal fields of Overton County, Tennessee. He left Tennessee about 1890 and drifted into the Coe colony. Prior to moving, he had already heard of the notoriety of the Coe Negroes. Allred was involved in a shooting on the ridge during the late 1890's and had to leave. He then lodged among the whites of the Cumberland River area of southern Kentucky, working for room and board. At present he lives at Meshack with Tommy Kirkpatrick in a tiny cabin located behind the main house. I first talked with Uncle George on August 14, 1961, and did not see him again until Christmas, 1962.

ALLEN, Cornelius V., b. ca. 1905 in Noah Hollow, Cumberland County. He still resides in that community with his wife, the former Ida Coe, daughter of Little John Coe. Cornelius is a total abstainer from the use of alcoholic beverages, and has never peddled moonshine whiskey. He is a farmer and resides in a neat frame structure which is as nice as any white neighbor's house. During my two visits to his home, in July and on October 12, 1963, Allen treated me cordially, told me what he knew about the older Negroes on the ridge, and suggested that I contact Bart Ballard, whose father killed two of the Coe Negroes. I was never able to get Allen to talk into the tape recorder, however.

ALLEN, Mrs. Cornelius V., b. ca. 1908 in the Coe colony. Mrs. Allen, the daughter of Little John Coe, gave the impression that she knew more than she was willing to tell about his elopement attempt with Nan Anderson. I was never able to develop a situation favorable for a recording session with the tape recorder. The July, 1963, visit proved virtually fruitless and would have been even worse had not their friend, W. T. "Bill" Rowe, accompanied me. As deputy sheriff, Rowe had befriended her people in times of trouble. On October 12, 1963, she consented to relate a portion of her recollections, and I wrote down many items with pen and pad. But even that attempt was hampered when her daughter stepped from the kitchen and told me to "lay off" the old stories about her ancestors. In 1956, Mrs. Allen had been persuaded by Miss Mary Ann Keen to sing the ballad of "Molly and Nan" and to relate a couple of stories about the elopement attempt. That tape came into my hands through the consideration of

D. K. Wilgus, to whom the tape had been submitted at Western Kentucky State College.

ANDERS, Everett, b. ca. 1915 in the Coe colony. He lives alone in the colony in a one-room shack. I never interviewed him with a tape recorder, but talked for over two hours with him during my visit during Christmas, 1962, to photograph cultural features on the ridge. He pointed out the remains of a moonshine still which had been destroyed only weeks earlier by Cumberland County officials.

ANDERS, Ray, b. 1910 in the Coe colony. He and his family are presently living in Burkesville where his children attend the recently integrated school system. Ray, a perfect gentleman, always treated me with utmost consideration. On two occasions we rode in his truck to Coe Ridge to look at the cultural features. As we traveled, he constantly gave brief historical accounts of many of the structures. I first recorded his historical traditions with a tape recorder on August 24, 1961, but talked with him on various occasions after that time.

ANDERS, Mrs. Ray (Fannie), b. 1908 in the Coe colony. Her repertory was expansive and did not exclude any area of traditional history. She learned most of her stories from her mother, Molly Coe Holman, who was the colony's storyteller, midwife, fortuneteller, and herb doctor. Mrs. Anders practiced all of these activities, too, at one time and even yet occasionally tries her hand at turning the cup. Aware of the excellent quality of her narrations, she expects some sort of remuneration for her services. I was able to satisfy her monetary desires by occasionally taking used clothing and fruits, and did so gladly. For other details of her life, consult the description which accompanies Ray Anders, her husband.

ANDERS, Ruthie, b. May 31, 1878, in the Coe colony; d. September, 1961. A daughter of Tom and Sett Coe, Ruthie married Frank Anders during the 1920's and left the Coe colony for Indianapolis. Due in part to old age, and perhaps to being intoxicated, she frequently had mental lapses during my interview with her on September 2, 1961. Nevertheless, she was able to relate a considerable amount of Coe history. That which she told agreed in the main with similar traditions collected from other informants. I went back to see her two weeks later, only to find that she had died the day before. She was buried in Indianapolis.

CARY, Royce, b. 1925 in Cumberland County, Kentucky. He lives in the Mud Camp community, but beyond that I know nothing of his background. I met him at Alexander's Grocery in Grider, where I was able to record his recollections for about twenty minutes. He was silenced by some of the white men in the store while he was talking about the times when local merchants would swap groceries for moonshine whiskey. He also told of the numerous times he had visited Coe Ridge in quest of whiskey and fun.

COE, Leslie, Jr., b. ca. 1900 in the Coe colony. He moved to Kansas City during the 1920's when a mass exodus from the colony occurred. I never met Mr. Coe; his traditions were recorded and sent to me by Loman D. Cansler, Jr., of Kansas City, Missouri, September, 1962. Coe stated on tape that he learned his historical traditions from older Negro generations who told the stories many times in his presence. The nature of the recorded materials indicates that his repertory is vast. He told stories which ran the gamut from slavery times to 1920, and his narrations exuded authority on the subjects.

COE, Lucy Robert, b. November 17, 1879, on Tooley

Branch, Monroe County; d. September 1963. She was the daughter of slave parents. Her mother was sold to a Southern slaver. While still a young girl, Lucy Robert married Robert Coe and moved to Coe Ridge, where she spent sixty-one years of her life. She left there in 1957, several years after Robert's death, and moved to Fountain Run, Monroe County. She lived there for five years, then moved to Tompkinsville, where she died in 1963. Lucy Robert was one of the informants who made the collecting project really worthwhile. She knew the older historical traditions and was not afraid to talk about them. Her narrations were colorful and often contained the curse words uttered by those who were contemporary with the incidents described.

COE, Tim, b. ca. 1920 in the Coe colony. He was the son of Chester and Ora Coe. He was not an informant in the strict sense of the word. It was he whom I contacted first when I made visits in June, 1961, for the purpose of establishing rapport with the Negroes. We talked for about one hour. During that time he related several stories concerning Coe history, and provided names and addresses for possible future informants.

KERR, Willa Ann, b. ca. 1885 at Meshack, Monroe County. She is descended from the Kirkpatrick Negroes who were held in bondage in Monroe County, just across the river from Turkey Neck Bend. Her repertory of stories about local slavery times is extensive, but she knew very little about the Coes. She lives with a white Richardson family in Glasgow, where she has been for several years now. Frequently she attends funerals in Cumberland and Monroe counties, when Richardson's Florists are in charge of floral arrangements.

TOOLEY, Alberta, b. 1928 in Tompkinsville, Monroe

County. She is the daughter of Kate Tooley and the niece of Lucy Robert Coe. Alberta and her child were residing with Lucy Robert at Fountain Run when I first talked with them. Alberta told some witch tales, but none were utilized in the present study. Her enthusiasm for Lucy Robert's stories, however, kept the latter busy talking at a rapid pace for nearly three hours. For the most part, Alberta's only interspersions were, "Aw, Aunt Lucy!"

TOOLEY, Kate Anders, b. ca. 1884 on Tooley Branch, Monroe County. She is the daughter of slave parents and the sister of Lucy Robert Coe. Early in life she married Wolford Tooley and moved to the Kingdom section of Tompkinsville. She was never a resident of the Coe colony, but knew its history mainly in terms of what she learned from her sister. To Aunt Kate goes much of the credit for information about prospective informants. I visited her on three or four occasions after the conversation in May, 1961, but always found her too sick to talk. She is afflicted with heart trouble and high blood pressure. She is now virtually blind and no longer recognizes me without first asking, "Who is it?"

TOOLEY, Mrs. Sarah Coe, b. October 7, 1910, in the Coe colony. She married Lee Tooley, son of Kate Tooley, and now lives at Fountain Run, Monroe County. Accompanied by Charlie Coe, I interviewed her at home on August 20, 1961. Two weeks later we met in Indianapolis and sought out Ruthie Coe Anders. Mrs. Tooley talked willingly on both occasions and told many of the stories which she had heard her father tell. She would not correspond with me, however. Two times I requested information by means of a letter, and both times she failed to answer.

WILBURN, Bully, b. ca. 1920 in the Coe colony. A

grandson of Tom and Mary Coe Wilburn, Bully is the son of Charlie Wilburn, who was one of the most respected Negroes to stem from the Coe clan. Bully left the ridge in the mid-1950's. None of his recollections are included in the present study, for they are not concerned with the areas covered in this work. Jokes, rhymes, and an occasional song comprised Bully's repertory. He was helpful in seeking out prospective informants.

WHITES

ALEXANDER, A. N., b. 1895 in Cumberland County, Kentucky. For several years he had been postmaster at Grider, Cumberland County, and proprietor of the general store there. His closest contact with the Coe Negroes came during 1938 when he campaigned for sheriff. He has known of them all his life, however, because of the stories told by people who loitered in his store. I first met him in June, 1961, when I went to Cumberland County for the purpose of establishing rapport with prospective informants. I interviewed him with a tape recorder on August 21, 1961, then revisited him on numerous occasions while passing through Grider.

BALLARD, Bart, b. 1875 in Cumberland County, Kentucky. He grew to manhood near Mud Camp, located near the Cumberland River. He is the brother of Molly Ballard, the white girl who attempted to elope with Calvin Coe. His father was responsible for the death of Oleson Wilburn and perhaps that of Joe Coe, two Negro men who were killed because of mistaken identities. Bart Ballard now lives in Marrowbone, Cumberland County, with his daughter and her family. I interviewed him on one occasion only, on October 12, 1963. He was willing to talk about his sister and the revenge taken by his father against the Negroes. Together we went to Molly's grave and copied the gravestone inscriptions.

CAIN, Emmit, b. ca. 1915 near Coe Ridge, Cumberland County. He is a close neighbor of the Richard Glasses and was visiting in their home during my first visit with them. Cain is a farmer and proprietor of a small country store in the hillcountry of southern Cumberland County. He has been a friend of the Coe Negroes across the years.

COE, Charlie, b. August 28, 1885, in Monroe County, Kentucky, on lands which originally were part of the Coe plantation on Kettle Creek. After marriage he moved to a farm near Tompkinsville where he raised his family and still resides. Within recent years Coe's first wife died. His second wife is in her late twenties. Constantly a friend to the Coe Negroes, he has extensive knowledge of that clan's tradition. He was very cooperative throughout the collecting project. In addition to answering questions, he went with me on a tour of the Coe plantation area. The most extensive interview with him occurred August 20, 1961, during our visit to the home of Mrs. Sarah Coe Tooley. I visited him and called him over the telephone many other times for the purpose of obtaining smaller bits of information.

COE, Tim, b. November 21, 1887, in Monroe County, Kentucky, on lands which originally were a part of the Coe plantation. He is the brother of Charlie Coe. After Tim Coe married a local girl, he settled on a farm in Turkey Neck Bend, not far from his homeplace. He knew much about the Coe Negroes and willingly related what he knew. Additionally, he and Mrs. Coe took me to visit Mrs. Etta Short and Mrs. Mattie Davidson at Tanbark. The only tape-recorded interview with Coe occurred August 22, 1961, but I visited him numerous times after that for the purpose of obtaining bits of information. Telephone conversations between the two of us were a common thing.

COE, Mrs. Tim, b. October 9, 1890, in the Turkey Neck Bend area of Monroe County. She is descended from the Richardsons, a pioneer clan from Virginia. During the times I talked with her husband, Mrs. Coe usually remained silent except to prompt his memory.

DAVIDSON, Mrs. Mattie, b. February 16, 1885, in Cumberland County on the Logan Prong of Kettle Creek. She is the sister of Mrs. Etta Short, another informant. Her former homeplace was occupied by Otley Coe's house at the foot of Coe Ridge until it burned in 1967. With her marriage, Mrs. Davidson moved to the farm on which she now lives with her widowed sister at Tanbark, Cumberland County. Her knowledge of the Coe Negroes is associated with the first and second generations on the ridge, plus some traditions of slavery times. She knew very little about the more recent Coes because her marriage removed her from intimate contact with them. The only tape-recorded interview with Mrs. Davidson occurred August 24, 1961; I never contacted her again.

GLASS, Richard, b. 1882 near the Red Bank community of Cumberland County. He married a local girl and spent his entire life in the community of his birth. Glass presently lives about one mile from the road which leads across Coe Ridge, and about two miles from the ridge itself. He was familiar with every generation who grew up on the ridge, but is afraid to talk much about them. He divulged some of his knowledge, but it is felt that he withheld a storehouse of information. Only at the insistence of his wife did Mr. Glass talk as much as he did. After two hours of narrations were recorded on tape from the Glasses, I left, satisfied with the visit. That was August 14, 1961. I stopped by their house at a later date to renew acquaintance and to reassure Mr. Glass that his controversial recollections were safely kept in my trust.

GLASS, Mrs. Richard, b. July 15, 1885. (The comments given for Richard Glass are applicable here.)

GRAVES, Green, b. 1895 somewhere near the Cumberland River in Monroe County. An interview with him was accomplished April 9, 1960, in the company of D. K. Wilgus, now with the University of California at Los Angeles. The tape has since been erased, and as a result much data have been lost. The purpose of that visit was not to record Coe traditions; thus what was recorded came rather accidentally. I do recall that his knowledge of the Coes seemed voluminous. Unfortunately, he died before I could return to record what he knew about the Coes.

GROCE, J. B., b. ca. 1905, Burkesville, Cumberland County. He was sheriff from 1946-49 and from 1954-57. He took part in several raids against the Coe Ridge moonshiners, especially during his first term of office. Because of his knowledge of the physical terrain of the ridge and of the habits of the Coe clansmen, Groce was often called upon by Sheriff Charlie Keen (1950-53) to assist in making arrests involving the Coes. Groce is exceedingly jovial and talked willingly into the tape recorder. He punctuated the narrations freely with colorful phraseology.

HAILE, Hascal, b. 1906 in the Vernon community of Monroe County. He spent his early years clerking in his grandfather's store, located on the banks of the Cumberland River at Vernon, where the Coes often came to purchase groceries and supplies. There also, Haile listened to the white men of the neighborhood talk as they loitered around the store. He had the utmost respect for the Negroes, but feared to talk too freely about them. I had talked with him on various occasions about local historical traditions, but I recorded his recollections about the Coe colony only on August 22, 1961.

KERR, Mrs. Myrtle, b. December 15, 1885, at Judio, Cumberland County. The great-granddaughter of Master John Coe, Mrs. Kerr has spent her entire life near her birthplace on the Cumberland River. Her ancestors came to Cumberland County from North Carolina at the beginning of the nineteenth century. After marriage, Mrs. Kerr moved to a farm located at the foot of Coe Ridge, where she still lives. From this vantage point she watched the Coes come and go from the ridge, often packing moonshine whiskey in bags. Mrs. Kerr has always been a friend to the Coes, and they have been friends to her. Her oral recollections reach back to the days when the Negro Coes were slaves on her ancestor's plantation, and her recollections further include most of their activities once they were established on Coe Ridge. I interviewed her on August 15, 1961, with a tape recorder and talked with her once after that time.

KIRKPATRICK, Price, b. ca. 1875 on Meshack Greek in Monroe County. His ancestors were perhaps the first people to settle in that portion of the county. He has been president of the People's Bank in Tompkinsville for many years. Much of his life has been spent doing research to prove that Abraham Lincoln was born in Monroe County, and oral tradition strongly corroborates this claim. Mr. Kirkpatrick never really knew the Coe Negroes, relating only what he had heard from others. He did, however, know Sue Ann Barton, the white girl who lived with Cal Coe and raised a large family by him. Kirkpatrick's traditional accounts of Coe history were recorded on August 21, 1961.

LOLLAR, Frank, b. ca. 1890 at Ellington's Landing, Cumberland County. He still resides in that community. He contributed one story about the Coe Negroes when, accompanied by Mr. and Mrs. Tim Coe, I visited the general store at Ellington's Landing.

MURLEY, Frank, b. ca. 1895. (See description given for Frank Lollar.)

MOORE, Mrs. Susie Taylor, b. ca. 1882 at Ashlock, Cumberland County. A widow, she resides alone in the community of her birth. She is a niece of George and Will Taylor, the Redheads. Of all the informants, Mrs. Moore alone held the Negro Coes responsible for the period of racial feuding.

POINDEXTER, Bill, b. June 25, 1882, in Turkey Neck Bend, Monroe County, d. 1963. His full name is William Richardson Poindexter, named by and for Dr. William Richardson who delivered him. Poindexter lived at Black's Ferry from the age of eight to twenty-one. He knew the Coes well during that period, for his father often made ox yokes for them. He told of three experiences his father, who was a patteroller, had related about that institution. At the time I talked with him in August, 1961, Poindexter lived at Ashlock, Cumberland County, near Mrs. Susie Taylor Moore, another informant who referred me to him.

ROWE, William T. "Bill," b. 1908 near Burkesville, Cumberland County. He served as deputy sheriff from 1950-57, under both J. B. Groce and Charlie Keen. This was during the period of intensive raiding against the Coe Ridge moonshining bastion. Rowe is a dignified, well mannered, soft-spoken gentleman, who took an active interest in my collecting project from the very first. It was he who helped me to establish rapport with Cornelius and Ida Coe Allen; they had learned to respect and trust him during his eight years in public office. Rowe also introduced me to J. B. Groce and shared a portion of his own recollections of the Coes during that visit.

SHORT, Mrs. Etta, b. April 26, 1879. (See comments for her sister, Mrs. Mattie Davidson.)

WELLS, Judge J. W., b. 1881 in Irish Bottom, Cumberland County. He still lives on a portion of the Wells homestead occupied during the late 1700's by his ancestors from Virginia. He served as judge of Cumberland County for one term and was the author of four books. One of the books, a collection of poems, brought his appointment as poet laureate of Kentucky in 1958. When I visited him, Wells was in the field riding a mule-drawn mowing machine. He was courteous enough to give me three hours of his time while the mules waited in the field. Although his knowledge of the Coes appeared extensive, he was hard to keep on that subject because of his broad knowledge of the history of Cumberland County in general. The visit with him on August 18, 1961, provided very few Coe traditions, but I was able to secure many recollections about logging and rafting.

WILLIAMS, Mrs. Edith, b. ca. 1888 in Barren County, Kentucky. In early womanhood she married and moved to Black's Ferry, Monroe County, where her husband operated a general store. Here, on the banks of the Cumberland River, Mrs. Williams watched the steamboats ply the waters of the upper Cumberland across the years and observed the log raftsmen on their way downstream to Nashville with their assembled rafts. It was these phases of local life about which Mrs. Williams was the most articulate. She knew the Coes, but was associated with them only as they came to her husband's store for food and supplies.

Appendix B: Tale Types, Motifs, and Migratory Legends

References accompanying each tale are keyed to the numbering system employed in Stith Thompson's *Types of the Folktale* and his *Motif-Index of Folk Literature*.

TALE TYPES

1862C   *Imitation of Diagnosis by Observation: Ass's Flesh*. P. 32 and note 18.

MOTIFS

D1318.5.2   "The corpse bleeds when murderer touches it." P. 146 and note 51.

E231   "Return from dead to reveal murder." P. 145 and note 50.

E334.2.2   "Ghost of person killed in accident seen at death spot." P. 145 and note 50.

E423.1.1   "Revenant as dog." P. 145 and note 50.

F500–529   "Remarkable persons." P. 71 and note 26.

F610.0.1	"Remarkably strong woman." P. 59 and note 56.
F617	"Mighty wrestler." P. 38 and note 33.
F618	"Strong man tames animals." P. 59 and note 57.
F624.3	"Strong man lifts cart." P. 152 and note 11.
J2412.4	"Imitation of diagnosis by observation: Ass's Flesh." P. 32 and note 18.
N10	"Wagers on wives, husbands, or servants." P. 38 and note 33.
X940(a)	"Remarkable lifter." P. 152 and notes 9 and 11.
X940(am)	"Strong man lifts a tree ten men have failed to budge." P. 152 and note 9, p. 153 and note 16.
X942(bp)	"Strong man carries sixteen-foot log from 300-year-old tree." P. 152 and note 10.
X973(a)	"Lie: Girl as remarkable wrestler." P. 59 and note 56.
X981	"Lie: Skillful marksman." P. 108 and note 58, p. 113 and note 70.
X981(ch)	"Man rolls barrel downhill, putting pistol bullet through bunghole each time it comes around." P. 113 and note 70.

MIGRATORY LEGENDS

Panther in the Yard. P. 68 and note 22.

Panther on the Roof. P. 68 and note 22.

Man Disguised As Woman Carried Gun Concealed in Basket. P. 117 and note 83.

Appendix C: Genealogical Charts

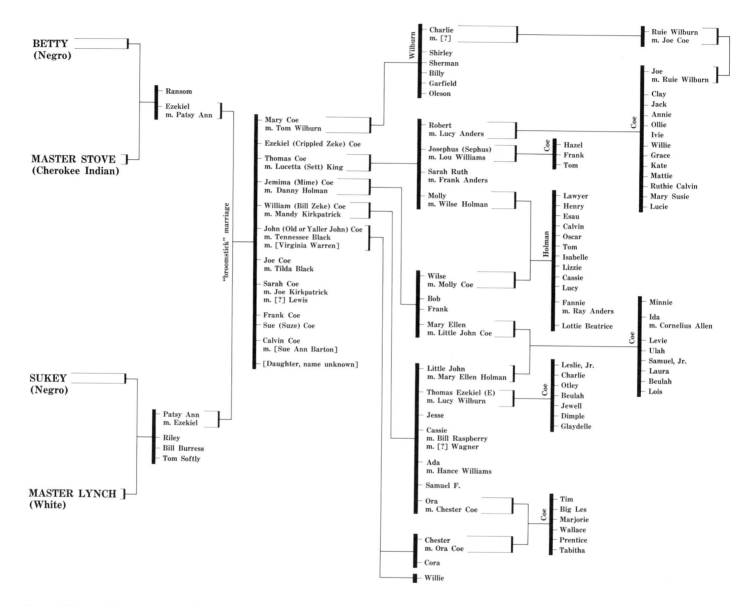

Coe Ridge Negro Families   214

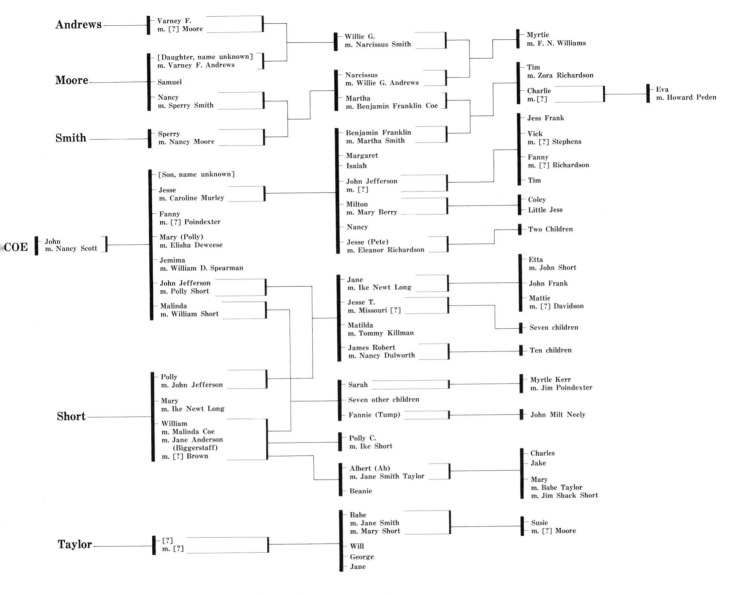

Bibliography

A. BOOKS

Andersson, Theodore M. *The Problem of Icelandic Saga Origins*. New Haven, Yale University Press, 1964.

Bancroft, Frederic. *Slave Trading in the Old South*. New York, Frederick Ungar Publishing Company, 1959.

Baughman, Ernest Warren. *Type and Motif-Index of the Folktales of England and North America*. Indiana University Folklore Series No. 20. The Hague, Mouton and Company, 1966. New York, Humanities Press, 1966.

Blegen, Theodore C. *Grass Roots History*. Minneapolis, University of Minnesota Press, 1947.

Boatright, Mody C., Robert B. Downs, and John T. Flanagan. *The Family Saga and Other Phases of American Folklore*. Urbana, University of Illinois Press, 1958.

Botkin, Benjamin A. *Lay My Burden Down: A Folk History of Slavery*. Chicago, University of Chicago Press, 1945.

Brewer, J. Mason. *Dog Ghosts and Other Texas Negro Folktales*. Austin, University of Texas Press, 1958.

Brown, William Wells. *Narrative of William W. Brown, A Fugitive Slave*. Boston, Anti-Slavery Office, 1847.

Chadwick, Hector M. and Nora K. *The Heroic Age*. Cambridge, England, Cambridge University Press, 1912.

Coe, Samuel F. *The Chronicles of the Coe Colony*. Kansas City, Kansas, privately published, 1930.

Coleman, J. Winston, Jr. *Slavery Times in Kentucky*. Chapel Hill, University of North Carolina Press, 1940.

Dobie, J. Frank. *Tales of Old-Time Texas*. Boston, Little, Brown & Co., 1955.

————, ed. *Legends of Texas*. Austin, Publications of the Texas Folk-lore Society, 1924.

Dorson, Richard M. *American Folklore*. Chicago, University of Chicago Press, 1958.

————. *Bloodstoppers and Bearwalkers: Folk Traditions of the Upper Peninsula*. Cambridge, Harvard University Press, 1952.

————. *Negro Folktales in Michigan*. Cambridge, Harvard University Press, 1956.

————. "The Debate over the Trustworthiness of Oral Traditional History," in Fritz Harkort, ed., *Volksüberlieferung: Festschrift für Kurt Ranke*. Göttingen, Verlag Otto Schwartz and Co., 1968.

Douglas, Byrd. *Steamboatin' on the Cumberland*. Nashville, Tennessee Book Company, 1961.

Drums and Shadows (see Writers' Project, Georgia).

Fedric, Francis. *Slave Life in Virginia and Kentucky: or, Fifty Years of Slavery in the Southern States of*

America, by Francis Fedric. An Escaped Slave. London, Wertheim, Macintosh, and Hunt, 1863. Washington, D. C., Microcard Editions, Microcard 326, Kentucky Culture Series No. 62.

Fenneman, Nevin M. *Physiography of Eastern United States.* New York, McGraw-Hill, 1938.

Fife, Austin and Alta. *Saints of Sage and Saddle: Folklore Among the Mormons.* Bloomington, Indiana University Press, 1956.

Fortes, Meyer. *The Dynamics of Clanship Among the Tallensi.* New York, Humanities Press, 1945.

Frank C. Brown Collection of North Carolina Folklore, The (see White, Newman Ivey, ed.).

Gomme, George Laurence. *Folklore as an Historical Science.* London, Methuen, 1908. Reprinted, Detroit, Singing Tree Press, 1967.

Gottschalk, Louis R. *Understanding History: A Primer of Historical Method.* New York, Alfred A. Knopf, 1950.

Hallberg, Peter. *The Icelandic Saga,* trans. by Paul Schach. Lincoln, University of Nebraska Press, 1962.

Hockett, Homer C. *Introduction to Research in American History.* New York, Macmillan, 1938.

——. *The Critical Method in Historical Research and Writing.* 3rd ed., New York, Macmillan, 1955.

Hyatt, Harry M. *Folk-Lore from Adams County, Illinois.* New York, Memoirs of the Alma Egan Foundation, 1935.

Johnson, Allen. *The Historian and Historical Evidence.* New York, Charles Scribner's Sons, 1926.

Kentucky Soil and Water: Conservation Needs Inventory. Frankfort, Kentucky Conservation Needs Committee, July, 1962.

Kittredge, George Lyman. *Witchcraft in Old and New England.* Cambridge, Harvard University Press,

1929. Reprinted, New York, Russell & Russell, 1956.

Knowlson, T. Sharper. *The Origins of Popular Superstitions and Customs.* London, T. Werner Laurie Ltd., 1930.

Leahy, Ethel C. *Who's Who on the Ohio River and Its Tributaries: The Ohio River from the Ice Age to the Future.* Cincinnati, Leahy Publishing Company [1931].

Liestøl, Knut. *Origin of Icelandic Family Sagas.* Oslo, H. Aschehoug and Company, 1930.

Loomis, Frederic B. *Physiography of the United States.* New York, Doubleday, Doran and Company, 1938.

MacRitchie, David. "The Historical Aspect of Folk-Lore," in Joseph Jacobs and Alfred Nutt, eds., *The International Folk-Lore Congress 1891, Papers and Transactions.* London, David Nutt, 1892.

McDermott, John F., ed. *Research Opportunities in American Cultural History.* Lexington, University of Kentucky Press, 1961.

McDougle, Ivan E. "Slavery in Kentucky, 1792-1865," *Journal of Negro History,* III:3 (July 1918).

Nevins, Allan. *The Gateway to History.* Boston, D. C. Heath and Company, 1938.

Nordal, Sigurdur. *The Historical Element in the Icelandic Family Sagas.* Glasgow, Jackson, Son and Company, 1957.

Paredes, Américo. "Folklore and History," in Mody C. Boatright, ed., *Singers and Storytellers.* Dallas, Southern Methodist University Press, 1961.

Parker, Donald D. *Local History: How to Gather It, Write It, and Publish It.* New York, Social Science Research Council [1944].

Patterson, Caleb Perry. *The Negro in Tennessee, 1790–1865[:] A Study in Southern Politics.* Austin, University of Texas, Bulletin Number 2205, February 1, 1922.

Perrin, W. H., J. H. Battle, and G. C. Kniffin. *Kentucky: A History of the State*. Louisville, F. A. Battey Publishing Company, 1886.

Raglan, Lord. *The Hero: A Study in Tradition, Myth, and Drama*. New York, Vintage Books, 1956.

Sauer, Carl Ortwin. *Geography of the Kentucky Pennyroyal*. Frankfort [Kentucky Topographic Office], 1927.

Sellers, James B. *Slavery in Alabama*. University, University of Alabama Press, 1950.

Sokolov, Y. M. *Russian Folklore*, trans. by Catherine Ruth Smith. New York, Macmillan, 1950.

Stief, Carl. *Studies in the Russian Historical Song*. København, Rosenkilde and Bagger, 1953. New York, Harcourt, Brace & World, 1957.

Taylor, Orville W. *Negro Slavery in Arkansas*. Durham, Duke University Press, 1958.

Thomas, Mrs. Jeanette (Bell). *Ballad Makin' in the Mountains of Kentucky*. New York, Henry Holt, 1939.

Thompson, Stith. *Motif-Index of Folk Literature*. Six volumes. Bloomington, Indiana University Press, 1956.

————. *The Types of the Folktale*. Helsinki, Suomalainen Tiedeakatemia Academia Scientiarum Fennica, 1961. Rev. ed., Hatboro, Pa., Folklore Associates, 1961.

Thwaites, Reuben G., ed. *Early Western Travels, 1748–1846*, Volume III, *François Andre Michaux's Travels West of Alleghany Mountains, 1802*. Cleveland, Arthur H. Clark Company, 1904.

Vansina, Jan. *Oral Tradition: A Study in Historical*

Methodology, trans. by H. M. Wright. London, 1965; Chicago, Aldine Publishing Co., 1965.

Wells, Judge J. W. *The History of Cumberland County.* Louisville, Standard Printing Company, 1947.

White, Newman Ivey, ed. *The Frank C. Brown Collection of North Carolina Folklore.* Seven volumes, Durham, Duke University Press, 1952-64.

Writers' Project, Georgia. *Drums and Shadows: Survival Studies Among the Georgia Coastal Negroes.* Athens, University of Georgia Press, 1940.

B. CENSUS SCHEDULES, MANUSCRIPTS, AND MAPS

The Population of the United States, Eighth Census. Washington, D.C., Government Printing Office, 1864.

The Statistics of the Population of the United States . . . Compiled from the Original Returns of the Ninth Census, June 1, 1870. Washington, D. C., Government Printing Office, 1872.

Microfilm Census Schedules for Cumberland and Monroe Counties, Kentucky, for the years 1850, 1860, 1870, and 1880.

Microfilm Slave Census Schedules for Cumberland and Monroe Counties, Kentucky, for the years 1850 and 1860.

Keen, Mary Ann. "The Coe Settlement of Cumberland County." Unpublished manuscript, submitted at Western Kentucky State College, Bowling Green, Kentucky, August 1, 1955, as a term project.

Peden, Mrs. Howard. "The Coe Family." Unpublished manuscript, located at the author's home on Morningside Drive, Glasgow, Kentucky.

United States Department of the Interior, Geological Survey map. Kentucky Topographic Series, 1954.

Land Areas of Kentucky and Their Potential for Use.

Agricultural and Development Board of Kentucky, Frankfort, 1953.

C. NEWSPAPERS

"Calvin Coe." *Burkesville Sesqui-Centennial* brochure, August 13–20, 1960.

"The Coe Clan of Pea Ridge." *Glasgow Times,* February 29, 1940.

"Coe Ridge Gained Fame as Hideout of Moonshiners." *Cumberland County News,* Sec. C, p. 4, August 16, 1960.

"Courier Was First Newspaper To Be Published in 1870." *Cumberland County News,* Sec. 13, p. 4, August 18, 1960.

Hardaway, Howard. "Coes of Cumberland Were Born to Fight." *Louisville Courier-Journal,* January 28, 1940.

"Interesting History of Coe Outlaws." *Glasgow Times,* December 1, 1932.

Leslie, John E. "Early Days of Monroe County." *Tompkinsville News,* August 28, 1954; reprinted, Sec. 3, p. 6, October 28, 1954.

"Newspaper Service in Monroe Since 1885." *Tompkinsville News,* 50th Anniversary Ed., Sec. 7, p. 1, August 28, 1954.

Pearl, Quinn. "Legendary Coe Ridge." *Louisville Courier-Journal Magazine,* December 12, 1954.

"Steamboats Played Important Part in History of City of Burkesville." *Cumberland County News,* Sec. B, p. 1, August 18, 1960.

D. PERIODICALS

Bohannan, Paul. "Concepts of Time Among the Tiv of Nigeria." *Southwestern Journal of Anthropology,* IX (1953), 251–62.

Cohen, Ronald. "Quantification." *African Studies Bulletin,* VIII:2 (Sept., 1965), 16–19.

De Laguna, Frederica. "Geological Confirmation of Native Traditions, Yakutat, Alaska." *American Antiquity,* XXIII (1958), 434.

Dixon, Elizabeth I. "Oral History: A New Horizon." *Library Journal,* 87:7 (April, 1962), 1363–65.

Dorson, Richard M. "Oral Tradition and Written History: The Case for the United States." *Journal of the Folklore Institute,* I:3 (Dec., 1964), 220–34.

Jones, G. I. "Oral Tradition and History." *African Notes,* II:2 (Jan., 1965), 7–11.

Jordan, Philip D. "The Folklorist as Social Historian." *Western Folklore,* XII:3 (July, 1953), 194–201.

Lach-Szyrma, W. S. "Folk-Lore Traditions of Historical Events." *Folk-Lore,* III (1881), 157–68.

Lowie, Robert H. "Oral Tradition and History." *Journal of American Folklore,* XXX (April–June, 1917), 161–67.

Morrissey, Charles T. "The Case for Oral History." *Vermont History,* XXXI:3 (July, 1963), 145–55.

———. "Oral History and the Mythmakers." *Historic Preservation,* XVI:6 (Nov.–Dec., 1964), 232–37.

Myres, John L. "Folkmemory." *Folk-Lore,* XXXVII (1926), 12–34.

Naroul, Raoul. "Data Quality Control." *African Studies Bulletin,* VIII:2 (Sept., 1965), 19–23.

Nutt, Alfred. "History, Tradition, and Historic Myth," *Folk-Lore,* XII (1901), 336–39.

Pendergast, David M., and Clement W. Meighan. "Folk Traditions as Historical Fact: A Paiute Example." *Journal of American Folklore,* LXXII (April–June, 1959), 128–33.

Vansina, Jan. "The Documentary Interview." *African Studies Bulletin,* VIII:2 (Sept., 1965), 8–14.

Walker, Wyman D. "Western Folklore and History." *The American West,* I:1 (Winter, 1964), 45–51.

Wells, Merle W. "History and Folklore: A Suggestion for Cooperation." *Journal of the West,* IV:1 (Jan., 1965), 95–96.

White, Helen McCann. "Thoughts on Oral History." *The American Archivist,* XX:1 (Jan., 1957), 19–30.

Zolberg, Aristide R. "A Preliminary Guide for Interviews." *African Studies Bulletin,* VIII:2 (Sept., 1965), 3–8.

Index

The Saga of Coe Ridge has been set on the Linotype in ten-point Century Expanded with two points spacing between the lines. Fourteen-point Century Italic was selected for display.

The book was designed by Jim Billingsley, composed and lithographed by Thos. J. Moran's Sons, Inc., Baton Rouge, and bound by the Nicholstone Book Bindery Inc., Nashville. Photographs by the designer were secured on location with the aid of the author. Spot drawings by the designer were based on field sketches by Maurice E. Coppock.

The paper on which this book is printed is designed for an effective life of at least three hundred years.

THE UNIVERSITY OF TENNESSEE PRESS : KNOXVILLE